The Road to Success

Learning How to Become an Effective Negotiator

Terry L. Boles—*The University of Iowa*
Lon D. Moeller—*The University of Iowa*
S. Beth Bellman—*The University of Iowa*

Kendall Hunt
p u b l i s h i n g   c o m p a n y

Cover image © Shutterstock, Inc.

Kendall Hunt
publishing company

www.kendalhunt.com

Send all inquiries to:
4050 Westmark Drive
Dubuque, IA 52004-1840

Copyright © 2012, 2020 by Kendall Hunt Publishing Company

Pak ISBN 978-1-4652-9823-2
Text ISBN 978-1-4652-9824-9

Printed in the United States of America
10 9 8 7 6 5 4 3 2 1

Dedication

Terry L. Boles

This book is dedicated to my sons,
Colby and Jeremy, who taught me how to become
a better negotiator and a better person.

■ ■ ■ ■

Lon D. Moeller

Thanks to my wife Linda and three daughters,
Jessica, Sarah, and Ashley,
who patiently supported me in turning a stack of notes
and PowerPoint slides into a book.
Their love and encouragement continues to be
a source of inspiration.

■ ■ ■ ■

S. Beth Bellman

Thanks to my family, friends, and students who
encourage me to be curious and inspire me to be a
life-long learner.

Acknowledgments

We were inspired to write this book because we felt that most of the existing negotiation texts are aimed at the graduate MBA level. Because our own institution, the Tippie College of Business at the University of Iowa, requires undergraduate management majors to take a negotiations course we wanted to create a book that would be more relevant to undergraduate students. We used learning to drive as a metaphor for learning to be a successful negotiator. We endeavored to create cases and interactive components of the book that focus on the types of negotiations that most undergraduates are likely to encounter, like negotiating an apartment lease, negotiation for a car, negotiating with roommates about household chores, salary negotiations for a first job, etc. Skills learned through experiential exercises will provide students a good foundation for negotiating in the business world.

Any book on negotiation represents more than the work of the authors. We were influenced by our training and experiences over our professional careers; and each of us brings to the topic a different perspective.

Terry L. Boles received her Ph.D. in Social Psychology at the University of California, Santa Barbara. She had the opportunity to do a two-year post-doctoral fellowship at Northwestern University's Kellogg Graduate School of Management in the Dispute Resolution Resource Center. Through this opportunity and others, such as participating in a six week seminar at the Institute on Negotiation and Dispute Resolution, held at the Center for Advanced Study in the Behavioral Sciences on the Stanford California campus, attending the annual meetings of the International Association of Conflict Management, her thoughts on negotiation teaching and research were influenced by a number of negotiation scholars. Among these she would like to acknowledge the positive contributions of the following individuals: Linda Babcock, Bruce Barry, Max Bazerman, Sally Blount, Bill Bottom, Jeanne Brett, Don Conlon, Rachel Croson, Carsten DeDreu, Michele Gelfand, Steve Goldberg, Rick Larrick, Beta Mannix, Kathleen McGinn, Lourdes Mundu-ate, Keith Murnighan, Maggie Neale, Mara Olekalns, Judi McLean-Parks, Madan Pillutla, Robin Pinkley, Jeff Polzer, Dean Pruitt, Etty Jehn, Ann Tenbrunsel, Cathy Tinsley, Leigh Thompson, and Laurie Weingart. Finally, she would like to acknowledge the mentorship, friendship, and loving support of Chuck McClintock, Nancy Hauserman, David and Judy Messick, Ron Schintler, Paul Weller and Sara Rynes-Weller.

Lon D. Moeller earned undergraduate and graduate degrees in Industrial Relations and Human Resources Management as well as a J.D. from the University of Iowa. While earning his graduate degree, he met several faculty members, including Anthony V. Sinicropi and Thomas Gilroy, who illustrated class lectures about labor-management relations with stories from their experience as labor mediators and arbitrators. His friendship with Professor Sinicropi led him to pursue careers in both academics and as a labor arbitrator following time in law practice. He would also like to acknowledge the lawyers and union representatives he has met along the way who taught him many of the negotiation lessons included in this book. Lastly, he would like to acknowledge the support of his colleagues in the Tippie College of Business, including Jay Christensen-Szalanski, Nancy Hauserman and Andrew Hosmanek.

S. Beth Bellman earned her Ph.D. in Interdisciplinary Studies: Decision Neuroscience from the University of Iowa, an MA in Personality and Social Psychology also from the University of Iowa, and her Masters in Education from Harvard University. She was formally introduced to the study of negotiation in a class she took as part of her Masters degree at Harvard Law School with Roger Fisher. She found herself immediately fascinated by the topic as it relied heavily on interpersonal communication and offered the potential for creating value. She was simultaneously studying the Social Psychology of Organizations with Richard Hackman and noticed the prevalence of negotiation in organizational settings and the role of social psychological principles at play in negotiation. Beth's understanding of personality psychology and social cognition grew as she pursued her doctoral studies. She was most interested in the application and implications of social psychological principles in business environments. Teaching negotiation is one specific way she is able to bring together some of what we know from the field of social psychology with a practical life and business skill. Beth would like to acknowledge the support of her colleagues in the Tippie College of Business including Jay Christensen-Szalanski, Amy Kristof-Brown, and Amy Colbert.

We would also like to thank our action editors, Melissa Tittle, and Torrie Johnson of Kendall Hunt Publishing, for their support and help throughout this project and Paul Carty for asking us to pursue the project.

Brief Contents

Contents

9 Objects in the Mirror May Be Closer than They Appear: Perceptions,
Biases, and Communication in Negotiation

About the Authors

Terry Boles, is Professor Emeriti at the Tippie College of Business, University of Iowa. She earned her Ph.D. in social psychology from the University of California at Santa Barbara and completed post-doctoral training at the Kellogg Graduate School of Management. Boles is a trained mediator, and has taught negotiation and conflict management at the undergraduate, MBA, and Executive MBA levels for over 25 years. Boles has also taught negotiation courses in Russia and Hong Kong. She is past president of the International Association of Conflict Management.

Lon Moeller is Professor Emeriti at the Tippie College of Business, University of Iowa and has held senior administrative positions in higher education. Moeller received his J.D. from the University of Iowa. He worked in private law practice, served as faculty ombudsperson and has conducted negotiation and conflict resolution training for corporate and non-profit clients. Moeller is a labor arbitrator and mediator and has been involved in extensive business negotiations and labor-management collective bargaining sessions over the years. He has co-authored three other books in the areas of entrepreneurship, business management and conflict resolution.

S. Beth Bellman is a Lecturer in the Tippie College of Business at the University of Iowa in the Department of Management & Entrepreneurship. She earned her Ph.D. in Interdisciplinary Studies: Decision Neuroscience from the University of Iowa. She has been teaching negotiation, primarily to undergraduate students, for the past seven years in person and online in both synchronous and asynchronous formats. She believes that teaching students about negotiations can improve both their business and personal relationships as they learn to become better communicators and to take an interest based approach to creating value.

Preface

Think about what it felt like the first time you sat behind the steering wheel of a car. It was exciting because driving a car allowed you to go to different places. Driving was frightening because of your new responsibilities and the possibility of making mistakes that could lead to an accident. The "rules of the road"—when to pass a car, deciding which car has the right of way at a four-way intersection, identifying the various road signs, and so on—were confusing when you started driving. But over time, and through hours of practice driving in different situations, you became confident in your ability to drive.

Good drivers anticipate bumps in the road. They watch for warning signs, ask for help with directions, and know that plans may need to change because of engine problems, road detours, or bad weather. Good drivers understand that new situations, such as the first time driving on a narrow mountain pass or driving in a foreign country, may require a changed approach to driving.

We have taught negotiation classes to a wide variety of undergraduate and graduate business students. Students are generally excited at the start of class to learn how to improve their negotiation skills. Some students are cautious negotiators and lack confidence in their abilities to negotiate. They are like the student driver starting a driver's education class. Other students are confident in their abilities in certain types of negotiations but are less confident in their abilities in other types of negotiations. They are like the driver who knows how to operate a car with an automatic transmission but who has no experience driving a vehicle with a standard transmission stick shift.

Good negotiators become good negotiators by understanding their own negotiation style, knowing how to prepare to negotiate, and developing a strategy aimed at accomplishing what they want to achieve. Every negotiation situation is different. There is no "one size fits all" approach that guarantees success to every negotiator in every situation. Different situations require different negotiation strategies, and no two negotiators are the same.

Although some people are better drivers than others, everyone can improve their driving skills. The same is true of negotiations. Negotiation skills can be taught and improved through practice. We have written this book to teach students how to become effective negotiators. Like a driver's education course, we will review some of the basic principles of negotiations—the "rules of the road"—on our road trip to negotiation success and give you, the reader, practice with learning how to negotiate in different situations.

Consider this book as your "driver's education course" for negotiations. In this book, we traverse the following topics on the road to becoming a successful negotiator:

- How to improve the skills needed to be an effective negotiator
- How to identify your conflict handling and negotiation styles and know when they will serve you well and when they will not
- Distributive bargaining and hardball tactics
- The role of concessions in negotiations and the influence of the fairness and reciprocity norms on negotiation behavior
- Integrative negotiations and strategies
- How to prepare a strategy for successful negotiations
- How to identify different interests in negotiations, brainstorm, and add value to negotiated agreements
- Negotiation leverage, power, and BATNAs
- How to deal with the emotions that arise during negotiations
- What it means to be an ethical negotiator
- Communication challenges in negotiation
- Gender and cultural differences in negotiations
- Impasse-breaking strategies and approaches, including mediation and arbitration

When you have finished reading this book, you will know what it takes to be an effective negotiator and will have had the chance to improve your negotiation skills through practice offered by the negotiation exercises, case studies, and discussion questions found in the online component of this book. When you see the   icon, go to the online component for interactive exercises, PowerPoint slides, review examination questions, and case studies.

We enjoy the chance to see how our students improve their negotiation skills during class. Understanding and applying the negotiation principles outlined in this book will put you on the road to negotiation success. Enjoy the ride.

Content Connections Reviewers

Michael Bochenek
Elmhurst College

Eugene Buccini
Western Connecticut State University

Solveg Cooper
Cuesta College—San Luis Obispo

Dennis Saley
North Carolina State University

Mark Davis
Harding University

Gaetan Giannini
Cedar Crest College

Earl Hill
Emory University

Stephen Humphrey
Florida State University

Mary Kern
Baruch College

Fengru Li
The University of Montana

Kathleen Mays
LeTourneau University

Kathryn Mercer
Case Western Reserve University

Kimberly Merriman
Penn State University—Great Valley

Leann Mischel
Susquehanna University

Gary Nichols
University of Central Florida

Nancy Oretskin
New Mexico State University—Las Cruces

Holly Schroth
University of California—Berkeley

Daniel Sierchio
Rutgers the State University of New Jersey

Eric Soares
California State University—East Bay

Morvarid Taheripour
University of Pennsylvania

Marc Weinstein
University of Oregon

Recognizing You Are on the Road: What is Negotiation?

Every driver encounters "first-time" situations—the first time driving in a large city, the first time driving on an interstate highway, or the first time driving on an icy road. Good drivers have gained the experience and developed the skills necessary to be successful in those situations.

Many first-time negotiators face similar problems. How many times have you walked into a store and been approached by a sales clerk who asks if he or she can help you find something? An inexperienced shopper may not understand that this innocent question frequently leads to a "hard sell." Sometimes an inexperienced shopper will buy something the shopper did not want to in order to get away from the pushy sales clerk. Experienced shoppers understand that this situation is a negotiation; if they are not willing to negotiate, they will tell the sales clerk, "I'm just looking, thanks."

In this chapter, we will help you recognize situations when you are "on the road," that is, situations that require negotiation skills, and identify the skills that are associated with effective negotiators.

CHAPTER OBJECTIVES

- To understand why people "hate to negotiate"
- To recognize "negotiation situations"
- To define what is meant by "negotiation"
- To understand what skills are necessary to be an effective negotiator

KEY TERMS

Negotiation
Zero-sum game

Fixed pie assumption
Traits of effective/successful negotiators

CHAPTER CASE

You will be graduating at the end of the semester. A new job awaits. You will need a new car. Your parents have offered to give you $2,000 to help pay for the cost of a car. You have $1,500 in your savings account. The car you want—a four-door sports utility vehicle (SUV)—is available brand new at the local car dealership for $32,000. You have also seen the same make of SUV advertised on a campus bulletin board for $24,000; however, this SUV is being sold "as is" (that is, with no warranties) and is three years old. Although you have an accepted job offer, it is not clear at the present time whether you will be assigned to Philadelphia, Atlanta, or a city in the Midwest—either St. Louis or Minneapolis. Two banks have indicated that they would be willing to loan you money to buy a new vehicle. You really don't want to spend more than $28,000.

You would likely view both of these situations—buying the brand new SUV from the car dealership or buying the used SUV from a private seller—as "negotiations." In both situations, the sellers have what you want (the four-door SUV) and you have something they want (the money needed to buy the vehicle). The sellers will try to persuade you to buy their SUV. You will do some research to determine the market value for both new and used SUVs so that you can persuade the sellers to lower their asking price.

There are other things you will need to consider in connection with your SUV negotiations. You should ask yourself: (1) Can I get the SUV I want for under $28,000? (2) What happens if I can't buy either SUV? (3) Does it matter how well I get along with the seller during the negotiation? (4) Are there certain features or add-ons for the SUV that I may be interested in? (5) What type of repairs or maintenance will the used SUV require? (6) Will the car dealership offer a maintenance or service plan for the new SUV? (7) How much should I first offer the seller? and (8) Should I have someone else, such as a family member or friend help with the negotiation? These are all reasonable questions that you would want to think about before buying a new vehicle.

Why Do Many People "Hate to Negotiate"?

Some people might jump into a car negotiation without thinking about the type of questions that must be answered for the negotiation to be successful. All they know is a starting point—how much money they want to spend—and the end point of wanting to buy a car. This is like taking a cross-country driving trip from New York City to Los Angeles without planning the route, getting the car ready for such a long trip, making hotel reservations along the way, or bringing enough music and audio books to help pass the time.

Many people hate to negotiate because of a past experience when they did not properly prepare for a negotiation. The car buyer who does not think about what he wants before stepping foot in a car dealership and who accepts the first offer made by the sales representative might "hate negotiations."

A negotiator who "leaves money on the table" or who constantly thinks she could have "done better" will likewise question her negotiation skills. Assume, for example, that you find an apartment that has all the features you are looking for—two bedrooms, new carpeting, and reserved parking. Because you like the apartment, you accept the landlord's $1,200 per month offer without looking at other comparable apartments in the area. If, after signing a year-long lease, you discover a comparable apartment that rents for $1,000 per month, you would have left $2,400 ($200 per month $\times$ 12 months) on the table.

Some people fail to anticipate that a situation will require negotiation skills until it's too late to change course. The decision to buy a car will require some type of negotiation. You would not go to a car dealership without expecting to be approached by a sales representative. In that case you will say, "No, I'm just looking" or "Tell me about your line of cars." The same is true when you want to buy a new house. You expect to look at price when you talk to real estate agents or start attending open houses to see what houses are on the market.

What about the situation when a co-worker wants to trade work days with you? She asks if you could cover her Friday night shift. Without thinking, and trying to be nice, you respond, "Sure, no problem." When all of your friends are going out on Friday, and you are stuck working, you question why you agreed to the shift change and wonder why you did not ask for something in exchange for the deal. *I hate to negotiate,* you think.

A final reason some people hate to negotiate is because they see negotiation as a **zero-sum game**, meaning that the only way they "win" in a negotiation is if the other person "loses." They don't like the win-lose aspect of negotiations. Under this **fixed pie assumption**, the negotiator assumes that what she wants is in direct conflict with what the other negotiator wants.[1] The pie is only so big, she reasons, so the negotiator believes she can get a large share of the pie only by taking more pie away from the other person.

There are **win-lose** situations in negotiations. If you are negotiating to buy a new bicycle and want to pay as little as possible and the seller wants to sell the bicycle for the highest price he can receive, your win (a lower price) is the seller's loss. Many times, however, people who carry this fixed pie assumption with them into every negotiation miss out on opportunities for both negotiators to win. Going back to our bicycle example, what if the seller also had a tire pump or spare tire that she was willing to include with the sale of the bicycle? Or maybe the bicycle seller also did maintenance work on bicycles and was willing to offer bicycle maintenance to you at a discounted rate. All of a sudden, this pie has expanded beyond the simple price of the bicycle to include no-cost bicycle accessories and discounted maintenance work for the buyer and a future customer for the seller.

Zero-sum game
a game where one person must win and one must lose. If negotiation is viewed as a zero-sum game, then it is assumed both parties want the same thing and only one can have it. There is no room for compromise or finding a solution that will satisfy both people.

Fixed pie assumption
this assumption is that the size of the resource to be divided (or the negotiation "pie") is fixed. This assumption is often false; as integrative negotiation can often increase the size of the pie by adding issues that allow both negotiators to find a way to agree to an outcome that satisfy both of their interests.

> **TAKE AWAY:** *People dislike negotiations for a variety of reasons, including a lack of knowledge about how to prepare to negotiate, the inability to identify when negotiation skills must be used to reach an agreement or resolve conflict, and the assumption that every negotiation is a win-lose proposition.*

Recognizing Negotiation Situations

Which of the following situations would you consider to be a negotiation?

- Whenever your roommate's friends come to visit for the weekend, they drink your soda in the refrigerator. No one has ever paid you back or offered to buy you new soda. You are getting tired of this routine, and know that one of your roommates has friends coming to visit during the upcoming weekend.

- You fly to a distant city for a callback job interview. You get to the city; your luggage does not. You are panicked because you need to look your best for the interview. The airline's customer service representative, however, is not giving you the answers you are looking for and it is doubtful you have enough time to purchase new clothes in time for the job interview

- August 16th is your scheduled wedding date. Your fiancé would like to have your wedding at her family's church, followed by a large reception at a local (and expensive) hotel. You would prefer to have a smaller "destination" wedding at the national park in Colorado where you met your fiancé. Your fiancé just texted you with information about the down payment required by the hotel for the reception.

- Your parents want you to graduate next May. You, on the other hand, are thinking about changing your major, which will require that you spend an additional semester at the university. You need to talk to your parents, but you have no idea how to tell them about the change in your graduation plans. They will be on campus next week for Family Weekend.

- You have taken your final group project for a class to a copy center to have the project bound and copied. When you pick up the copy job, you are short five copies and the copy center employee forgot to include the table of contents page that you left with the order. The final project is due today at 5:00 P.M., and the copy center manager wants you to pay for the extra cost to get the order right. The clock on the wall of the copy center says 4:00 P.M.

- The pizza delivery driver brings the wrong order to your apartment —you ordered three combination pizzas and the pizza delivery driver brought you three vegetarian pizzas. Your friends are coming over in 10 minutes to watch the Super Bowl football game. The pizza delivery driver is asking you to pay full price plus a tip and is waiting on your doorstep.

- You live in a second story apartment. On the first floor lives an elderly couple who generally go to bed each night around 10:00 P.M. You like to study after 10:00 P.M. The past two days, the couple has placed notes on your door demanding that you "quiet down" at night. You do not think you have been particularly noisy and prefer to study at home rather than go to the university library. The couple has, you feel, avoided talking to you when you have asked to talk about their concerns.

- The professor for your online statistics course has a deadline of 5:00 P.M. for each of the assignments in her course. The online statistics course is being offered by a university located in Florida, which is in the Eastern Time Zone. You live in Milwaukee, Wisconsin, which is in the Central Time Zone. When you attempt to submit your first statistics assignment to the online course website (at 4:00 P.M. Central Standard Time), you receive a message that says your assignment is "late" and will not be accepted for grading. Your professor never told you that 5:00 P.M. meant 5:00 P.M. in the Eastern Time Zone. You need to do well in this course, and cannot afford to receive a grade of zero on this first assignment. You have emailed the professor about this "misunderstanding."

- You are driving home from on campus next Friday following the end of the semester. Five people can fit into your car for the drive home. You have found four students from your campus who live near your home in New Jersey, and who agreed to split the cost of gas for trip to New Jersey. This morning, your best friend from high school left a voice mail message asking if you could pick her up on your way home – she knows you have a car, and her university is located an hour away from your campus, but directly on your way home to New Jersey. Your best friend's voice mail message says she "knows she can count on you," and "won't be able to get home if she can't ride with you." Now what?

- Ever since your first-year at the university, you have worked as a cashier at a local grocery store, working twenty hours per week (usually on the weekends). The store manager is a graduate of your university and has consistently given you finals week off so that you could study and prepare for your final examinations. This semester, however, the store manager has scheduled you to work your regularly assigned shifts during your scheduled final examination week at the university. You really do not think you can work your regular twenty-hour workweek and have the time to study for your final examinations. You have a meeting with the store manager this afternoon to talk about your work schedule.

■ ■ ■ ■

A Definition of "Negotiation"

By now, you have probably realized that each of the preceding situations seems to be a negotiation. But why? What exactly is a **negotiation**?

To some people, a negotiation is similar to a high stakes game of poker.[2] Others define a negotiation as an "interactive communication process"[3] or a problem-solving exercise that occurs "when parties are trying to find a mutually acceptable solution to a complex conflict."[4] Some describe negotiation as a "ritual of participation,"[5] whereas others see negotiation as "haggling."[6] Despite these different definitions, we know it "takes two people to negotiate."[7]

Negotiation
a process that helps two or more people work together to achieve goals and solve problems.

"... In reality, no one *wins* negotiations. Business negotiations are not a competitive activity. They are a creative activity if done well."

—Requejo, W. H., & Graham, J. L. (2008). *Global negotiations: The new rules* (p. 5). New York: Palgrave MacMillen.

We define "**negotiation**" in this book to mean a process that helps two or more people work together to achieve goals and solve problems. Negotiation involves two or more people who work to achieve individual and joint outcomes. A negotiation is not an argument or a debate, although to some negotiators a negotiation can feel like it. There is a certain amount of give-and-take to any negotiation, meaning that the parties to a negotiation expect to make concessions and further expect the other side to move off of his or her initial position as the negotiation progresses. A negotiation is also less than a game to win or lose than many people think. Although it is important to get your way, it is equally important to remember that your reputation and the way you negotiate also factor in to your success at the negotiation table.

> **TAKE AWAY:** *Effective negotiators understand that negotiation is a problem-solving activity that requires the active participation of both negotiators in order for a deal to be reached.*

Many people don't see negotiation situations develop until it is too late to do any planning. Without proper planning, your chances of being successful in negotiation diminish. If you were taking a long road trip, you would plan your route, identify places to stay along the trip, and watch your gas tank to make sure you did not run out of gas before you reached your destination.

Similar planning is important for effective negotiations. Planning for a negotiation means thinking not only about what you want but also about the negotiation style that best fits the specific negotiation situation. Consider, for example, how you might negotiate with a street vendor in another country. You won't likely see that person again, and your relationship with him may not be important to you. On the other hand, you may have limited money with which to buy what the vendor is selling from his stand.

The outcome of your negotiation—how much money you spend—matters. Your negotiation will probably be competitive, since this is likely a one-time business transaction. You might make an offer for a low price, and the vendor might counter with a high price. He may reject your attempt to "split the difference." When you threaten to walk away, suggesting that the vendor just lost a sale, he may lower his price within the range of what you were willing to spend. At that point, you would probably have a deal. Think about whether this competitive negotiation style would work when you have asked that "special someone" to go on a date to watch a movie. In this second case, the relationship matters. The specific movie you end up watching may not be as important to you as spending the time with your "special someone." A good negotiator in both cases understands that the strategy and approach must be changed depending on the situation. We discuss different negotiation styles, and how they fit different negotiation situations, in the next chapter.

> ". . . I believe that negotiating is not a game. It's a business relationship in action. And nothing can kill a negotiation more quickly and more completely than a me-against-you attitude. While the 'gotcha' approach may work in a single transaction, it is hardly likely to produce a successful, ongoing business relationship. Over time, both partners have to win. Otherwise, the loser will drop out."
>
> —Williams, M. (1987, September 1). How I Learned to Stop Worrying and Love Negotiating. *Inc. Magazine.* Retrieved from http://www.inc.com/magazine/19870901/3846.html.

What Makes Someone a Good Negotiator?

One way to understand how to be an effective negotiator is to study people who have a reputation of being good negotiators. Rackham observed 48 negotiators who were identified as being "effective" negotiators in 102 labor-management negotiation sessions.[8] He found that skilled negotiators:

- Spend over three times as much time as average negotiators anticipating common ground issues during the planning stages of a negotiation;
- Establish settlement ranges rather than a fixed settlement point;
- Avoid the use of "irritators"—words or phrases that are intended to persuade but that serve only to irritate the other negotiator—in face-to-face negotiations;
- Tend to make fewer counterproposals during the early stages of face-to-face negotiations;
- Avoid defend/attack behaviors during negotiations;
- Are concerned about avoiding misunderstandings during the negotiations;
- Ask nearly twice as many questions during negotiations compared with average negotiators; and
- Share internal information—feelings, perceptions, emotions, and so on—about what's going on in her or his mind with the other negotiator.

Rackham's study suggests that skilled negotiators view negotiations as a partnership with the other negotiator and not as a competitive game. Less

Traits of effective/ successful negotiators
genuine, flexible, ethical, an active listener, and curious. This is not an exhaustive list, but a negotiator who has these five traits is well on their way to being a successful negotiator.

skilled or average negotiators use irritators to persuade the other person to see things their way. Telling the other negotiator that you have made a "generous," "reasonable," or "fair" offer is an irritator because the underlying message is that the other person is not generous, reasonable, or fair. Skilled negotiators understand what they want to accomplish in a negotiation. They think about what they can offer the other negotiator to reach an agreement. Skilled negotiators ask questions aimed at identifying what is important to the other negotiator, work to exchange information with the other person, and avoid making personal attacks.

TAKE AWAY: *Rackham's study emphasizes that effective negotiators tend to use more "cooperative" type skills in negotiation than confrontational or competitive tactics. Cooperative people can, therefore, be effective negotiators.*

Through our study of negotiations and our observations of a variety of negotiations students, we have identified five traits as being important for negotiation success. A good negotiator is genuine, flexible, ethical, an active listener, and curious.

1. **Genuine:** You have to be yourself at the negotiations table. We all have different strengths and weaknesses in negotiation. Trying to copy someone else's approach to negotiations will not lead to success. A cooperative person can be effective in price-only business transactions. Competitive negotiators can likewise be effective in situations that require relationship-building skills. What is important is that you understand and work with your general tendencies at the bargaining table when analyzing a negotiation situation and preparing a strategy.

   Inexperienced negotiators frequently try to imitate the style of negotiators who they know to be successful. One of the authors learned about the value of developing his own style shortly after graduating from law school. He worked for a law firm that was known for its expertise in representing employers in collective bargaining sessions with labor unions. The author's mentor advised him of the best way to be a good negotiator, which included walking out on the labor union during negotiations. This trick, according to the author's mentor—let's call him Charlie Smith—"always worked" because it made the labor union reevaluate

Senator Dan Quayle: " . . . I have as much experience in the Congress as Jack Kennedy did when he sought the presidency . . ."

Senator Lloyd Bentsen: "Senator, I served with Jack Kennedy, I knew Jack Kennedy, Jack Kennedy was a friend of mine. Senator, you are no Jack Kennedy . . ."

—1988 Vice Presidential Debate. (1988, October 5). Commission on Presidential Debates. Retrieved from http://www.debates.org/index.php?page=october-5-1988-debate-transcripts.

its position and make concessions to management. The author decided to use this trick when he started representing management clients in labor negotiations. In his first labor Xnegotiations, the author timed his walk-out during the third bargaining session. After receiving the union's proposal, the author decried how "unreasonable" the labor union had been and started walking toward the door. As he neared the door, the author turned around to see the labor union's negotiation team laughing—not the response the author anticipated. At that point, the labor union's chief negotiator, paraphrasing the previous exchange between the candidates at the 1988 Vice President Debate, told the author, "I know Charlie Smith, Charlie Smith is a friend of mine, you are no Charlie Smith. Now, get back here and start negotiating."

The moral of this story is that we have our own negotiation style. Although we can learn from other people, copying someone else's approach won't lead to negotiation success. An effective negotiator has to be genuine.

2. **Flexible:** Even the most experienced negotiator knows that the best-planned negotiation strategy may have to change. Sometimes a competitive negotiation with "strangers" becomes a problem-solving negotiation with "friends." Think about a time when you were trying to find someone to share the cost of gas for your drive back home following the end of the semester. You posted a sign in your residence hall indicating that you were looking for riders. A student called to ask about riding back with you. Since you didn't know this student personally, your first offer was to have him pay at least half of the cost of gas. You also expected the other student to have someone pick him up at your house, rather than make a special trip to drop him off at his home. What if in talking to the student you discovered that you had mutual friends or were in the same academic major. You actually like this person. When he asks if you could drop him off at his house since his family will be on vacation when you arrive, you say, "No problem." All of a sudden, what was once a transaction with a stranger has the feel of a conversation with a "friend."

> "I've learned not to push a losing argument to the end because it allows the other person to become even more locked into his position . . . If you find yourself unable to persuade the other party, it's time to back off for a while and design another approach. At the end of the process you want to be able to describe the outcome as mutually satisfying—that both parties used give and take."
>
> —Sports Agent Leigh Steinberg, quoted in Strout, E. (2002, September). The closer. *Sales & Marketing Management, 154*(9), reprinted in Lewicki, R. J., Barry, B., & Saunders, D. M. (2007). *Negotiation: Readings, exercises and cases* (5th ed., pp. 283–289, 286). New York: McGraw-Hill Irwin.

3. **Ethical:** While you don't have to be best friends with the other negotiator, it is important that you be able to trust what the other negotiator tells you. You can trust a good negotiator to keep her or his word during a

"Never lie when negotiating, because lies catch up with you. Be direct."

—Former United Nations Ambassador Bill Richardson, quo quoted in Richardson, B., with Ruby, M. (2005). *Between worlds: The making of an American life* (p. 219). New York: Penguin Group.

negotiation. It is also important that you don't lie during negotiations and that you negotiate with an understanding of the different options that are fair to you and to the other negotiator. As stated by famous sports attorney Bob Woolf:

Just never compromise on your principles. You've got to develop a reputation for being smart and honest—so people know you won't renegotiate, you won't play tricks. You can't play tricks, because you'll probably be going back to these people again—or to someone they know. Your good reputation is incredibly important.[9]

4. **Active Listener:** Active listening means listening to understand what the other person has to say.[10] A good negotiator listens to understand and asks questions to check on that understanding.[11] If you worked at a shoe store, you would need to be an active listener to sell shoes. You would ask customers what type of shoe they were looking to buy, ask them to try on some shoes they were interested in, and then ask questions about the look and fit of the shoes. Based on the answers to these questions, you might look for a different style of shoe or find a different size of shoe for the customer. At the end of this conversation, you would hope for an outcome that was a win for both you (a sale and possibly a commission) and the customer (a stylish pair of shoes).

"The main thing in any negotiation is to never assume you know the other side's position. Listen first. Don't do anything. Just sit there and listen."

—Paul Tagliabue, Former National Football League (NFL) Commissioner, quoted in Greenfeld, K. T. (2006, January 23). The big man. *Sports Illustrated Magazine.* Retrieved from http://sportsillustrated.cnn.com/vault/article/magazine/MAG1108538/index.htm.

5. **Curious:** One of the difficult things in negotiation is to identify what you want and to determine what the other person may want. "Why" you want something is called an interest. We hope that you are able to negotiate "better deals" after you read this book. Better deals are those that satisfy as many of the negotiators' (yours and theirs) interests as possible. Many negotiators don't continue to look for new options to a negotiation once they reach an initial agreement. This is why being curious helps a negotiator ask questions that will help put the many pieces of a negotiation into place.

Former star of the *Hardball* television program, Chris Matthews, offered a study of successful politicians in his book, *Life's a Campaign.* Successful politicians, Matthews notes, understand the "deep human need to be paid attention to"[12] and are naturally curious people.

People think of politicians as big talkers. The folks who win elections are big listeners. They know the way to a stranger's heart is to display some spark of interest in them. It's not all pretense. The best of them are genuinely curious about other people, including those citizens who can't vote.[13]

"In all my years of doing deals, a few rules and lessons have emerged. Most important, always try to put yourself in the other person's shoes. It's vital to understanding in depth what the other side really wants out of the deal."

—Business Executive and Entrepreneur, Wayne Huizenga, quoted in Sebenius, J. K. (2001, April). Six habits of merely effective negotiators. *Harvard Business Review*, p. 89.

In the next chapter, we will look at how to identify your basic negotiation style and discuss a "situational" approach to negotiations.

CHAPTER SUMMARY

In this chapter we explored different reasons why many people fear or hate to negotiate. We also reviewed different definitions of "negotiation" to help you better identify the existence of situations when negotiation skills are needed. We closed the chapter by looking at the type of skills that distinguish effective from less effective negotiators.

Questions/Exercises

1. Identify a negotiation in which your actions, or the actions of the other person in the negotiation, was motivated by a "fixed pie assumption."

2. You are studying in London as part of a two-week study-abroad program. There are three other students living in your London flat, all of whom you know from your home university in the United States. You want to do well in your course but also want to see as many of the historic sites in London as you can. Rather than buy souvenirs, you prefer to take pictures of the different places you have been and then post your pictures on your social networking site.

   Your roommates like to do things as a group. One roommate is on a strict budget and prefers visiting as many free places (e.g., museums) as possible. The other roommate likes to party and buy new clothes and seems to have quite a lot of money to spend while in London. The third roommate is still suffering from jet lag and favors taking afternoon naps.

   You have proposed to visit three sites that are in relatively close proximity after class today: Harrods department store, the Victoria and Albert Museum, and the Natural History Museum. For dinner, you suggest going to a restaurant that offers Japanese ramen noodles fare. As you can guess, your roommates are not in complete agreement with you. Not everyone wants to go to three places in one afternoon. One student "hates museums," while another "hates to shop." One roommate wants to go to out for Italian food, another wants to visit an American-styled barbecue restaurant, and the third roommate prefers to eat at an upscale restaurant near Harrods.

What makes this situation a negotiation?

3. Think about someone you know who you consider to be a good negotiator. This may be a parent, someone you have worked for, a politician, a businessperson you have seen on television, or a friend of yours. What specific skills or characteristics make this person a good negotiator?

4. In the movie *Erin Brockovich* (2000), attorney Ed Masry meets with another attorney who represents a company that Mr. Masry is suing on behalf on his client. During this meeting, the company's attorney advises Masry that the company is willing to settle the lawsuit for $250,000, the $250,000 is "more than a fair offer," and the offer was "final and more than fair" (https://www.youtube.com/watch?v=5Jdk3riKKwo). Why might the company's offer (and its attorney's justification) to Masry be viewed as an "irritator"?

5. Your accounting firm has done the auditing work for a local company for nearly 25 years. Last week, you received a letter from the new chief financial officer of the company, demanding that you cut your auditing rates by 25%. Yesterday, when you called the chief financial officer to talk about her letter; she said, "Can't you read? Your auditing fees are way too high for us. If you don't cut them by 25%, we will have to bid out the auditing work. In fact, I know that there is another accounting firm in town whose auditing rates are 25% lower than your rates." After this call, you are furious. Who does the chief financial officer think she is? She is totally ignoring the good work your firm has done for her company over the past 25 years. There is no way your firm can cut its auditing rates by 25% without creating a precedent with the firm's other clients. You also think her claim about another accounting firm in town whose auditing rates are 25% lower than the rates your firm charges is a bluff.

You have a meeting with the chief financial officer next week. Based on these facts, do you consider this to be a negotiation? Assuming that this situation will require negotiation skills, how do you propose to prepare for this meeting with the chief financial officer?

Endnotes

1. Thompson, L. L. (2009). *The mind and heart of the negotiator* (4th ed., p. 179). Upper Saddle River, NJ: Prentice Hall.

2. Carr, A. Z. (January–February, 1968). Is business bluffing ethical? *Harvard Business Review, 46,* 143–153; MacMillan, D. (2008, June 19). How to win at poker and business. *BusinessWeek.com.* Retrieved from http://www.businessweek.com/managing/content/jun2008/ca20080619_339630.htm.

3. Shell, G. R. (2006). *Bargaining for advantage: Negotiation strategies for reasonable people* (p. 6). New York: Penguin Group.

4. Lewicki, R. J., Barry, B., & Saunders, D. M. (2010). *Negotiation* (6th ed., p. 3). New York: McGraw-Hill Irwin.

5. Ury, W. (1993). *Getting past no: Negotiating with difficult people* (p. 111). New York: Bantam Books.

6. Condon, B. (2009, June 8). Haggle economy: buyers strike back. *Forbes, 183,* 26–27.

7. Bell, J. (2009, September 8). NFLPA leader chides league: let's start negotiating CBA. *USA Today.com.* Retrieved from http://www. usatoday.com/sports/football/nfl/2009-09-08-nflpa-dsmith_N.htm.

8. Rackham, N. (1980). *The behavior of successful negotiators.* London: Huthwaite Research Group Ltd in Lewicki, R. J., Saunders, D. M., & Minton, J. W. (Eds.). (2007). *Negotiation: Readings, exercises, and cases* (5th ed., pp. 171–182). New York: McGraw-Hill Irwin.

9. Hopkins, M. S. (1989, February 1). How to negotiate practically anything. *Inc. Magazine. com.* Retrieved from http://www.inc.com/magazine/19890201/5526.html.

10. McGookin, S. (2007, September 17). Talking sense. *Forbes.com.* Retrieved from http://www.forbes.com/2007/09/17/ross-negotiations-statecraft-lead-cx_sm_0917ross.html.

11. Reeves, S. (2005, July 5). The ABCs of negotiating. *Forbes.com.* Retrieved from http://www.forbes.com/2005/07/07/careers-negotiating-work-cx_sr_0707bizbasics.html.

12. Matthews, C. (2007). *Life's a campaign: What politics has taught me about friendship, rivalry, reputation and success* (p. xiv). New York: Random House.

13. Matthews, C. (2007). *Life's a campaign: What politics has taught me about friendship, rivalry, reputation and success* (p. 45). New York: Random House.

2

What Type of Driver Are You?: Negotiation Styles, Motivations and Assumptions

Remember when you learned to drive? You may have been fearful of getting behind the wheel, and when you did, you were overly cautious. As a result, you were likely to proceed slowly and to experience many stops and starts before finding a level of comfort when driving. On the other hand, you may have been the overconfident and reckless type of driver and started pedal to the metal, showing little regard for the rules of the road or your own safety. If so, you likely received some serious admonition from your driving instructor or, worse, a warning or ticket from the local police. Our point is that regardless of the rules of the road, we don't all drive the same way. Each of us brings our own personality or disposition to our driving style, and we have to learn to share the road with those who may drive differently. So it is with our negotiation or conflict handling styles.

CHAPTER OBJECTIVES

- To analyze and understand your conflict handling and negotiation style
- To know when your style will serve you well and when it will not
- To learn how to use the different styles strategically
- To understand social motives and how they may affect negotiation strategy
- To understand how the nature of your relationship with the other will affect your conflict handling and negotiation style
- To understand the role that assumptions and stereotypes play in the negotiation process

KEY TERMS

Conflict handling styles
Accommodation
Avoiding
Compromise
Competing
Problem solving/collaboration
Dual-concern model

Social motives
Win-win
Win-lose
Stereotypes
Assumptions
Self-fulfilling prophecy

CHAPTER CASE

Negotiating the purchase of a used car is a common example of the kind of negotiation many people don't like. But contrast that with negotiating with your friends about where to have dinner or where to go on Spring break. Consider further negotiating with your partner or a family member, what is important to you now? It's likely that each of these scenarios elicits a different feeling in you and a different approach to the negotiation. Why is that? Can you identify and name the factors that change the way we feel about and approach negotiations? Imagine negotiating with a team that you value being a part of and are committed to producing quality results versus a team that you are required to be on and frankly lack commitment to the results.

■ ■ ■ ■

Conflict Handling Styles

Conflict handling styles
the different approaches that individuals take to resolve conflicts or to handle negotiations. Most people have a preferred style, but a good negotiator can adapt their style to the situation.

Win-lose
an outcome of a negotiation where one person gets what they want and the other person receives nothing (or very little).

Some people avoid conflict at all costs and avoid confrontation whenever possible. *Avoiders* may view the negotiation process in and of itself as a conflict to be avoided, and by doing so, they are unlikely to achieve their goals. Others love the challenge of a conflict or negotiation opportunity and treat the situation as a game to be won. *Competitors* excel in **win-lose** situations and may use a variety of contentious or hardball tactics, such as posturing, deception, threats, and false promises to achieve their goals. Moreover, they have a tendency to view conflict and negotiation situations as win-lose even when they are not. That is, some cling to their competitive style regardless of the situation.

Some people are *accommodators* and prefer to give in or give the other what they want in order to keep the peace. Everyone likes an accommodator, but one has to question whether the accommodating person can ever achieve personal goals if always putting the relationship with the other above his or her own goals and objectives.

Others prefer to *collaborate* when faced with a conflict or negotiation situation. Collaborators often see such situations as a problem or challenge to be solved. As such, they gather information from all parties involved in the conflict and seek to achieve an outcome that everyone is happy with, or more pragmatically, one that everyone can live with. It is not the case that collaborators don't care about their own outcomes and interests; they do. However, they are less likely to view conflict and negotiation as win-lose situations. Rather they work to find mutually acceptable win-win outcomes.

Finally there are the *compromisers*. Compromisers are those people who value equality and fairness. They believe in give and take, and as a result, they are willing to accept outcomes that are somewhere in the middle. They rarely, if ever, achieve their high goals but are content to know that the other side also had to make concessions in order to reach agreement.

What Type of Negotiator Are You?

If you were forced to select one negotiation or conflict handling style as most resembling your own, you could probably do so without difficulty. Each of us is likely to have a style that comes naturally and with which we are comfortable. Nevertheless, you may be able to think of situations where you deviated from that style, either because you thought the situation called for it or because you felt another style might be more effective in helping you achieve your goals.

There are a number of conflict style assessments that you can take online or in a pamphlet form, and your instructor may require you to take one of these.[1,2] What these assessment tools have in common is that they ask you to imagine a conflict situation and then ask you to choose one of two behavioral responses to that situation. There are a series of such questions that pit each possible response style with each of the others. You end up with a score on each of the five styles, and the style with the highest score is considered your dominant style. It is likely that you will have at least one other style that you score quite high on as well and others that you will score lower on. Just because you have a dominant style doesn't mean that you will always use it or that you never use your less preferred styles. Most of us are flexible and can adapt our negotiating style as the situation demands.

After filling out one of these assessments students often ask, "Which one is the best?" or "Which one is right?" or "What does it mean if I score high on both Competition and Accommodation?" To answer that question, we turn to Figure 2.1, which depicts the **dual-concern model** based on the work of

Dual-concern model

a two-dimensional model that plots conflict handling styles as a function of level of concern for own outcomes and interests (Assertiveness) and as a function of the concern for the other's outcomes and interests (Cooperativeness).

FIGURE 2.1 The Dual Concern Model

Pruitt.[3] This model assumes negotiators have two areas of concern when they negotiate. First, they have a concern (which can be high or low) for their own outcomes, and second they have a level of concern for the other's outcomes. Figure 2.1 plots the five styles on a two-dimensional space, where the y-axis is the level of assertiveness, or level of concern you have for your own interests and outcomes, and the x-axis is the level of cooperativeness, representing the level of concern you have for the other person involved in the conflict or negotiation.

In this figure we can see that each negotiation style has its place as a function of level of concern for own and other's interests and outcomes. It is not that some styles are good and others are bad. Rather, each makes sense in certain situations. Let's work our way through this figure and see why this is so.

First, imagine a situation where you have little concern for your own interests and outcomes and little concern for the other person's as well. It is somewhat challenging to think of such situations where there is no self interest, but often petty or irrelevant issues arise that simply are not worth our effort to resolve. For example, you may be indifferent toward a discussion about the type of logo to adopt for your service organization or where to hold your meetings. Your indifference about these issues, as well as your indifference as to whether others get what they want, may lead you to avoid the discussion altogether. It simply isn't worth your time and effort. In such (rare) cases, **avoiding** is an appropriate strategy.

On the other hand, if you have a high level of concern for either your own or the other person's interests and outcomes (you really care where the meetings for your service organization are held), then avoiding is clearly a suboptimal strategy. By avoiding the issue, you are forgoing the necessary communication and information sharing to understand the other's point of view, as well having the opportunity to express your own, both of which are critical to resolving the conflict. In sum, *avoiding is a good strategy* when neither you nor the other person cares much about the issue, or if one or the other of you is very angry at the moment and need a cooling-off period. *Avoiding is a poor strategy* when you care about an issue but don't speak up or when you consistently use this strategy to sidestep the conflicts in your life.

Second, in situations where you have high concerns for your own interests and outcomes and little concern for the other's (think, buying a car from a used car dealer) then **competing** is an appropriate strategy. It makes little sense to be concerned about how well the dealer is doing in the negotiation over the price of a car you want to buy; it is, after all, your money, and you want to spend as little of it as possible. Furthermore, you can rest assured that the used car dealer will accept an offer only if it is in the dealer's best interest to do so. As we will discuss more fully in the next chapter, competing makes sense when the situation is viewed as a **zero-sum game**, with one person winning and the other losing. Zero-sum situations are often referred to as a **fixed pie situation**, suggesting that the resource to be divided is fixed.

Avoiding
a conflict handling style where the individual is uncomfortable with conflict and avoids confrontation altogether. This style only makes sense if the issue is unimportant to both negotiators. Avoiding the conflict rarely makes it go away.

Competing
a conflict handling style where the negotiator looks out for his or her own interests and cares little about the relationship with the other person. Competitors like to "win" and they do well in one-time negotiations, but less so when there are multiple issues and the relationship with the other is important.

Interestingly, strong competitors often see all situations as win-lose zero-sum and hence, use that strategy regardless of the situation.

It is easy to imagine, however, situations where you have concerns for both your own and the other's outcome (you and your friend want to attend a movie that you will both enjoy). In such situations it would be harmful to the relationship to use a competitive strategy where you force your will on your friend. You might win in the short run but lose in the long run (no one wants to be friends with a selfish bully). Thus, *competing is a useful strategy* when you need to stand firm (when something is important to you) and maintaining a good relationship with the other is of low or little importance. *Competing is a poor strategy* if the situation is not zero-sum and there is the possibility of both parties doing well by working together. Competing is not likely to payoff in the long term if you use this strategy repeatedly with someone you care about or will need to interact with in the future.

Third, let's consider **accommodating** as strategy. The **dual-concern model** implies that accommodating is appropriate when concern for other's outcomes is high and concern for your own outcomes is low. Generally accommodation can be thought of as "giving in," so it is helpful to think of situations where accommodation makes sense. As the dual-concern model suggests we are more willing to accommodate in situations where we have little self-interest. Negotiators who use accommodating as a consistent strategy would have little or nothing to show for their efforts, and humans are rarely that altruistic. Rather, accommodating makes sense in the context of a long-term relationship.

Think of a marriage or other close relationship. You may be willing to accommodate your significant other on an issue she cares passionately about (agreeing to attend the art museum opening with her tonight) because you know that when something is important to you, she will accommodate your wishes in the future (attending the car races with you next week). Accommodating then, can be a practical strategy as long as you engage in turn taking over time. To do this, one needs to do some internal bookkeeping such that concessions are reciprocated. Obviously, when only one person

Accommodation
a conflict handling style where the individual gives in to the other. This is not an effective style in a one-time negotiation; however, if there is an ongoing relation-ship between the negotiators, one can (and should) accom-modate the other if the issue is relatively unimportant and the relationship matters a lot.

accommodates this will result in an asymmetry that is likely to harm the relationship.

Surprisingly to some, accommodating can make sense in a business setting. Imagine your long-term supplier calls and informs you that he is going to be a week late with a delivery and requests that you not penalize him for this delay. To accommodate the supplier you would need to be in a situation where waiting will not hurt your own outcomes; say, for example, you have plenty of the supplier's inventory still on your store's shelves. So, in this instance you are willing to grant the supplier's request because you realize that sometime in the future you may need to call your supplier and request a rush delivery without charge. The supplier then will be much more willing to say yes to your request due to your prior accommodating behavior. Obviously, this would not be an effective strategy if there was no opportunity for reciprocity. In sum, *accommodating is an effective strategy* when concern for your own interests and outcomes is low and there is an ongoing relationship with the other person. *Accommodating is an ineffective strategy* if concern for your own outcomes is high **or** if you don't have an ongoing relationship with the other person.

Fourth, **collaboration** (sometimes referred to as **problem solving**) is most likely to occur when there is high concern for both one's own and others' interests and outcomes. Think of working on a group project where there are conflicting ideas about the best way to proceed. If team members value one another's inputs, they will give them serious consideration and work together to find a mutually beneficial solution, rather than treating the situation as one to be won at the expense of the others' ideas. This style requires time to work through and consider interests and creative outcomes. Some people are problem solvers by nature and enjoy the challenge of finding mutually beneficial solutions. They may instinctively care about the interests of others. Thus, collaboration is an effective strategy when the stakes are high (you care very much about the outcome) and maintaining a positive relationship is equally important.

Collaboration may not be the best strategy when the issue is a trivial one or if the person across the table is not also willing to collaborate. Collaboration requires both parties to share information and work together, which usually requires a certain level of trust and respect between negotiators. If these are missing, collaboration will be difficult. In sum, *collaboration is an effective strategy* when the stakes are high and the relationship is valued. *Collaboration will be difficult* if the other person is unwilling to adapt to the strategy or if there is a lack of trust.

Fifth, is the **compromise** conflict handling style. Compromisers often engage in give and take to keep the peace. Or they may be very concerned with fairness and equality. Compromise may be the only effective strategy when you are negotiating over a single issue, such as price, for example. If you are hoping to pay only $10 for a widget and the seller is asking $20, you are likely to engage in a series of concessions where you end up somewhere

Problem solving/ collaboration this style works best when negotiators care a lot about their own interests AND they value the relationship with the other negotiator. This strategy works well when there are multiple issues to be negotiated and negotiators have different preferences and priorities over the issues.

Compromise is meeting someone halfway. If there is only a single issue to be negotiated and the negotiators' positions are diametrically opposed, compromise is probably the only feasible solution. Compromisers value equality and fairness.

in the middle, say $15. Thus, compromise in this case leaves you with only half of what you would have liked to achieve in the negotiation.

Some negotiators confuse compromise with collaboration. That is, they might judge the $15 agreement as a **win-win** because each party gave up an equal amount. But this isn't really true as each person gave up something to reach agreement. As we will see in Chapter 3, collaboration is more likely to occur when there are multiple issues to be negotiated. When negotiating over a single issue, compromise is often the best you can do. In sum, *compromise is an effective strategy* when the resource is fixed and getting something is better than getting nothing. *Compromise is a poor strategy* when there are multiple issues and the situation is not zero-sum.

Many people see compromise in a positive light, especially if they position themselves with a high opening offer so that they will end up where they wanted to be anyway. In a *For Better or Worse*[4] comic strip, Michael and his mother are negotiating over a time for him to come home on a weeknight. He starts with 11:00 P.M. and she counters with 8:30 P.M.; they make concessions until they agree on 10:00 P.M. Each walks away saying, "I love it when I win." Presumably, each expected to end up at 10:00 P.M. when they positioned themselves with their respective opening offers.

Not everyone sees compromise as a positive outcome. In the *Calvin and Hobbes*[5] comic strip, after they agree to a 50/50 split of the winnings of an art project, Calvin walks away saying, "A good compromise leaves everybody mad." Some view a compromise as a glass half full; others see it as half empty.

Win-win
an outcome of a negotiation that gives both parties what they want.

TAKE AWAY: *Most of us have a preferred style of negotiating. Good negotiators can access the situation so they know when their style will be appropriate and when they need to switch to one that is more appropriate given the situation. Over time, experienced negotiators gain a level of comfort with several different styles.*

■ ■ ■ ■

Social Motivational Orientation

Negotiation is often about the division of resources between two or more parties. In some situations a person in power or control may get to make the decision about how to divide resources and the other person has no say over the matter. What are your motives if you get to decide how to divide resources between you and another person? This is a question that has generated a significant amount of research in social psychology for over 40 years, beginning with the early work of Messick and McClintock.[6] Before discussing this research in more detail we would like you to go to the online component to this chapter and fill out an instrument called a "9-trial Decision Task." This task will ask you to make a series of nine choices that will determine the goods you and someone else will receive. An example of this decision task is displayed below:

9-Trial Decision Task

Choose one letter:	A	B	C
You Get	500	500	550
Other Gets	100	500	300

In this example if you choose "A," you will get 500 goods and the other person will get 100; if you choose "B," you will get 500 and the other person also receives 500; and if you choose "C," you will receive 550 and other person will receive 300. All the trials you will do will have this same basic structure. Please proceed to the website now.

How did you do on this 9-trial task? How did you feel about taking it? One of the first things students usually say is that they would have done better (or enjoyed the task more) if they had known what the *goal* of the task was. Another common response is, "Who is the other person?" These are reasonable questions that in most situations would help us decide what the "right" choice is. However, in this task, there is no right choice. Rather, the creators of the task were interested in knowing how people will respond in the absence of information about a goal and who the other person is. The underlying assumption is that in the absence of such information people will go with their base instincts. That is, people will make assumptions about the goal of the task. Some will assume that the goal is to choose the option that gives them the most, others will assume that the goal is to get more than the other person, and others will assume that goal is to maximize the total which in this task is the option that gives both parties an equal amount. Others say that the choice they made would be different if the other person was their toughest competitor in a business situation than if the other person was their mother, and we hope that is true. But in the absence of this information what *did* you assume?

The online component of this chapter will give you a score on the three social motives that were measured in this task: individualism, competition, and cooperation (sometimes referred to as the pro-social choice). If you chose the individualist option every time, you would have scored 9/9 on individualism and 0 on the other two social motivations. Sometimes people will choose only 6/9 of any one particular social orientation. For research purposes, if 6 out of 9 are chosen consistently, then you will be classified as an individualist, a competitor, or a cooperator. If you did not score at least 6 out of 9 for any one orientation, then the researchers would consider you unclassifiable; that is, you would not be classified as having a dominant orientation. Most people, however, do have a dominant social orientation, just as they may have a dominant negotiation style. As it is with negotiation styles, so it is with social motivations—none are normatively good or bad, but each will be more appropriate in different situations and with different people. So if your score shows you to be a competitor—that is, you consistently chose the distribution that maximized the difference between you and the other person—then you will need to be aware that this social motivation may get you in trouble if the goal of a particular situation is to maximize joint gain or if the other person is someone with whom you wish to cultivate a positive relationship.

Individualism, cooperation, and competition are only 3 of 9 possible **social motives** that an individual may display. A circumplex of these motives, based on the work of McClintock and van Avermaet,[7] is shown in Figure 2.2. In this figure, social motives are plotted as vectors on a two-dimensional space; where one dimension is maximizing or minimizing own outcomes and the other is maximizing or minimizing the other's outcomes. The other motives are less commonly displayed in social interaction. For example, pure altruism is rare outside of family ties.[8] Aggression is a more extreme, and

Social motives reveal one's preferences for distributions of resources between oneself and another person. The three primary social motivations studied are cooperation, competition and individualism.

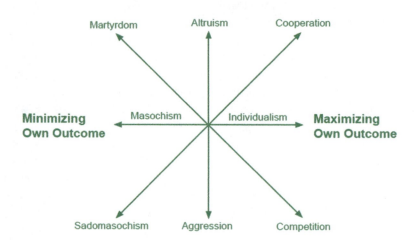

FIGURE 2.2 A Circumplex of Social Motives

hence less socially acceptable, form of competition. Masochism (desire to harm oneself) and sadomasochism (desire to harm self and others) are pathological motives that fall more into the realm of clinical psychology than normal social interaction.

Research on social motives has shown that one's social orientation can affect negotiation strategy and outcomes. Cooperative people tend to make more concessions,[9] yet they have also been shown to work better together in maximizing the pie.[10] The more cooperators there are in a group increases the likelihood that more problem solving information will be exchanged.[11] Cooperators use more integrative (win-win) strategies, offer more proposals, and use less contentious tactics than competitors do.[12] They tend to reciprocate cooperative behavior in negotiation more than individualists and competitors do.[13] Not surprisingly, competitors, and to a lesser extent individualists, tend to do better in distributive (win-lose) negotiations. Distributive bargaining and integrative negotiations are discussed in detail in Chapters 3 and 4.

■ ■ ■ ■

Relationships: What about the Other?

Considerable time and space have been allotted in this chapter to consider the appropriateness of various negotiation styles partly as a function of our relationship with the other person. Why is it so important to consider this relationship?

Our relationships with others can vary along a dimension from a complete stranger on one end to our closest family member on the other. If the person you are negotiating with is a complete stranger, you are likely to be less open with the information you share until you have determined that this person is trustworthy. This determination of trust could take several interactions between the two of you. We discuss the role and importance of trust in Chapter 8, but suffice it to say, in the absence of trust, it will be difficult to achieve collaborative win-win outcomes.

When we know someone well, we have a history of prior interactions that will guide us in our choice of negotiation strategy. If you know, for example, that your sister always lies to get her way, then you may be as self-protective and as competitive with her as you would be with a complete stranger. Alternatively, a competitive interaction with a close valued friend is likely to make you uncomfortable, because you might risk the relationship by doing so.

There are clearly other types of relationships between these two extreme endpoints. In some situations you may not know the person you are negotiating with, but you may know that she belongs to the same sorority that you belong to and this common group membership may lead you to be more trusting than you would if she were in a different sorority. On the other hand, you may be more willing to share more information with someone who belongs to any sorority than you would be with someone who wasn't in the Greek system. Shared group membership may lead negotiators to make assumptions about possible shared values that in turn may lead us to treat the person as a trusted other even if we don't know him or her well.

If shared group membership is irrelevant to the situation being negotiated, it could be a mistake to assume that shared values in one context will naturally extend to other contexts. This is why in all negotiations we must consider both the relationship and the situation when developing our strategy.

The Role of Assumptions in Negotiation

Individuals make **assumptions** about how others may behave based on a variety of criteria. The assumptions could be based on one's prior interactions with an individual, in which case the assumptions may be quite accurate. In other cases where we know little about the other person we may make assumptions based on their gender, their ethnicity, their group memberships, their national culture, and so forth. In such cases our assumptions could be wrong. For example, some may adhere to the stereotype that women are always relationship-oriented and thus unlikely to behave competitively. Accordingly, such a person might prepare for an open sharing of information in the negotiation and be unpleasantly surprised when the woman does not reciprocate and instead uses competitive tactics to achieve her goals with little regard for her negotiation counterpart.

Assumptions are often made about individuals based on stereotypes, or other imperfect information. In negotiation it is important to check out your assumptions before assuming they are true.

Stereotypes

beliefs about a group or culture that are based on generalized knowledge that are assumed to be true of any individual from that group or culture. The problem with stereotyping is that the central tendency of any group is usually not true of any one individual from that group, yet people interact with the person as if it was true.

Self-fulfilling prophecy

a situation where you assume something is true of an individual (like, they are competitive) and you treat them in a way consistent with that assumption (you act competitively toward them) and by doing so bring out the very behavior you assumed to be true (they act competitively toward you because you acted competitively toward them).

Similarly, we may have strong stereotypes about people from other cultures. **Stereotypes** can be thought of as statistical average of a group's tendencies applied to an individual from that group. As such, stereotypes may provide some helpful information if we know nothing at all about the other person. Yet, it is important to realize that although some stereotypes may be based on a kernel of truth, it is risky to assume that the broad stereotype will apply to any given individual. Think of your stereotype of the "American negotiator." Who comes to mind? When we ask those in our classes, a common response is John Wayne. Why? We would argue that John Wayne exemplifies the tough, yet fair-minded rugged individualism that captures the stereotype of the American spirit. Notice the qualities of the John Wayne stereotype. First, he is male; second, he is tall; third, he is strong; fourth, he is usually armed; fifth, he wears a cowboy hat; and sixth, he is astride a horse. Suppose further that someone held this stereotype of the American negotiator and made a number of assumptions about how he would negotiate and prepared for the negotiation based on those assumptions. What would this person do if upon arriving at the negotiation, the petite American Olympic gymnast Shawn Johnson was waiting at the negotiating table? Needless to say, constructing a negotiation strategy on assumptions one makes based on a stereotype would be misguided at best in this case and potentially disastrous if one does not make a quick recovery. We need to have a plan B in our back pocket if our assumptions turn out to be wrong.

Too often negotiators proceed with the negotiation process as if the assumptions were true and as a result find themselves in a **self-fulfilling prophecy**.[14] A self-fulfilling prophecy occurs when we hold an assumption such as "I expect this person to be competitive." If I believe this assumption is true, then I will prepare a competitive strategy and use competitive tactics with this person to protect myself from being exploited. As a result, the person will also behave competitively toward me for the same reason. I observe the other person's competitive behavior and it confirms my prior assumption. Note that I can elicit this behavior whether the person is a competitor or not.

As negotiation teachers we would never tell you not to make assumptions. Assumptions play an important role when there is a lack of information on how another may behave. A good piece of advice, however, is to *treat assumptions as hypotheses to be tested.*

TAKE AWAY: *Test your assumptions about the other party early in the negotiation process; if they aren't verified, you should discard them.*

CHAPTER SUMMARY

■ ■ ■ ■

In this chapter we covered negotiation styles and when each type may be appropriate as a function of the dual-concern model. We also described the concept of social motivation and presented an online task that classified you as either an individualist, a competitor, or a cooperator as a function of your preferences for resource allocations between you and another person. We then gave examples of when those motivations may lead to different negotiation strategies and outcomes. The importance of considering the nature of your relationship with the other person you are negotiating with was emphasized. We discussed the role that assumptions and stereotyping may play in negotiations and when both can get you into trouble if they are incorrect.

Questions/Exercises

1. Using the dual-concern model, identify and explain the negotiation/conflict handling approach that would be most appropriate for the following situations first presented in Chapter 1:

   a. Whenever your roommate's friends come to visit for the weekend, they drink your soda in the refrigerator. No one has ever paid you back or offered to buy you new soda.

   b. You fly to a distant city for a callback job interview. You get to the city; your luggage does not. You are panicked because you need to look your best for the interview. The airline's customer service representative, however, is not giving you the answers you are looking for.

   c. Your parents want you to graduate next May. You, on the other hand, are thinking about changing your major, which will require that you spend an additional semester at the university. You need to talk to your parents, but you have no idea how to tell them about the change in your graduation plans. They will be on campus next week for Family Weekend.

   d. You have taken your final group project for a class to a copy center to have the project bound and copied. When you pick up the copy job, you are short five copies and the copy center employee forgot to include the table of contents page that you left with the order. The final project is due today at 5:00 P.M. and the copy center manager wants you to pay for the extra cost to get the order right. The clock on the wall of the copy center say 4:00 P.M.

   e. The pizza delivery driver brings the wrong order to your apartment—you ordered three combination pizzas, and the pizza delivery driver brought you three vegetarian pizzas. Your friends are coming over in 10 minutes to watch the Super Bowl football game. The pizza delivery driver is asking you to pay full price plus a tip and is waiting on your doorsetp.

   f. You live in a second-story apartment. On the first floor lives an elderly couple who generally go to bed each night around 10:00 P.M. You like to study after 10:00 P.M. The past two days, the couple has placed notes on your door demanding that you "quiet down" at night. You do not think you have been particularly noisy and prefer to study at home rather than go to the university library. The couple has, you feel, avoided talking to you when you have asked to talk about their concerns.

2. If you are more interested in maximizing the relative difference between your own and another's outcomes than you are in maximizing your own outcome you would be considered a/an:

   a. cooperator

   b. individualist

   c. competitor

   d. unclassifiable

3. If two negotiators are both "avoiders," what will be the challenges they face if they are trying to resolve a dispute?

4. Which type of negotiation style would be best suited to resolving a dispute if both parties felt strongly about the outcome and were interested in maintaining a positive relationship with the other?

5. Explain the difference between collaboration and compromise.

Endnotes

1. Thomas, K. W., & Kilmann, R. H. (1974). Thomas-Kilmann Conflict Mode Instrument, XICOM, New York.

2. Russo, E., & Eckler, M. (1994). *The conflict strategies inventory.* King of Prussia, PA: Organizational Design and Development Inc.

3. Pruitt, D. G. (1991) Strategic choice in negotiation. *American Behavioral Scientist, 27,* 167–194.

4. Johnson, L. (1992, February 27). *For Better or Worse.* Universal Press Syndicate.

5. Waterson, B. (1993, May 1). *Calvin and Hobbes.* Universal Press Syndicate.

6. Messick, D. M., & McClintock, C. G. (1968). Motivational basis of choice in experimental games. *Journal of Personality and Social Psychology, 44,* 294–309.

7. McClintock, C. G., & van Avermaet, E. (1982). Social values and rules of fairness: A theoretical perspective. In V. J. Derlega & J. Grezlak (Eds)., *Cooperation and helping behavior* (pp. 43–71). New York: Academic Press.

8. Trivers, R. L. (1971). The evolution of reciprocal altruism. *The Quarterly Review of Biology, 46,* 1–35.

9. Langner, C., & Winter, D. (2001). The motivational basis of concessions and compromise: Archival and laboratory studies. *Journal of Personality and Social Psychology, 81*(4), 711–727.

10. Olekalns, M., & Smith, P. L. (1999). Social value orientations and strategy choices in competitive negotiations. *Personality and Social Psychology Bulletin, 25*(6), 657–668.

11. Weingart, L. R., Brett, J. M., Olekalns, M., & Smith, P. R. (2007). Conflicting social motives in negotiating groups. *Journal of Personality and Social Psychology, 93*(6), 994–1010.

12. Olekalns, M., & Smith, P. L. (1999). Social value orientations and strategy choices in competitive negotiations. *Personality and Social Psychology Bulletin, 25*(6), 657–668.

13. Van Lange, P. A. M. (1999). The pursuit of joint outcomes and equality in outcomes: An integrative model of social value orientation. *Journal of Personality and Social Psychology, 77*(2), 337–349.

14. Merton, R. K. (1968). *Social theory and social structure.* New York: Free Press.

3

Driving the Short Trip Across Town: Principles of Distributive Bargaining

When you are taking a short trip across town, you may check to see if you have your wallet and driver's license, and maybe a coat if it is cold, but other than that you jump in the car and you are off on your trip. If you are getting ready to drive across the country, however, you will likely be more systematic about what you take along. You'll need maps (or a good app on your phone) and hotel reservations, and you'll probably get the car tuned and the tires checked and aligned before heading off. So it is with different types of negotiations. Distributive negotiations, which we cover in this chapter, tend to be like the short, quick trip across town. They are likely to be one-time interactions over a single issue (such as price) with individuals who you do not share a close relationship with. These negotiations are often characterized as zero-sum win-lose situations. They can still be important and require preparation, but they are not as complex as the multi-issue, mixed-motive types of negotiations that we call integrative, which will be discussed in Chapter 4.

CHAPTER OBJECTIVES

- To understand the characteristics of distributive bargaining
- To be able to identify hardball tactics and to know how to counter them
- To understand the role that reference points play in negotiation
- To know when you should make the first offer
- To understand the role of concessions
- To understand fairness norms

KEY TERMS

Distributive negotiations/bargaining
Claiming value
Single-issue negotiations
Contentious or hardball tactics:
    highball/lowball, intimidation,
    bogey, nibble, chicken, and good
    cop/bad cop

Reference points: AL, BATNA, RP, and
    objective information
Bargaining zones and zones of
    potential/possible agreement
Norm of reciprocity
Fairness norms

Distributive bargaining is what most naïve negotiators think of when they think of negotiation. Simple buyer/seller negotiations are typically distributive in nature. Imagine a flea market, a garage sale, or an online sale or swap meet where a seller wants as much money as possible for an item and the buyer would like to pay as little as possible. A savvy buyer would usually not begin a negotiation over price with the seller until she had some idea of the value of the item. Instead, the buyer might scout out if there are similar items for sale and use this information to her advantage. If, in fact, there are good alternatives that she can buy from other sellers, then the buyer would have leverage in this negotiation—if the seller won't accept her offer, she can buy the item from another seller. If the item is unique and rare, and the buyer feels she must have it no matter what, then the seller will have the advantage,

---

Box 3.1

Bargaining

Versus Negotiation[1]

What is the difference between bargaining and negotiation? You may have noticed that in the text, we tend to use the terms "bargaining" and "negotiation" interchangeably. However, some would argue that they have different connotations. Bargaining often brings to mind haggling, such as haggling over the price of a car which many find offensive. Haggling can make one appear unseemly. Still, definitions of bargaining often include the word "negotiation": a "Bargaining—the negotiation of the terms of a transaction or agreement."[2]

Negotiation, on the other hand, seems more nuanced and sophisticated. Negotiations are often perceived as more formal occasions where negotiators are expected to behave in rational and unemotional ways: "Negotiation—the act or process of conferring or discussing to reach agreement in matters of business or state."[3]

What is important, in our opinion, is that both bargaining and negotiation are *processes* that interdependent people engage in to achieve some goal. Goals can be about preferred distribution of resources, services, or behaviors that one will provide the other. Some goals may be as simple as maintaining positive relationships. We also assume that individuals engage in the process because they believe they will be better off than they would if they didn't bargain or negotiate.

especially if he knows that the buyer cannot obtain the item elsewhere and he is aware that the buyer really wants the item.

Although this example seems simple and straightforward, it captures many of the important aspects of distributive bargaining that need to be understood if one is to excel in this type of negotiation.

Characteristics of Distributive Bargaining

We begin with the underlying assumptions and/or characteristics of **distributive bargaining**. The **first** is the assumption is that there is a fixed amount of resources to be divided. This is referred to in the negotiation research literature as the **fixed pie** or **zero-sum** assumption. It is the negotiators' job to come to some agreement about how to slice the resource pie, and what one party gains, the other party loses. As such, it is not surprising the two negotiators may view the other as an adversary or opponent, as each will attempt to claim the biggest share of the pie. Distributive bargaining then constitutes the **"claiming value"** dimension of negotiation.[4]

A **second** assumption about distributive bargaining is that the interests of the parties are diametrically opposed. If this assumption is true, it follows that it is not possible for both parties to achieve their goals; that is, "If you get what you want, then it is not possible for me to get what I want."

Third, distributive bargaining is more likely to occur when negotiators are negotiating over a **single issue**. Why is this so? Imagine for a moment that there are several issues to be negotiated between the two parties. For example, two businesspeople could be negotiating over the price, quality, and delivery time of a product. A seller might want the highest price, not too many specifications on quality, and plenty of time to deliver. The buyer wants the lowest price, a guarantee on quality, and a rush delivery. One could say that the buyer and seller still had diametrically opposed preferences over the three issues. However, if pressed, the seller may agree to the buyer's demand for quality and rush delivery in order to maximize price. Likewise, a buyer may agree to pay top dollar in order to get a guarantee on quality and an early delivery. When there is more than one issue to be negotiated, there is the possibility that negotiators may weight (or rank) the issues differently. Accordingly, they may be able to reach agreement by making trade-offs among the issues. A caveat here is that some very competitive negotiators may see all three issues as distributive ones and be unwilling to make trade-offs regardless. We will discuss multi-issue negotiation in more detail in the next chapter. Suffice it to say, when there is only a single issue to be decided (such as price), the negotiation is much more likely to take on a distributive tone.

A **fourth** assumption, that may not always hold, is that the relationship between the two parties is not a strong one. We are more likely to engage in distributive bargaining with a car salesperson because: (1) we have no prior relationship with the salesperson; (2) we value getting a good price for

Claiming value
this is the amount of the resource being negotiated that is claimed by a negotiator. Negotiators who focus on claiming value are looking to claim as much as possible for themselves.

Single-issue negotiations
a negotiation where there is one issue being negotiated—like the price for a car. These negotiations are often referred to as "distributive" negotiations in that the resource being negotiated (usually money) must be divided or distributed in some way.

Contentious or hardball tactics
these are tactics that negotiators may use to claim as much value for themselves as possible. These tactics are used to undermine, fool, or confuse the other negotiator.

ourselves more than we value the relationship with the salesperson; and (3) if we can't get the price we want, we are willing to walk away because there are other car dealers we can give our business to. We are less likely to engage in hard-nosed bargaining with those whose friendship we value. As suggested in assumption one, those engaged in distributive bargaining often see themselves in a win-lose battle and view the other as an opponent. When the relationship between parties is strong, people may prefer either to avoid the negotiation altogether or to accommodate the other party to preserve the relationship. This is not to imply that those in a close relationship never engage in distributive bargaining; but if they do, they either are willing to risk hurting the relationship because the issue is important to them or believe that the relationship is so strong or that the issue is so minor that the relationship will survive.

A **fifth** characteristic of distributive bargaining is that negotiators may be willing to engage in **contentious** or **hardball tactics** to achieve their goals. We discuss these tactics, and how to deal with them, in the following section.

> **TAKE AWAY:** *Distributive bargaining is more likely to occur when the resource to be divided is fixed, there is only one issue, the relationship is short term, and negotiators' positions are diametrically opposed.*

Contentious and Hardball Tactics

We have all been at the mercy at one time or another of someone who uses hardball tactics. These individuals often resort to such tactics either because they have worked successfully in the past and no one has ever called them on it or because they are feeling desperate and use them as a last resort. We discuss these tactics here, not because we encourage you to add them to your negotiation repertoire, but because you need to be aware of them when they are being used against you. And once you've identified their use, you need to know how you are going to respond.

Highball/Lowball

Negotiators using this tactic begin the negotiation by making an extreme first offer (either a high or a low offer, depending on whether they are the seller or buyer). They do so because they assume it will undermine your confidence in what you think is an appropriate value and that you will not counter with the value you initially intended but move in their direction instead. This tactic can be successful if you are uncertain of the value of the item or issues being negotiated. If you have done your homework and are well prepared, then these extreme offers should not sway you off course. Those who make extreme offers run the risk of the other negotiator simply walking away believing that the negotiator isn't acting in good faith.

What can you do when someone wants to play **highball/lowball**? What you *don't* do is immediately counter with a concession. Instead, you should ask the negotiator to justify the extreme offer. Ask for objective information to support the demand being made. If the negotiator counters with a statement that the offer is "fair," ask why it is fair. Tell the negotiator that a more reasonable offer will need to be made before you will counter.

Highball/lowball
a contentious tactic where a negotiator makes a first offer that is extremely high (if they are the seller) or low (if they are the buyer), in the hopes of convincing the other negotiator that their own goals are unachievable.

TAKE-AWAY: *BE prepared. If you are not, you will not recognize a highball or lowball offer when you see one.*

Box 3.2 The Power of the "Flinch"

In his book, *Secrets of Power Negotiating for Salespeople,* Roger Dawson identifies a series of negotiating rules or "gambits" for successful sales negotiations. These gambits include things such as asking for more than you expect to get, never saying yes to the first offer, playing the reluctant seller, concentrating on the issues and not on the personality of the other negotiator, using a higher authority, avoiding confrontational negotiating, and never offering to split the difference among others. One of the more interesting suggestions Dawson makes is that of "flinching." A flinch means that a negotiator should "react with shock and surprise" when receiving a first offer. The other negotiator is generally watching for your reaction to his or her proposals. A flinch signals that the other negotiator has gone too high or too low. According to Dawson, "a concession often follows a flinch," because the other negotiator may have knowingly thrown out a high or low proposal simply to see your reaction.

Dawson, R. (1999). Secrets of power negotiating for salespeople: Inside secrets from a master negotiator (pp. 40–43). Franklin Lakes, NJ: Career Press.

Intimidation

Think of the schoolyard bullies you encountered in your youth. Their goal was to intimidate others so that they could "rule" the playground. In negotiation, **intimidation** can take many forms. As on the playground a negotiator can use threats to intimidate you. They can try to undermine your confidence in your position by presenting false information that suggests your goals are unobtainable. They can show anger or make you feel guilty or weak. All of these intimidation tactics are rooted in the bully's desire to make you feel powerless.

How do you deal with bullies and their intimidation tactics? Ideally you would avoid negotiating with such people in the first place. This requires gaining as much information as possible before the negotiation about the individual you are going to be encountering. Have others in your organization

Intimidation
a tactic that seeks to undermine the other negotiator's confidence, often by providing false or dubious information.

interacted with the person before? Does the person have a reputation for using intimidation? Learn everything you can so that you will be prepared if the person uses intimidation. Surprisingly, calling people on the tactic can be quite effective. If someone is threatening you, consider responding with the following: "Is that a threat? It sounds like a threat to me. You should know that I refuse to deal with individuals who threaten me. I will agree to continue this negotiation only if you agree to halt all such behavior immediately." Believe us, most bullies are never confronted in such a way. You also have power in the negotiation; otherwise, they would not be negotiating with you. You need to let them know that to achieve their goals they will have to change their ways; otherwise, you will walk away. Moreover, if you do walk, you can make sure that others are aware of the behavior and the intimidating individual's reputation will suffer as a result.

Bogey

Bogey
a contentious tactic where a negotiator pretends something or some issue is important to him or her, but it is not. This tactic is often employed so that the negotiator can then "concede" on the issue (which really isn't a concession at all) and get something of value in return.

Bogeys are issues that negotiators pretend are important to them when they really aren't. People use this tactic because they are trying to claim value on all issues—even unimportant ones. Needless to say, this can hurt relationships if you were to make a concession to someone on what you were convinced was an "important" issue and then later learn that it wasn't. Bogeys can actually come back to haunt negotiators who use them. Imagine you are involved in an employment negotiation and you pretend that working in Chicago is really important to you even though you may be quite satisfied to work in the New York City or Dallas office. If the recruiter really believes your bogey, he or she may say, "Okay, I'll give you a position in the Chicago office if that is important to you, but you'll have to accept a lower salary because I already have senior people in the Chicago office. If you had been willing to go to Dallas, I could have given you a higher-level position. But, I want to make you happy, so Chicago it is!" And there you stand shell-shocked, knowing you blew the chance for a better position and that where you were located wasn't that important to you. It is hard to take a bogey back once it is on the table.

Nibble
this is a tactic that attempts to "nibble" away an agreement that has already been struck. After selling you a big ticket item at a reduced price the other negotiator may then try to add on extras like an extended warranty, which brings the price back up to what you would have originally paid.

Nibble

A **nibble** is first getting commitment on the price of an item and then asking the other person to toss in a little more. This tactic is more likely to be used when purchasing big-ticket items. You might purchase a nice suit and ask the salesperson to add a tie or scarf for free. Surprisingly, people often fall for the nibble, perhaps because they fear losing the sale. Another reason is that the requested add-on is usually a small percentage of the cost of the original item.

If the nibbling technique is so effective, how can a negotiator respond to it? The first key is to recognize nibbling as a tactic to get something from you without a corresponding concession, or put another way, "to get something for nothing." Next, stick to your last offer. "Calling" the other negotiator on use of a nibble may cause him or her to back off the request. If you worry that you might jeopardize the deal if you don't give up something extra, hold something of little value back and throw it out in response to a nibble.

Chicken

Playing **chicken** is going head to head on a destructive path and waiting to see who "chickens" out first. An often-used example is that of two hot-rodders out on a lonely dirt road driving toward one another at top speed. If one doesn't chicken out, both are dead. This is the ultimate high-stakes bluff. The nuclear arms race between the United States and the Soviet Union in the 1950s and 1960s was an example of playing chicken. The only defense was to be able to pose a threat equal to the one you are confronting. In the end, someone must offer a proposal that allows both negotiators to back down without losing face.

It is hard to imagine a negotiator going to this extreme to achieve individual goals. However, groups and collectives often do so. Management and labor unions involved in contract negotiations are known to use this tactic, believing that their bluff will not be called. Management threatens to move the factory out of the country, and the union threatens to strike. If the bluff is called, the bluffing party loses face if they don't follow through; if it isn't called, the bluff will pay off. It is only a matter of time, however, until the tactic backfires. This extreme tactic is more likely to occur when parties feel they have exhausted all other options. If you find yourself in a game of chicken, it is probably time to take a hard, realistic look at the situation and ask yourself if the risk you are taking is worth any potential gain.

Good Cop/Bad Cop

This tactic is a somewhat transparent one where two negotiators conspire beforehand to break the other party down. One negotiator (the "**bad cop**") puts on a tough act, and then an apparently more reasonable negotiator (the "**good cop**") comes in and offers a softer alternative that was probably the goal (of both the "good cop" and the "bad cop") all along. This tactic might work well with the uninitiated, but most people who have watched enough police programs on television are not likely to take the bait. The best defense in this situation is to call them on it, or simply ignore the tactic.

Chicken
an extreme tactic that forces the other to show his or her hand. The nuclear arms race is an example of the game of chicken.

Good cop/bad cop
when negotiating with a partner, one takes the hard line and puts extreme pressure on the other side, leading them to believe that a deal may not even be possible, then the "good cop" comes in and makes a concession that allows the cop duo to receive what they had hoped for all along.

TAKE AWAY: *When involved with distributive bargaining, beware of hardball and contentious tactics that others may use to achieve their goals. Recognize them for what they are, and don't let them fluster you.*

■ ■ ■ ■

Reference points
there are many reference points in the negotiation process. They serve as benchmarks for a negotiator to assess how well they are doing in the negotiation. One may be the goal for the negotiation, another the bottom line, or what one can get elsewhere, or what someone else received.

AL
stands for aspiration level. This is a high target that a negotiator sets for him- or herself for the negotiation.

BATNA
stands for the "Best Alternative to a Negotiated Agreement." A BATNA is a reference point that is outside of the negotiation. It is what you will get if you don't get agreement in the current negotiation it might be the status quo, or another outside offer. Having a good BATNA gives you power in the negotiation.

Reference Points in Negotiation

How do you decide whether a negotiated outcome is a good outcome? Without a frame of reference, it is hard to make such evaluations. This is why setting, understanding, and respecting the reference points you set are key to being a successful negotiator. We turn to the most important of these next. For simplicity, we use examples of a single-issue negotiation over price, but all of these reference points can encompass multiple issue negotiations as well.

Aspiration Level

Your **aspiration level** (**AL**) is your ideal outcome. It is what you are aiming to achieve. It is based on your goals and objectives for the negotiation. It should be optimistic, but realistic. Research has shown that those who set higher ALs generally do better than those who simply set general or "do your best" goals.[5]

Your AL is what brings you to the bargaining table. It should be based on your preparation about what you can reasonably expect to achieve. Emphasis is placed on the word "reasonable" here. You do want to aim on the high end of what is reasonable, but you need to guard against being overly optimistic and pricing yourself out of the market. If you cannot provide objective information to justify your high aspiration, it will be difficult to achieve. For example, if you are selling your 10-year-old Honda Civic with 185,000 miles on the odometer and your aspiration is to obtain enough money from the sale to put a 20% down payment on a new $50,000 Lexus, you are highly unlikely to achieve this AL. Why? Because justifying that you need that much to buy a Lexus is not going to be a convincing objective argument for the buyer. Buyers will rely on objective information such as the price quoted by Kelly Blue Book for a private sale of a 10-year-old Civic in your zip code with the same number of miles that yours has. Not only will you not achieve your aspiration in this example, but you may not reach agreement at all due to the lack of a positive settlement zone (which we discuss later in this section). So our advice for setting your AL is to "aim high, but keep your feet on the ground."

BATNA

BATNA is an acronym for Best Alternative to a Negotiated Agreement, a phrase first coined by Fisher and Ury in their seminal book on principled bargaining called *Getting to Yes*.[6] Your BATNA represents your fallback position, that is, what you are going to do if you don't get an agreement in the current negotiation. It is an alternative that exists outside the current negotiation. If you have an outstanding offer on your 10-year-old Honda Civic, that offer is the BATNA for any further negotiations you may engage in to sell your Civic.

Often your BATNA may not be very attractive to you, which is likely why you are continuing to negotiate with someone else. Still, having a BATNA, even if it isn't a great one, is better than having no BATNA at all. Why? Because without a BATNA, you are more likely to accept a suboptimal outcome. A BATNA can be a source of power in negotiation. It keeps you from accepting a poor outcome, and it gives you the power to walk away from the table if the offer on the table isn't as good as or better than your BATNA. Entering into a negotiation without a BATNA is like being the emperor with new clothes[7]—you are leaving yourself exposed for exploitation. Entering a negotiation without identifying your BATNA leaves you vulnerable to not achieving good outcomes. This is analogous in our short trip driving example to leaving the house without your cell phone in case of emergency, there's no good fall back.

The Emperor's New Clothes[8]

At times, negotiators have a tendency to overestimate the value of their BATNA. That is, they consider hypothetical alternatives—like the potential buyer out there who has a passion for owning 10-year-old Honda Civic and is willing to pay premium dollar for one. Good luck on finding that person, because if you turn down a reasonable offer now, finding this type of buyer will be your only option.

If your BATNA isn't good, you should search for other alternatives that may be better. This often involves brainstorming or exploring new avenues you hadn't considered before. Perhaps you can give your old Honda Civic to a charity and receive a tax credit that will compensate for the lost income from the sale. As you will see repeatedly in this book, having a BATNA is a key component of your negotiation toolbox. For one, it helps you decide what your reservation price should be.

RP

stands for "reservation price," which for a buyer is the most he will pay or for a seller the least she will accept. In preparing for a negotiation you should establish what your RP will be before coming into the negotiation so you don't pay too much (the winner's curse) or accept too little.

Objective information

all the reference points set in a negotiation should be based on objective criteria. A BATNA, for example, isn't what you hope or dream you can get elsewhere, it is what you already *know* with certainty that you can get elsewhere.

Reservation Price

Your **reservation price (RP)** represents your bottom line; it is the least you will accept if you are a seller and the most you are willing to pay if you are a buyer. A number of criteria can contribute to where you set your RP. As we mentioned previously, your BATNA is one of them. You should set your RP at some level above your BATNA; otherwise, why engage in another negotiation? So if your BATNA is a tax credit for $3,000, your RP for selling your 10-year-old Honda Civic may be $3,500.

Another is **objective information** such as the list price for a 10-year-old Honda Civic on a number of automotive websites. Others may use some general formula such as selling the car for at least 35% of what they originally paid for the car. This approach could get you in trouble if the buyer doesn't find that argument persuasive. Objective information based on research or market value provides a good source of data upon which to base your RP.

Your RP might also depend on your understanding of the other person's BATNA. If that person has located another Honda Civic at a dealer, you might want to try to find out how much the dealer is asking for the Honda Civic. Accordingly, you set your RP at a price point that is more attractive than what the buyer can get at a dealer.

Generally, we advise that you should not change your RP once you have begun the negotiation. If it was based on good preparation, your BATNA, and good information about the other negotiators alternatives, it would be unwise to accept something less than your RP. One exception to this rule is if you learn information in the negotiation itself that suggests your assumptions (about their BATNA, for example) are wrong.

Bargaining Zones

The bargaining zone will be between the two initial offers of the buyer and seller. Presumably each will begin at a level slightly above (if seller) or below (if buyer) their AL, because each expects that there will be a series of concessions before agreement is reached. We discuss concession making later in this chapter.

Settlement Zone or Zone of Potential Agreement

If negotiators are behaving rationally and respect the RPs they set, then there will be a positive settlement zone if the buyer's RP is higher than the seller's RP. It is as simple as that. However, in debriefs of classroom negotiations we often discover that a positive settlement zone existed yet no agreement was reached. There are a number of possible reasons for this outcome. One may be that there is a lack of trust between negotiators, and if one believes that the other isn't negotiating in good faith, that person may prefer to settle for his or her BATNA rather than deal with someone deemed untrustworthy.

Sometimes negotiators learn information during the negotiation that they did not have when they set their RPs, which causes them to change it, and as a result a positive settlement zone no longer exists.

To examine the relationship between these reference points for a buyer and seller, we turn to a number of graphic depictions. Suppose the potential buyer of a 10-year-old Honda Civic LX Sedan with four doors and 185,000 miles has done his homework and believes its value is $3,200. The only other Honda Civic LX he has found in the area is at a dealer who is asking $4,000 for one with 165,000 miles. Thus, the buyer's BATNA is $4,000, and he sets his RP at $3,600 because if he can't get the car for that price, he would rather pay $4,000 and get one with fewer miles. His AL is to purchase the car for less than $3,000. He decides $2,800 is not an unreasonable amount, so he will start by offering $2,500. The buyer's reference points in this situation are depicted in Figure 3.1.

FIGURE 3.1 Buyer's Reference Points

You, the seller, have also done your homework and know that there is a dealer in your area selling the same make and year of Honda Civic with slightly fewer miles for $4,000 and this may be the potential buyer's only alternative. The trade-in value for your car is listed as $1,800, and the private party price is set at $3,200. Your BATNA is the $3,000 tax credit that you can get by giving the car to charity, and based on this, you set your RP at $3,300. Your aspiration is to get $3,800 for your car, so you decide to make your opening offer $4,200. The seller's reference points are depicted in Figure 3.2.

FIGURE 3.2 Seller's Reference Points

Now we combine the reference points of buyer and seller to examine the bargaining zone as illustrated in Figure 3.3.

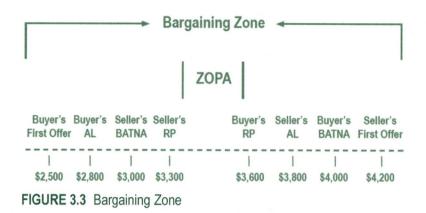

FIGURE 3.3 Bargaining Zone

Bargaining zone
the bargaining zone is the distance between the two negotiators opening offers. This is the zone in which bargaining takes place.

If buyer and seller stick to their preparations, then you as the seller will ask for $4,200 for the car and the buyer will counter with $2,500, which defines the **bargaining zone**. At this stage you may feel there is no point in continuing the negotiation, as you are facing a rather large bargaining zone (from $2,500 to $4,200) and it may seem that that there is no potential for agreement. Only by going through the negotiation process often called the **negotiation dance**, which involves a series of concessions and information exchanges, will the parties know if agreement is possible. For example, the buyer may say your $4,200 asking price is unreasonable, as he can buy a car from the dealer for less than that with fewer miles. You may counter that you can get more than the $2,500 she is offering by donating your car to a charity. So each of you may make a series of concessions until the difference between your offers is $300. You are asking for $3,600, and the buyer is offering $3,300. You have now entered the **zone of possible agreement (ZOPA)**. You could end up accepting the $3,300 offer, you could hold firm and get $3,600 for the car (the buyer's RP), or you may end up somewhere in between. Because a positive zone of agreement exists doesn't mean you will always reach agreement, but it follows that if each of you respects your planning and reference points, you should reach agreement. However, one party may feel he has conceded more than the other party and refuse to budge. Or because the two opening offers were so far apart, one party may lose confidence or desire in the ability to reach an agreement.

Zone of potential/ possible agreement
this zone is defined by the reservation prices of the seller and the buyer. If a buyer's RP is more than the seller's RP—there is a positive bargaining zone. If the buyer's RP is less than the seller's RP there is no positive bargaining zone and agreement will be unlikely.

If instead the buyer had set his RP at $3,300 (the most he would pay) and you, as seller, had set your RP at $3,600 (the least you will accept), no positive settlement zone would exist, and you would likely reach an impasse, unless one of you violated your RP and accepted an offer below it (or above the RP the buyer said he would pay). This is an example of a negative bargaining zone.

TAKE AWAY: *Reference points allow you to set goals and bottom lines in negotiation. They help you know when to walk away or when to accept the deal and be satisfied. If these are well defined going into a negotiation, you will never accept an outcome that isn't in your best interest.*

Information Gathering

How do you learn about the other side's BATNA or reservation price? Sometimes you can learn the BATNA of the other side before the negotiation begins, if that information is public. This is usually not the case. You could, of course, ask the other person, and some inexperienced negotiators may actually tell you. Generally, it is not a good idea to reveal one's BATNA, especially early in the negotiation. If you do, you are anchoring the negotiation outcome closer to your RP than your AL. You certainly never want to reveal your BATNA if it is not a good one. If the other negotiator learns this, he or she will have the competitive advantage, knowing you will likely agree to an offer only slightly better than your BATNA. For the same reasons, you should not reveal your RP, as doing so indicates to the other how little you are willing to accept and you will be unlikely to receive an offer any higher than that.

Assuming the other person is as smart as you are and knows enough to not reveal these reference points directly, how then can you determine the other person's RP? There are indirect ways you can learn where they may be. One way is through the pattern of concessions. When concessions get smaller and smaller in magnitude, you can usually assume that the negotiator is reaching his or her RP. Of course, it is possible to strategically fake this through your pattern of concession making, so you need to be sensitive to other cues. Is the person showing consistency in the way the issues are discussed and questions are answered? If not, this may be a signal that the negotiator is using hardball tactics. It is also possible to detect truthfulness by paying attention to the other negotiator's body language. Those who are faking or misrepresenting typically have a hard time looking you in the eye when they do so, or they may show other signs of being uncomfortable such as pacing nervously or tapping a pencil on the desk.

Is there ever a time when it makes sense to reveal your BATNA or RP? It may make sense when the other person is no longer making concessions and you are at an impasse. You may get movement if you reveal that your current BATNA is better than what they are offering. Of course, this better be true, because if it is not, you risk their response being, "Well, take your BATNA then." You also may want to reveal your BATNA if you believe it is better than the other person thinks it is. But a word of caution: once the other negotiator knows this, he or she also knows how much (or little) has to be offered to get you to say yes—and this is much more likely to result in an outcome nearer your RP than your AL.

■ ■ ■ ■

Who Should Make the First Offer?

This question leads to a lot of discussion the first week in the classroom. Some students make a strong case for being the one to go first as an example of first-mover advantage. By beginning the negotiation, you have the opportunity to set the tone for the negotiation and provide an anchor that the other side must now work hard to move. This argument makes sense if you know the lay of the negotiation land. If, on the other hand, you have a great deal of uncertainty about the worth of the product or service you are negotiating over, it would be foolish to make the first offer. Why?

Imagine you want to buy a cotton blanket at a street stall in a Mexican market; you don't speak Spanish and know very little about the Mexican culture. You are at an immediate disadvantage in this situation because (1) you don't speak the language, so you can't ask questions or understand answers; (2) you have no idea what the cost of labor is in this country; and (3) the only frame of reference you have is what a similar blanket would cost in the United States. Despite these reasons for not doing so, you still believe there is an advantage to making the first offer. You decide that the blanket would be a real bargain at $20 and so you offer $20. The stall owner smiles, takes the $20, wraps the blanket, and wishes you adios. Now do you still feel you got a good deal? You should be happy as you felt the blanket would be a steal at $20, but now you have the feeling you should have offered less. This is often referred to as the "winner's curse"; you got what you wanted, but you paid too much for it. In markets that we don't understand, we would be far better to stand back and watch others negotiate or at a minimum negotiate with several vendors before buying.

Other students take the position during the first week of our negotiation class that you should always let the other go first. That way you won't be the one who paid $20 for a blanket that your friends got for $12. Still, first offers can anchor the negotiation, and if you have good knowledge of the value of the item, you might not want to allow the other to set an anchor that will be difficult to move away from.

So who should make the first offer in a negotiation? The fact is, like many other questions in behavioral science (and in the law), the answer is "it depends." If you are lacking knowledge of the market price for something, you should not make the first offer; if you have good information about the market price of what you are negotiating for, it might be to your advantage to do so, especially if you believe the other party is not knowledgeable. If both parties are knowledgeable, then it probably makes little difference which one makes the first offer because neither will be overly influenced by it.

Box 3.3 Don't Take the First Offer You Receive

One of the authors heard this story from a business school dean who described the following negotiation as "the best and the worst negotiation he ever did." The heiress of a large family had died and mandated that a large portion of her wealth should be endowed to various colleges and universities. However, she did not specify how much would go to specific universities. Rather, those who wanted to make a case for receiving a portion of the endowment had to present their case to her attorneys for consideration. The dean did a considerable amount of homework, he knew what some other colleges had received, and he felt he could justify the amount he was going to ask for. He decided to ask for $10 million, which was more than others had received, but he felt he could justify the amount. On the day of his meeting with the attorneys he walked into their office and made his best case for an award of $10 million. The attorneys said, "Yes." End of negotiation.

The dean said, "I knew I should be thrilled, I got what I asked for, an amount I really didn't think I could get; but I'll always wonder if I had asked for $15 or $20 million if they would have said yes to that as well." There is something about the negotiation *process* that allows us to feel confident we have done the best we could.

Box 3.4 The Employment Negotiation

One of the most important (and most dreaded) negotiations new graduates face is the negotiation of an employment contract. Why? To begin, the outcome of this negotiation is likely to impact the life of the recent graduate for some years to come. For example, it may determine the size of future pay raises. Assume that everyone in a particular work unit is going to be allocated a 4% raise in a given year. Although this seems an egalitarian way to distribute scarce resources, a closer look will suggest this may not be so. Imagine that in a given year a company offers three new hires a starting salary of $35,000. One negotiation avoider is thrilled with the offer and accepts it immediately without negotiation. The second new hire negotiates for a $38,000 salary based on her internship experience and good references. A third, who has a good BATNA (an outstanding offer of $38,000), negotiates for $40,000. Now consider the 4% raise offered the following year. The non-negotiator will receive a raise of $1,400, bringing his salary to $36,400, whereas the individual who negotiated a $40,000 salary will receive a raise of $1,600, bringing her current salary to $41,600. What was a $5,000 difference upon hiring is now a $5,200 difference and will continue to grow every year, such that at the end of 10 years (assuming a 4% raise every year), the difference is $7,117. At the end of a 30-year career, the non-negotiator will be making $109,153 and the negotiator $124,746; a difference of $15,593. Moreover, this is assuming that both parties are offered and accept a 4% raise every year. This assumption is probably false, as the person who negotiated for more upon hiring is likely to continue to negotiate for more every year, leading to a difference that will be much larger.

TAKE AWAY: *Unless one is completely indifferent toward monetary outcomes,* **negotiation matters!**

Overcoming Fears of Negotiating

When provided with the employment negotiation example in the preceding box, few can deny that failing to negotiate leaves "money on the table." Yet many people are still reluctant to engage in a negotiation over salary, especially when it may be the first job offer received. Let's examine some of the reasons people might give for not negotiating and consider whether those reasons are valid.

Reasons for reluctance to negotiate salary:

1. They will think I am greedy.
2. I'll appear too aggressive.
3. They won't like me and will decide not to hire me.
4. I don't have any basis for asking for more.
5. I don't have a BATNA.

On the surface, these may seem like legitimate concerns, and at times, they may be valid. When we examine them more closely, however, their validity is questionable. Looking out for yourself in any negotiation is your responsibility. Asking for more money does not mean you are greedy, nor do you have to be aggressive in doing so. Moreover, in years of teaching negotiations and discussing salary negotiations, not a single person (even at the executive level) has reported that a firm decided not to hire him or her simply because they asked for more. The firm may not be able to meet your asking price, but it is highly unlikely that once the negotiation has reached the stage of your being offered a position at a certain salary that the offer will be rescinded.

Obviously, you will be more comfortable asking for more if you can provide objective criteria to support your ask. This requires homework on your part. Go to your college career center and find data on the range of salaries offered for certain positions in different areas of the country. Your career services center can also provide information about what past years' graduates received in salary in different occupations. If you can show that the salary offer is below the mean for your training and experience, you do have an objective basis for asking for more. Even if the employer gives you an average salary offer, you may be able to provide criteria that show you deserve to be paid better than average. You may have done an internship, served as president of a student organization, or graduated in the top 10% of your class, experiences that would increase your value to the firm. Don't overlook the advantages you may have over others vying for the same position.

There is no question that if you have a job offer from another firm, this will increase your leverage in being able to ask for more. A BATNA gives you power at the bargaining table. What if you don't have one? There are two answers to this question. One is, "Go out and get one." Even if this means finding a temporary low-paying position, at least you will know what you will do if you don't reach agreement in the current negotiation. The other answer is that you always have a BATNA, and it is the status quo. Neither of these, the low-paying job or the status quo, may be attractive alternatives, but they may be your best alternatives at the moment. The more you can improve your alternatives away from the table, the better you'll be able to do at the negotiating table.

Norms and Their Relationship to Concessions

Although it would be nice if everyone met your aspiration price, most of us know that we will have to make at least some concessions during the negotiation. In fact, by engaging in the concession-making process, when agreement is reached, we have more confidence that we have done the best we could—unlike in the situation when someone accepts your first offer, in which case you'll always wonder if you could have done better. Concessions are rooted in the **norm of reciprocity**. This norm, which is fairly universal, is that if you make a concession to me, then I am obligated to make a concession to you. If you share information with me, then I should be equally forthcoming. Those who violate the norm of reciprocity do so at their own risk. That said, there is still an opportunity to achieve your goals while respecting this norm. You do not necessarily have to make concessions of equal size, especially if your first offer was not extreme.

> **Norm of reciprocity** a nearly universal norm which says that "if you do something nice for me, then I must do something nice for you." This norm plays an important role in negotiations both for concession making and for information sharing.

Do not get caught in the trap of being the only one to make concessions. If you begin with a fairly ambitious, but justifiable, asking price and the other negotiator balks and says, "That is ridiculous—you have to come down," don't immediately respond with a slightly less ambitious offer. If you do, you have effectively given something up without getting anything in return, a unilateral concession. You should first ask the other negotiator to explain why he or she believes your offer to be too high. If the negotiator continues to object to your fairly ambitious asking price, demand reciprocity. Ask for a counteroffer in exchange for a change in your asking price.

Fairness Norms

Everyone wants to be treated fairly and with respect. On the other hand, everyone may not agree on "what's fair." Most people will resist an ultimatum that says "take it, it's fair." Their first response is likely to be "fair to whom?" Most people don't like answers forced on them, even good answers. They'd prefer to decide for themselves what is fair. That is why telling another negotiator that you have given a "fair" offer is often considered an example of being an "irritator," which the Rackham study, discussed in Chapter 1, suggests effective negotiators should try to avoid.

Fairness norms
there are many norms of fairness. The most commonly used are equity, equality and need.

Four **fairness norms** are commonly used for deciding the distribution of resources: equity, equality, need, and precedence (sometimes referred to as maintaining the status quo). Suppose a group of students who have been working together on a group project are asked by their professor to come up with the fairness norm they want to be used for distributing 20 extra points for their project. Smart Sue, who claims she did most of the work on the project, will argue for an equity fairness rule. That is, she feels that the person who contributed the most to the project (Sue in this case) should receive more points than those who contributed less (12 points for Sue, 2 points each for the rest). Lazy Lucy, who contributed very little to the project, argues for an equality rule—share and share alike; she argues that everyone in the group should receive the same number of points (5 points for everyone). Mousy Mark argues that he needs the points more than the others because they are all A students and will pass the class regardless, whereas he may get a D in the course if he doesn't receive more of the points (17 for Mark, 1 for everyone else). Daring David feels things should be done the way they have always been done; the men should receive more points than the women (6 each for David and Mark; 4 each for Sue and Lucy). Needless to say, these students are going to have a great deal of difficulty in deciding what is fair, especially after the work is done. A better strategy would be to decide on the fairness norm first; then each could adjust the inputs accordingly.

Although the previous example is somewhat tongue-in-cheek, it illustrates nicely that not everyone is going to agree on what is fair. A norm that people can agree on is that individuals should engage in good faith negotiations. As such, they agree not to engage in personal attacks or make extreme demands or ultimatums. They should honor commitments, be honest, share relevant information, and be willing to make concessions.

CHAPTER CASE

We've talked a lot about used cars as examples in this chapter. Cars represent a major lifetime purchase that most people will do on average 5-7 or more times. This case is an opportunity for you to think about what steps you would take, based on what you know now, to prepare to purchase a used or new car.

You've decide on the make, model, and year or age of the car you are interested in. Name and describe the reference points you will need to determine prior to the negotiation. Then identify at least two sources where you will begin to research your desired vehicle and determine the numbers for the reference points you identified. What is your BATNA? Identify something you can do to strengthen your BATNA. Identify your opening offer based on your reference points. In order to have a positive bargaining zone, give an example of what the sellers RP might be. Give one example of what the sellers RP might be if there were a negative bargaining zone.

CHAPTER SUMMARY

Distributive bargaining is most likely to occur when relative strangers are negotiating over a single issue. There is a fixed pie of resources to be divided. Hence, this type of bargaining is often referred to as zero-sum or win-lose. Negotiators are more likely to use hardball tactics in distributive bargaining situations. Good negotiators learn how to not fall prey to these. Reference points such as aspiration level, BATNA, and reservation prices play an important role in negotiations, as they define the bargaining and settlement zones of the negotiation. A good negotiator sets these parameters before the negotiation begins. Concessions play an important role in negotiation and help the negotiator understand if or where settlement will occur. Norms of reciprocity and fairness influence concession making and judgments of the appropriateness of outcomes.

Questions/Exercises

1. Barbara and Nakeisha are negotiating over the price of a widget. Their pattern of concessions is as follows:
   Nakeisha begins by asking $25 for her widget.
   Barbara offers $3 for the widget.
   Nakeisha counters with $20.
   Barbara offers $6.
   Nakeisha counters with $15.
   Barbara offers $8.
   Nakeisha counters offers $10.
   Barbara offers $9.
   Which negotiator—Nakeisha or Barbara—is more likely to be believed when she says her last offer is her final offer? Why?

2. You are shopping for a new couch at the local furniture store. You look to spend between $1,000 and $2,000 for a new couch. The sales manager believes she can sell you a new couch for somewhere between $1,500 and $2,500. Based on these facts, is there a positive or negative bargaining zone when it comes to the sale/purchase of a new couch?

3. Give an example of someone using a nibble as a negotiation tactic. How would you counter such a tactic?

4. You are driving through a small town in New Mexico. As you pass the town square, you see a man selling hand-crafted picture frames. You stop your car and approach the man. All you have in your pocket is $25. You don't want to spend all of your money because you will soon need to put gas in your car. The most you can spend on the picture frame (and still have enough money to put gas in your car) is $15. You have never met this man before nor do you intend to return to this town once you leave. The man cannot sell the picture frame to you for anything less than $20. Your conversation with the man goes as follows:

   You: How much for the picture frame?

   The Man: This is a hand-crafted picture frame. You will not find another like it anywhere in the world. I can't sell you this picture frame for anything less than $50.

You: Fifty dollars? Are you nuts? I saw a similar picture frame in Santa Fe that was going for $10. Tell you what, I will give you $10.

The Man: I am offended. My time alone in making this picture frame is worth $50. However, because it is late in the day, I will sell this picture frame to you for $40.

You: This is going nowhere. I guess I will buy the picture frame I saw in Santa Fe. Take care. (You start walking away).

The Man: Wait, wait. We can make this work. I can sell this to you for $25.

You: Sorry, the best I can do is $15.

The Man: That will not work. Have a good trip.

a. What characteristics suggest this is a distributive negotiation?

b. Do you have a strong BATNA? Why or why not?

c. Identify the hardball tactics that were used in this negotiation.

5. We have talked a lot about used cars as examples in this chapter. Cars represent a major lifetime purchase that most people will do on average 5-7 or more times. This case is an opportunity for you to think about what steps you would take based on what you know now, to prepare to purchase a used or new car.

You have decide on the make, model, and year or age of the car you are interested in. Name and describe the reference points you will need to determine prior to the negotiation. Then identify at least two sources where you will begin to research your desired vehicle and determine the numbers for the reference points you identified. What is your BATNA? Identify something you can do to strengthen your BATNA. Identify your opening offer based on your reference points. In order to have a positive bargaining zone, give an example of what the sellers RP might be. Giveone example of what the sellers RP might be if there were a negative bargaining zone.

Endnotes

1. Based on WordNet 3.0, Farlex clipart collection. © 2003–2008 Princeton University, Farlex Inc.

2. Bargaining. (2000). In *The American Heritage Dictionary of the English Language* (4th ed.). Houghton Mifflin Company. New York.

3. Ologies & -Isms. (2008). The Gale Group, Inc.

4. The concepts of claiming value and creating value are discussed in detail in the work of Lax, D., & Sebenius, J. (1986). *The manager as negotiator: Bargaining for cooperation and competitive gain.* New York: Free Press.

5. Latham, G., & Locke, E. (1991). Self-regulation through goal setting. *Organizational Behavior and Human Decision Processes, 50,* 212–247.

6. Fisher, R., & Ury, W. (1981). *Getting to yes.* Boston: Houghton Mifflin.

7. Andersen, H. C. (1837). *Fairy tales told for children.* C.A. Reitzel: Denmark

8. Illustration by Vilhelm Pedersen, Andersen's first illustrator.

The Adventure of of Cross-Country Driving: Principles of Integrative Negotiations

We compared **distributive bargaining** in Chapter 3 to taking a short driving trip across town. When thinking about integrative negotiation, we compare it to taking a cross-country driving trip. On a cross-country driving trip, there will be many more vehicles on the road and multiple on and off ramps. Unlike the short driving trip across town, extensive preparation is required for a cross-country driving trip; you will need to plan your driving route plus have an understanding of the terrain and the driving and weather conditions you might encounter. A cross-country driving trip can provide opportunities to see new things and meet new people. The same is true of an integrative negotiation; you will need a well-stocked negotiation toolkit to take advantage of the opportunities that an integrative negotiation presents.

CHAPTER OBJECTIVES

- To recognize the fundamental differences between distributive bargaining and integrative negotiation
- To analyze situations for integrative potential
- To develop a repertoire of integrative strategies and tactics
- To learn how to "not leave money on the table"
- To learn how to quantify the issues and options in a negotiation by doing a multi-attribute utility analysis
- To learn how to make Multiple Equivalent Simultaneous Offers (MESOs)

KEY TERMS

Integrative negotiation	Interests	Claiming value
Principled negotiation	Priorities among issues	Multi-attribute utility
Mutual gains bargaining	Bundling issues	analysis
Win-win negotiations	Compatible issues	MESOs
Positions	Creating value	

CHAPTER CASE

Your sister knows you are taking a negotiation course, and asks for your help in preparing for a meeting she will be having soon with a sales representative at the local car dealership Three years ago, your sister entered into an agreement to lease a brand-new car. She agreed to lease the car from the local car dealership for four years. Under the terms of the lease agreement, your sister pays a monthly lease payment to "rent" the car from the car dealership, which continues to own the car. Your sister is responsible for paying for her own car insurance, and to pay for the regular maintenance on the car. As part of the lease agreement, and in order to reduce the amount of her initial down payment on the lease, your sister agreed that she would pay a penalty of .25 per mile (instead of the car dealership's standard mileage penalty of .10 per mile) for any mile over a total of 60,000 miles that the car was driven during the term of the lease agreement. Your sister agreed to a higher mileage penalty in her car lease because (at the time) she anticipated driving approximately 10,000 miles per year. Due to a change in her job, including a move across the country to a new city, your sister has been required to drive more than what she had planned when she signed the lease agreement with the local car dealership. She currently has driven the car 65,000 miles, has another year left on her lease, and will likely put an additional 15,000 miles on the car before she is ready to return it to the car dealership at the end of her lease. At this rate, your sister will have to pay the car dealership an additional $5,000 dollars as a mileage penalty (if not more, depending on how much she drives the car) when the lease ends. To further complicate the situation, your sister and her partner are in the process of adopting a baby, and it will be difficult to get a new baby and a car seat in and out of her two-door car that she leases from the car dealership. Your sister has asked you to develop a negotiation strategy that will allow her to return the car to the car dealership, avoid paying the mileage penalty, and get a new (and larger) car with similar monthly lease payments. Is there anything you can do that will allow the car dealership and your sister to both "win" in this negotiation?

■ ■ ■ ■

Principled negotiation a term used by Fisher and Ury in *Getting to Yes,* which advocates deciding and negotiating on issues based on their merits (and the importance of those issues to each negotiator) rather than haggling over each issue, assuming that both negotiators have the same level of interest in achieving their stated position for each issue in the negotiation.

What Is Integrative Negotiation?

Integrative negotiation comes in different guises: some refer to it as win-win bargaining, others call it mutual gains bargaining, interest-based bargaining, or principled negotiation. The terms differ somewhat according to the training and background of those who use them. The term "**principled negotiation**" was first introduced by Fisher and Ury.[1] They contrasted a principled negotiation approach to a positional one. Interest-based bargaining is an approach that is increasingly used in collective bargaining between employers and labor unions. Before negotiation begins, both labor and management negotiation teams receive training on how to approach the contact negotiations based on the interests of both sides.

"**Win-win,**" unfortunately, is a greatly overused term that has come to mean that everyone is equally satisfied with the outcome, or that both parties gained equally during a negotiation. **Mutual gains bargaining** assumes reciprocity in information sharing and sufficient give and take such that both parties mutually benefit from the negotiation.

A classic story used to illustrate integrative negotiation is the story of two sisters who are fighting over the last orange in the house. Each insists she must have it, but in the interest of keeping peace in the family, the sisters decide to split the orange and cut it in half. One sister takes her half of the orange out on the porch of the family home, eats the pulp, and tosses the peel of the orange half in the trash. The other sister grates the peel of her half of the orange for a cooking recipe and disposes of the pulp of her half of the orange. Each sister settled for half of what she wanted. Had each sister shared information with the other, both would have had 100% of what they wanted. Integrative negotiation requires sharing critical information so that the interests of the parties can be met, even though their positions ("I must have the whole orange") cannot. Integration of interests allows negotiators to create value and increase the size of the negotiation pie, so that both negotiators can benefit from the negotiation.

At its core, **integrative negotiation** is about integrating the *interests* of both parties involved in the negotiation or dispute. To the novice, integrative negotiation sounds a little bit like wishful thinking. How is it possible to integrate interests, when on the surface parties appear to want very different things? Perhaps the best way to understand integrative negotiation is to compare and contrast it with distributive bargaining.

Win-win negotiations
integrative negotiation, principled negotiation, and mutual gains bargaining are all forms of win-win negotiations.

How Does Integrative Negotiation Differ from Distributive Bargaining?

Single versus Multiple Issues

Distributive bargaining is most likely to occur when negotiators are bargaining over a single issue, often price. As we observed in the previous chapter, in distributive bargaining, parties usually have incompatible positions (sellers want more money, and buyers want to pay as little as possible), and if an agreement is to be reached, one or both parties must give up their position. That is, the best one can do in such situations is to compromise while claiming as much value as possible. Negotiations such as this are often referred to as a fixed pie, meaning that they can be sliced only one of two ways: either the pie is split evenly, or one side gets the bigger piece. The negotiator who receives the bigger piece is said to have claimed more value. Distributive bargaining is all about claiming value when resources are fixed.

Integrative negotiation, on the other hand, is about trying to grow the fixed pie in order to create value. This does not mean that negotiators are no longer interested in claiming value; they are. However, to the extent that more value is created, the more of the resource pie there will be to share. One way to turn a distributive situation into an integrative one is by adding issues.

Mutual gains bargaining
another term for integrative negotiation that is often used in collective bargaining. The focus is on both parties doing the best they can in the negotiation.

Integrative negotiation
a negotiation where parties attempt to integrate their interests. To do so, parties must be willing to share their interests, and be able to prioritize the issues to be negotiated, so they can concede on low-priority issues in order to claim more value on high-priority issues.

For example, if in addition to negotiating the price of a car, a car buyer could also negotiate financing, extended warranty, and complimentary oil changes, then the car buyer may be able to move away from his or her initial position on price. That is, a car buyer may be willing to pay a higher price if that means low-interest financing, an extended warranty at no cost, and free oil changes for a year. The car dealership may be willing to make these concessions in order to be able to report to the home office that the price of the car did not have to be discounted. When there are multiple issues on the table, there is an opportunity for negotiators to make trade-offs among them.

In returning to the negotiation case study at the start of this chapter, it appears that your sister has very little leverage that she can use to negotiate with the car dealership. Under the terms of the lease agreement, she will have to pay for the mileage penalty. To avoid increasing the mileage penalty, your sister may need to keep her car in the garage and find other ways to get to and from work. With a new baby joining the family soon, the thought of taking a bus to work, or traveling with a new baby by taxi or car service do not seem to be attractive options. What may interest the sales representative at the car dealership to work with your sister and her situation? For example, the sales representative may understand that there is great market demand for the type of car your sister is leasing – that is, there are many people who would like to buy your sister's leased car from the car dealership. The sales representative could, therefore, work with your sister to end her current lease, and sell her

Box 4.1 An Example of "Expanding the Pie" in Negotiations

Sports agent Drew Rosenhaus represented professional football player Clinton Portis. Portis was drafted by the Denver Broncos and was the 2002 National Football League (NFL) Rookie of the Year. He was still under contract with the Broncos for an additional two years. Portis' contract was at the NFL salary minimum, with no incentives. He felt that his play on the field "outperformed" his contract. While Portis wanted to renegotiate his contract, the team had little interest in giving him a new contract. The only negotiation issue between the Broncos and Portis was Portis' salary. The parties were at an impasse. Rosenhaus, however, looked to expand the pie by looking for a team that might trade for Portis and sign him to a new and more lucrative contract. Another team, the Washington Football Teams, was having difficulty signing one of its players, cornerback Champ Bailey. Rosenhaus convinced Washington to trade Bailey for Portis. Denver was happy with its new cornerback (Bailey) and signed him to the new contract he wanted. Washington was happy with its new running back (Portis) and signed him to a new contract. A negotiations standoff became a win-win situation for both players by adding parties and issues to the negotiations. As Rosenhaus noted, "It was a win for everybody."

Rosenhaus, D., & Rosenhaus, J. (2008). Next question: An NFL super agent's proven game plan for business success (pp. 161–172). New York: The Berkley Publishing Group.

car to an interested buyer (which would benefit the car dealership and may provide a commission sale to the sales representative). Your sister could then return the car and pay her mileage penalty. However, your sister would still need a new car to meet her family's needs. Your sister could negotiate a new lease agreement with the sales representative and ask the sales representative to reduce the extra miles she has driven her current vehicle (5,000) from the mileage allowance of her new car lease. If that occurred, your sister would avoid having to pay the mileage penalty under her current car lease.

While there are quite a few "ifs" in this proposed response to your sister's situation, it is also apparent that this situation could involve an integration of the interests between your sister, the sales representative and the car dealership.

Table 4.1 summarizes the major differences between distributive bargaining and integrative negotiations.

TABLE 4.1 A Comparison of Distributive Bargaining and Integrative Negotiation

Negotiation Factors	Distributive Bargaining	Integrative Negotiation
Number of issues	Single issue	Multiple issues
Nature of relationship	One-time interaction	Expect multiple interactions with the same person/party
Negotiator focus	Positions	Interests
Strategy	Do not share information	Share information about needs or interests
Tactics	Hardball	Build trust and ask questions
Goal	Claiming value	Creating and claiming value

Positions versus Interests

Taking a **position** in negotiation is like drawing a line in the sand and telling the other negotiator that you will not cross it. It is giving an ultimatum to the other side. In essence, a positional bargainer is saying, "my way or the highway." If both parties to a negotiation hold equally strong positions, then the likelihood they will reach an impasse is high because neither is able or willing to make any concessions. Positions are by their nature non-negotiable. To achieve an integrative solution, one has to understand the **interests** that lie beneath the position.

Let us consider an employment negotiation in a difficult economy. A new college graduate who has accumulated considerable student loan debt over the past four years, is getting married next week, needs to buy a car, and wants to buy a home soon may take the position that he needs a salary of

Positions

a position is a stand taken in a negotiation, like "I must have a salary of $100,000." Positional bargaining can lead to impasses if a negotiator will not move from his or her position.

> Keep in mind that behind seemingly opposing positions can lie identical, or at least compatible, interests. It's surprising how often, in negotiations, both parties want the same thing but are blinded to that fact by the positions they have assumed. Interests—yours and the other party's—should remain your focus throughout the course of the negotiation."
>
> —Sports Agent Leigh Steinberg, in Steinberg, L., & D'Orso, M. (1998). *Winning with integrity: Getting what you want without selling your soul* (p. 147). New York: Times Books.

Interests are the underlying reasons for the position a negotiator takes. For example, the reasons for an applicant's asking for a starting salary of $60,000 are unpaid college loans, need for a new house and new car, etc. *Positions* are singular; *interests* are multiple.

at least $60,000 in order to accept a job offer. The recruiter, on the other hand, cannot offer the new graduate a cent more than $50,000 due to the company's salary guidelines for newly-hired employees. If each person sticks with their respective positions, the company will lose a highly qualified candidate and the potential employee misses the opportunity to work for the company for which he is most qualified. The two hold incompatible positions and there is no zone of positive agreement.

However, if the recruiter and potential employee were to look beyond their positions and share their underlying **interests** (which can be thought of as the reasons they hold the positions they do), it might be possible to strike a deal. If the graduate shares with the recruiter the information about the outstanding student loan debt and the urgency to buy a car and home, he may learn that the company has a policy of paying up to two years of an employee's student loans. He may also learn that the company can help with acquiring a low-interest car and home loan from a local bank. Learning this, the potential employee realizes that he can accept the $50,000 salary if his other interests are met. If parties stick to their **positions** and never discuss their interests, opportunities will be lost and value left on the table.

TAKE AWAY: *Positions are singular; interests are multiple. There is only one way to fulfill a position, but there may be multiple ways to satisfy the underlying interests. Sharing your interests and asking about the other negotiator's interests will increase the likelihood of reaching an integrative solution.*

Is the Negotiation a One-Time Interaction, or Will There Be Multiple Encounters?

If the negotiation is a one-time deal with a person you never expect to interact with again, you are likely to engage in positional bargaining and make few, if any, concessions. On the other hand, if this is going to be one of many ongoing negotiations, positional bargaining is not likely to pay in the long run. That is, you may achieve your goals in the short run, but the relationship may be so damaged by your insistence on having your position met that any future negotiation with the same person may be a battle as the other attempts to reach parity.

Even a car-buying negotiation, which most consider a one-time deal and accordingly put little value on the relationship with the car salesperson in order to push for the best deal possible, could backfire in the long run if there is only one car dealer in town. Negotiators have long memories, especially if they think they were exploited or not treated fairly. So before claiming all the value on the table, consider whether you will be negotiating with this person in the future. If so, you can allow the other negotiator to save face by leaving something on the table for him or her to claim.

> **TAKE AWAY:** *You never know when you may need to negotiate with someone again, and next time, they may be in the driver's seat. Don't burn your bridges.*

What "Tools" Are Required in the Negotiation Toolkit to Be a Successful Integrative Negotiator?

First, Know Yourself, Your Interests, and Your Priorities

As in any negotiation, a negotiator needs to be prepared. This begins with a solid understanding of what you need from the negotiation. It means identifying the issues to be negotiated and understanding your priorities among them. Rarely will all issues be equally important to you. Being able to prioritize issues gives you a better handle on where you must remain firm, and where you are willing to make concessions or trade-offs.

Second, Know the Other; Take That Person's Perspective

Perspective taking means stepping into the other negotiator's shoes and trying to view the negotiation from their perspective. What is the negotiator trying to achieve? What issues are going to be most important to this person? Why are many negotiators unwilling to engage in perspective taking? Most likely their reluctance stems from a distributive fixed-pie mind-set. That is, a negotiator may feel that taking the other's perspective is the same as taking the other's side, and that doing so will reduce one's own outcomes. In integrative negotiation, nothing could be further from the truth. If the goal of negotiation is getting the other negotiator to say "yes" to your proposals, you need to understand what needs to be in those proposals in order for that person to say "yes." This means, at least for a while, you need to analyze the negotiation situation as if you were the other negotiator so that you have a good handle on what issues he or she is likely to place a high priority on and which less so.

Engaging in this process may also help you identify issues that are important to the other side that are unimportant or irrelevant to you. The normal tendency would be to take those issues off the table. But wait! If an issue is perceived to be important to the other person and it is not to you, that gives you the opportunity to concede on that issue in order to claim value on an issue that *is* important to you. Research has shown that negotiators who take the perspective of the other side are better at coordinating and problem solving with others.[2]

> **TAKE AWAY:** *Seeing things from the other negotiator's perspective gives you opportunities to create value by including issues that are of low priority to you but important to the other negotiator and that can be traded for issues that are of high priority to you.*

Third, Gather Information: Ask and Answer Questions

In negotiation, information is like gold. The negotiator with good information about the issues and about the person across the table will reap the benefits of information gathering. Some information gathering can and must take place before the negotiation begins. What can you learn about the person you will be negotiating with? If you don't know the person, perhaps you can find someone who does. To the extent that you can reduce uncertainty about the negotiation behavior and style of the other negotiator, the more prepared you will be for the negotiation.

If the person you are negotiating with is representing a firm or other constituency, you may be able to learn more about the organization that person represents by checking trade journals, the company's website, and so on. Making yourself knowledgeable about the firm and the way it does business before the negotiation begins will reduce unpleasant surprises during the negotiation process.

Still, some information simply can't be known beforehand, like the other negotiator's reservation price, alternatives away from the table (their Best Alternative to a Negotiated Agreement - BATNA), or priorities over the issues. This is when it is good to know how to ask pertinent questions. Research has shown that negotiators who ask questions about priorities and preferences among the issues do better in negotiations than those who do not.[3] Questions about preferences and priorities are less likely to put the other negotiator on the defensive, whereas questions about reservation prices and BATNAs might.[4] Table 4.2 summarizes the type of questions asked during a negotiation.

In addition to asking questions, you should also be prepared to answer questions about your interests and priorities. Unlike in distributive bargaining, where you may want to keep information hidden from the other side due to fear of exploitation, in integrative negotiation you would be at a disadvantage if you did *not* share information. Getting information from both sides out on the table can turn the negotiation into a joint problem-solving adventure rather than a distributive battle.

Fourth, Develop Reciprocity—Share Information about Interests and Priorities

In Chapter 3 we discussed the vital role that the norm of reciprocity plays in the negotiation process, especially as it relates to concession making in distributive bargaining. In integrative negotiations it plays an equally important role in information sharing. To reach outcomes that maximize gain for both parties, all critical information about interests and priorities over issues needs to be shared. That said, it would be a foolish negotiator who laid all of his or her cards on the table at once.

TABLE 4.2 Types of Questions to Ask in Negotiation and the Reasons for Asking[5]

Type of Questions to Ask	Reason for Asking	Example
Open-ended questions	To encourage the other to open up and share information about positions, interests, issues, priorities, and potential settlement options	"Can you share with me which issues are most important to you and why?"
Close-ended questions	To move the other from talking about things in general and to force them to be more specific	"Which issue is most important to you?"
Questions that seek clarification	To pinpoint differences or correct possible misunderstandings	"Am I correct in understanding that you are unable to make the final decision about this matter?"
Leading questions	To get the other party to confirm your position or your understanding of an issue	"Can you see why I am unable to make any further concessions?"
Questions that uncover underlying concerns	To signal that you want to shift from a distributive approach to an integrative one	"Can you help me understand why accepting my offer doesn't meet your needs?"
Questions that seek creative solutions	To generate proposals that meet the needs of both parties	"Is there another way to think about the problem we face?"

Why? Because one of the first things a negotiator must determine is whether the other party also sees the negotiation as an integrative one, and if not, he or she must work to convince the other that both would be better off by sharing information.

Here is where the norm of reciprocity shines. Reciprocity builds the trust that is required to feel comfortable in sharing information about interests and priorities. Start small; begin by sharing some non-critical information and see whether the other negotiator reciprocates. If so, you can respond by sharing more information and observing if it is also reciprocated. Using this "back and forth" type of - strategy—each of you going back and forth, and trading information— you will be able to get all the relevant information on the table; the task then becomes one of joint problem solving rather than concession making.

Fifth, Think about the Negotiation Holistically Rather than Piecemeal

Priorities among issues
when there are multiple issues in a negotiation a nego- tiator should be able to prioritize among them.

Another key to successful integrative negotiation is keeping the big picture in mind. Too often, negotiators get caught up in the minor details and can't see the forest for the trees. Yes, issues are important, and you want to be sure that all the issues are on the table. But we know that all issues are not equally im- portant to you, nor will they be to the other negotiator. However, you should not assume that you and the other negotiator always want different things on every issue.

When there are multiple issues, they will likely fall into three different categories. **First**, are the strictly distributive issues—where you and the other negotiator hold completely different positions on the issue and the issue is equally important to both of you. In an employment negotiation, this issue might be salary (you want $60,000, and the employer wants you to accept $50,000). **Second**, are the integrative issues; these are the issues where you still want different things, but your priorities among them are different. For ex- ample, in an employment negotiation, a high-priority issue for you may be to have all your moving expenses paid (the employer would prefer to pay none) and a lower-priority issue may be the date you start working (the employer wants you to start on June 1, but you would rather wait until August 1). The employer, however, may put a high priority on the starting date and much low- er priority on moving expenses, as paying them may be standard in their indus- try. Thus, these two issues, when packaged together, become integrative ones. You give the employer what the company needs on starting date (because it is a lower-priority issue to you) in return for having your moving expenses fully paid (which is a lower priority issue to the company). **Third** are the compat- ible issues where both parties' preferences are aligned. This realization often comes as a complete surprise to negotiators, as an assumption many make is that each will have opposing preferences for every issue.[6] Thank goodness this isn't always the case. You may prefer to work in Chicago because you have family there, and the employer may want you to work in Chicago because your skill set best matches those needed in the Chicago office. You may want to be placed in the information technology department, and because it is the skill set the company needs, that is exactly what the employer wants as well.

Compatible issues
when there are multiple issues in a negotiation there is a tendency to think that the parties want different things on all the issues. There may, how- ever, be several compatible issues in the negotiation. In an employment negotiation both parties may want the job candidate to be in a certain location and doing a certain type of job. Recognizing compatible issues can help negotia- tors build integrative agreements.

Because of these combinations of preferences and priorities over the issues, it is possible to package or bundle them together to create value in the negotiation. If you negotiated these issues independently and you assumed you wanted different things on each, you may have ended up compromising on each issue, leading to a deal where you split the difference on salary, you got half your moving expenses paid, and you end up working in Des Moines, Iowa in the human resources department. This outcome doesn't meet your interests or those of the employer. On the other hand, if you share preferences and priorities and bundle the issues, you may still end up splitting the difference on salary (a distributive issue that is equally important to you both, so you receive a starting salary of $55,000), but you will trade starting date for moving expenses (the integrative issues; you start June 1 and get 100% of your moving expenses paid) and you will be employed in Chicago in the information technology department (the compatible issues). This packaged deal will be much more attractive to you both and doesn't leave value unclaimed as it would be if you split the difference on every issue.

This example illustrates the value of sharing information in integrative negotiations. In the last section of this chapter, we will focus on an integrative strategy that requires you to quantify your preferences and priorities over the issues. This method helps you see where the trade-offs may be when there are multiple issues to integrate and will keep you from leaving value unclaimed.

Bundling issues when there are multiple issues in a negotiation it is often helpful to "bundle" like issues together and offer them as a package. For example, in an employment negotiation a recruiter might make an offer that bundles benefits, retirement, and vacation days together.

Finally, Be Patient and Trust the Process

By now, it should be abundantly clear that integrative negotiation takes time and patience. The overeager negotiator who wants to jump in unprepared and start claiming value immediately will not fare well in these types of negotiations. Because integrative negotiation takes time and commitment to the process, you need to evaluate the situation first to determine whether it calls for integrative techniques. A glance at Table 4.1 should help you decide. If there are multiple issues, you have interests that must be met, and the relationship with the other negotiator is ongoing, then it is important to take the time to prepare for an integrative negotiation. If, on the other hand, it is a negotiation with only a single issue and is clearly a one-time transaction with someone you do not expect to interact with in the future, then it is unlikely you will engage in the integrative process. If the issue is terribly important to you, however, you might consider how you can turn what appears to be a distributive situation into an integrative one by adding issues to the negotiation.

Quantifying the Issues and Possible Outcomes: Reaching the Pareto Frontier

As noted previously, multiple-issue negotiations are more complicated, but they also provide more opportunities for both parties in the negotiation to find value. The key when there are multiple issues is to remember that the two parties to the negotiation may value those issues differently. Let's take the example of a typical purchaser/supplier negotiation. Suppose a large business needs a supplier of office supplies. Price will obviously be an important issue for both parties, but price isn't the only issue. Other issues may include the time to delivery, quality control of the product, after-sale service, and exclusivity of the purchaser/supplier business relationship. Imagine that in preparing for the negotiation, the purchaser and supplier rank ordered the issues from most to least important to them.

Purchaser Rankings of Issues	*Supplier Ranking of Issues*
1. Price	1. Exclusivity
2. Quality guarantee	2. Price
3. On-time delivery	3. After-sales service
4. After-sales service	4. Time to delivery
5. Exclusivity	5. Quality guarantee

What we can see from the rankings alone are opportunities for the parties to make trade-offs among the issues. Immediately we notice that an agreement to use the supplier's products exclusively is more important to the supplier than price. That is, there is value to the supplier of being the only supplier of office supplies to the purchaser. This will allow the supplier to be more flexible on price. The reason the supplier ranked the issues of delivery time and quality guarantee so low may be because they already have a good quality control process in their factory and a good supply of product, so providing both of these come at low cost to the supplier.

While the purchasing company cares a lot about price, it is also interested in a quality guarantee and a promise of on-time delivery. So even though a cheaper price is better for the purchasing company, it may be willing to pay more if there is a guarantee of quality and on-time delivery of the product. Also, by ranking exclusivity last we can assume the purchaser is fairly indifferent about this issue as compared to the others. Thus, we see the opportunity for the two parties to make trade-offs among the issues. The supplier may be willing to offer on-time delivery and a guarantee of quality *if* the purchaser will agree to use the supplier's product exclusively. The purchaser may agree to pay more for the after-sales service if a lower purchase price of the products can be agreed on. This process of trading off low-priority issues for higher-priority ones is often referred to as *logrolling*.

Creating value value is created when parties make trade-offs among issues rather than simply compromise on all issues. Creating value is often called "expanding the pie."

We have used the phrase "leaving money on the table" quite liberally up to this point. What exactly does it mean, and how do you know if you have maximized gain or left money on the table? In the office equipment example, we see how, at a minimum, ranking the issues can help the negotiator see the opportunity for making trade-offs and **creating value**. However, the value created is subjective and not quantifiable. One technique for quantifying a negotiation is using a decision process that is like a **multi-attribute utility analysis**.

This approach involves (1) identifying the issues, (2) prioritizing the issues by weighting them, and (3) identifying the options within each issue and quantifying those to represent your preferences. Let's return to the supplier/purchaser example and apply this technique. To begin, rather than ranking the issues, we ask the purchaser and the supplier to weight the set of issues, the constraint being that the weights must add up to one. This forces negotiators to go beyond a ranked preference order and forces them to value the issues *relative to one another.*

Purchaser Weighting of Issues	*Supplier Weighting of Issues*
.50 Price	.40 Exclusivity
.30 Quality guarantee	.25 Price
.10 On-time delivery	.15 After-sales service
.075 After-sales service	.10 Time to delivery
.025 Exclusivity	.10 Quality guarantee

We learn a lot more about the parties' priorities among the issues when we use this process. We see for the purchaser price is as important as all the other issues combined. And that after-sales service and exclusivity really matter very little. For the supplier, being the exclusive supplier of the office supplies is as important as price and after-sales service are together. And the time to delivery and a quality guarantee are equally (un)important. If negotiators went only this far in quantifying the negotiation, they would have a more sensitive instrument for making trade-offs and creating value. But we can do even better by also looking at the options within each issue and valuing them such that the preferred option receives 100 points and the remaining ones are given points according to the negotiator's subjective value. Unlike the weights, these values are not constrained to add to one.

Table 4.3 shows the next two steps. The first is the values that each party places on the options within each issue, and the second is a column showing the values multiplied by the weights for that issue. Now we can look at the quantified subjective value for each negotiator for every possible outcome. If the purchaser was given his or her top preference for every issue, it would be worth 100 points to the purchaser and 9.5 points to the supplier. If the supplier was given his or her top preference for every issue, it would be worth 100 points to the supplier and 2.475 points to the purchaser. It is unlikely that either side would agree to either of these extreme outcomes.

However, we can consider some packages the negotiators could offer one another. This is part of what is known as a **MESO strategy**. MESO stands

Multi-attribute utility analysis
a process of weighting the issues in a negotiation (weights must add to one) and then assigning a numeric value to the options within each issue. This process forces a negotiator to prioritize the issues and allows the negotiator to quantify the issues and option, thereby helping him or her see where the trade-offs might be.

MESO
an acronym for "Multiple Equivalent Simultaneous Offer." If a negotiator has done a multi-attribute utility analysis of the issues then he or she can bundle some of the issues and offer two bundles simultaneously that are of equal value to him or her. This signals a willingness to be flexible in the negotiation; it also helps discover where the trade-offs in the negotiation might be.

for multiple equivalent simultaneous offers. Why would a negotiator want to do this in a negotiation? The idea is that one negotiator can offer the other a choice between two (or more) "bundles" that the negotiator is basically indifferent between, based on the previous utility analysis. For example, the purchaser could say to the supplier, "I will present to you two offers, and you tell me which one you prefer."

TABLE 4.3 A Multi-Attribute Utility Analysis of a Negotiation

Issues (and options within each issue)	Purchaser's Value of Options		Supplier's Value of Options	
Price (per product)	**.50**	**(Ps W × V)**	**.25**	**(Ss W × V)**
a. $0.50	100	50	0	0
b. $0.75	25	12.5	50	12.5
c. $1.00	0	0	100	25
Quality guarantee	**.30**		**.10**	
a. 100%	100	30	20	2
b. 80%	50	15	25	2.5
c. 60%	0	0	100	10
On-time delivery (delivery on the day promised)	**.10**		**.10**	
a. 100%	100	10	25	2.5
b. 80%	80	8	50	5
c. 50%	0	0	100	10
After-sales service	**.075**		**.15**	
1. Free for 30 days	25	1.875	100	15
2. Free for 60 days	50	3.75	20	3
3. Free for 120 days	100	7.5	0	0
Exclusivity	**.025**		**.40**	
a.. Purchaser will use supplier's supplies exclusively	25	.625	100	40
b. Purchaser will use supplier's supplies exclusively for the first 6 months	50	1.25	75	30
c. Purchaser has the right to purchase other suppliers' office supplies	100	2.5	10	5

Offer A: "I can give you $1.00 per product if you agree to give me 100% quality guarantee, 100% on-time delivery, after-sales service free for 120 days, and the right to use other supplier's office supplies

OR

Offer B: "I'll buy the office supplies for 50 cents product, and I'll agree to accept 60% on the quality guarantee, 50% on-time delivery, and 30 days of free after-sales service and will buy office supplies from you exclusively."

Notice that these two simultaneous offers from the purchaser are very close in subjective value. A = 50, B = 52.5.

Now consider the supplier's response. Option A is worth 34.5 points to him, and Option B is worth 75 points. The supplier would strongly prefer Option B. What the purchaser learns from the supplier's response is that the price must not be the most important thing to the supplier, because he prefers Option B to A, and Option B pays half as much per product. The purchaser may not know which of the other issues is most important to the supplier, but through a series of such offers, he could narrow it down.

The supplier could also make a MESO offer to the purchaser. He could offer:

Option C: Exclusivity, 30 days free after-sales service, 100% quality guarantee, 100% on-time delivery, and 50 cents per product.

OR

Option D: No exclusivity, 120 days free after-sales service, 60% quality guarantee, 50% on-time delivery, and $1.00 per product.

Option C is worth 59.5 points to the supplier, and Option D is worth 50 points.

This is a no-brainer decision for the purchaser, as Option C is worth 92.5 and Option D is worth only 10. Now we can see how making MESO offers can create value. The supplier is indifferent between C and D, whereas the purchaser can gain 92.5 with Option C.

What is the highest joint value that can be created in this negotiation? The following two outcomes provide nearly the same joint value, but the supplier would prefer the first and the purchaser would prefer the second.

1. 50 cents per product , 100% quality guarantee, 100% on-time delivery, free after-sales service for 30 days, and exclusivity is worth 92.5 to the purchaser and 59.5 to the supplier, for a joint total of 152.
2. 50 cents per product , 100% quality guarantee, 50% on-time delivery, free after-sales service for 30 days, and exclusivity is worth 82.5 to the purchaser and 67 to the supplier, for a joint total of 149.5.

We can compare these two outcomes to an outcome where negotiators did not bundle or make packaged proposals and simply compromised on every issue. That is, they agreed on the middle option for each issue. A pure compromise would give the purchaser 40.5 and the supplier 53, for a total of 93.5. Outcomes 1 and 2 and the compromise solution are plotted in Figure 4.1. The plot makes it abundantly clear that both supplier and purchaser are better off with Option 1 or Option 2 than they are with the compromise solution. One can think of the shaded area between the two lines as the money left on the table by not making trade-offs and bundling offers through integrative negotiation.

Another way to think about creating value is that any line further to the "northeast" in a graph such as the one in Figure 4.1 creates value. The point on the line indicates who claims the most of the value created. In the examples plotted in Figure 4.1, both Option 1 and Option 2 favor the purchaser. Outcomes on the same line that moved further to the "west" (left) would favor the supplier. Once negotiators have agreed on an outcome where no party can do better without the other doing worse, they are said to have reached the Pareto frontier. This would be true of both Options 1 and 2. The compromise solution, however, is dominated by any outcome in the shaded area to the "northwest." Both parties would prefer an outcome in the shaded area to the compromise solution. The unshaded area between the two lines

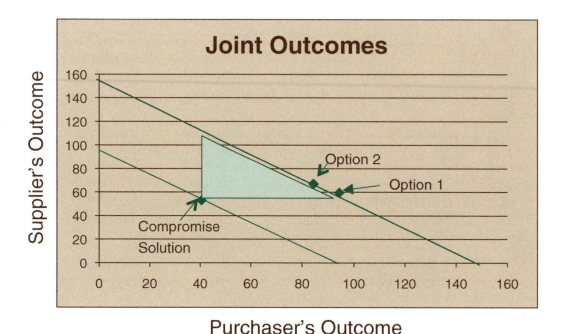

FIGURE 4.1 Plot of Joint Outcomes: Option 1, Option 2, and the Compromise Solution

is Pareto dominated by the shaded area. The area below the shaded area (to the right) would be better for the purchaser, but the supplier would not accept outcomes in that area because they are even worse than the compromise solution. Likewise, the purchaser would not move from the compromise position to the area above the shaded area (to the left) because it would make them worse off.

CHAPTER SUMMARY

In this chapter we differentiated integrative negotiation from distributive bargaining. We discussed the distinguishing characteristics of integrative negotiation situations. Typically, they involve multiple issues, and it is assumed that parties will value the issues differently. Also, the relationship with the other person must be considered, because these are typically not one-time interactions. We examined the difference between "positions" and "interests" and learned how to uncover the interests of the other party. One way is taking the other's perspective; another is asking good questions. We learned a system for quantifying a multi-issue negotiation and showed how bundling offers can create value over simply compromising on every issue. We learned about the Pareto frontier and how outcomes that fall below it leave money on the table.

Questions/Exercises

1. You are an athletic director at a large, publicly funded university. Due to **a recent economic** downturn, your athletic department has had to cut its operations budget by 25%. That budget cut has been offset by a $15 million gift the athletic department received last year from one of the university's major donors. The donor's only condition for the $15 million gift was that the university name its soon to be completed basketball arena after the donor's family—the Stanwick Basketball Arena. Yesterday, you received a telephone call from the university president. She told you the donor's granddaughter was accused of paying a classmate $20,000 to write her term papers when she was a student at another university. Although the granddaughter denies the allegations, newspapers are reporting that she did return her degree. The president tells you the university's faculty senate is demanding that the university not name the basketball arena after the Stanwick family. Local news and television reporters have been calling your office asking about the "hypocrisy" of naming a university facility after a family that is known for academic misconduct. The president asks you to "gently persuade the donor to take the family name off of the basketball arena." You like the donor, need his continued financial support for the athletic department, and don't want to anger him. Is this an integrative or distributive negotiation? Why?

2. You are the owner of Baker's Point Resort, a business located on the shores of Spirit Lake in northwest Iowa. Baker's Point Resort rents boats and fishing gear. It is open from May 15 until September 15. Baker's Point Resort is organized as a limited partnership—you are the general partner and handle all of the day-to-day decisions for the business, and your sister is the primary investor and limited partner.

   This year you have decided to start selling live bait—night crawlers and minnows—for fishing. When your grandfather opened Baker's Point Resort in 1960, the business sold live bait; however, Baker's Point stopped selling live bait in 1978, when your uncle ran the business. You have checked the old bait house and all the equipment and tanks still work.

   The largest live bait wholesaler in Iowa—Bernita's Fine Bait Shop—is located in nearby Estherville, Iowa. The next closest bait shop is Minnow World, located in Jackson, Minnesota. You have scheduled a call to talk to the owner of Bernita's Fine Bait Shop about purchasing live bait for the upcoming fishing season. Based on a quick review of "live bait" websites, you have a general sense that the "going rate" for night crawlers is $2.25 per dozen and $1.50 per dozen of minnows. You estimate that each month you will need 30 dozen night crawlers and 25 dozen minnows. Your expected price range for night crawlers is between $2.00 and $2.25 per dozen and $1.25 and $1.50 per dozen for minnows. If you can't reach an agreement with Bernita's Fine Bait Shop, you will have to contact Minnow World; however, you have no idea about the prices they charge for live bait

or even if they sell more than minnows.

   Since Baker's Point Resort is located approximately 15 miles from Bernita's Fine Bait Shop, you will likely have to pay for the transport of your minnows and night crawlers. The store in Estherville that stocks fishing gear for Baker's Point charges $25 per delivery for its delivery charge. You do not want to pay more than $25 per delivery and would hope the delivery charge for Bernita's Fine Bait Shop would be in the $15 to $20 range since you know Bernita's sells live bait to three other fishing resorts on Spirit Lake. You would also prefer that deliveries be made on the first Friday of the month.

   During your meeting with the owner of Bernita's Fine Bait Shop, you will negotiate over (1) price per dozen for minnows and night crawlers and (2) the delivery charge per monthly shipment of minnows and night crawlers. What is your Best Alternative to a Negotiated Agreement (BATNA) in this negotiation with Bernita's Fine Bait Shop? How would you evaluate the strength of your BATNA? List five questions that you plan on asking the owner of Bernita's Fine Bait Shop when you start the negotiation.

3. Harlan Sanders, better known as "Colonel Sanders," was the founder of the Kentucky Fried Chicken restaurant chain. Colonel Sanders started selling chicken from a gas station he operated in Corbin, Kentucky. He eventually created his recipe of "11 secret herbs and spices" for the coating of the chicken, and developed a special way of cooking the chicken, using a pressure cooker.

   Attorney John Y. Brown, Jr., and financier Jack Massey, approached Sanders in 1963 about selling the Kentucky Fried

Chicken business to them. The sale of Kentucky Fried Chicken was completed in 1964. The details of that negotiation are summarized below:

When the two men [Brown and Massey] called on him [Colonel Sanders] in Shelbyville in October, 1963, and made their offer, the Colonel answered without hesitation that a sale was out of the question. He made mildly disparaging remarks about city slickers. Brown and Massey argued that the Colonel should have time to enjoy life now, and that if he died before selling out much of his estate would probably go for taxes. They offered him two million dollars, some stock in the proposed new company, and a continuing relationship with Kentucky Fried Chicken, as the company's adviser and living image. They promised that quality control would be their byword, and they swore that no one would ever tamper with the chicken recipe. The Colonel knew that the proposal was logically sound, but somehow it didn't seem right. Could a father sell his child? For the next several weeks, the Colonel meditated while Brown wooed him. They crisscrossed the country, counselling with daughters, grandchildren, nephews, preachers, bankers, accountants, franchisees—everyone who was close to the Colonel or would be affected by the sale. Finally, on January 6, 1964, the Colonel gave in and signed a contract. The deal was to be completed on March 6th, when the stock would be transferred and the Colonel would be given a down payment of five hundred thousand dollars. Under the terms of the contract, the Colonel retained Canada, and the new company got the rest of the world minus England, Florida, Utah, and Montana—four areas that the Colonel had already disposed of. In addition to his two million, the Colonel got a lifetime salary of forty thousand dollars a year (increased since then to seventy-five thousand); he turned down ten thousand shares of stock. The next two months were tense ones for Brown. As the new team prepared to take over, the Colonel was increasingly fidgety, and cross as could be. He had built up this company single-handed, and now here he was turning it over to people from outside the food business—a lawyer and a financier, neither of whom knew a drumstick from a pig's ear. Brown expected every day that the deal would fall through, but when March 6th came the Colonel gritted his teeth and took the money.

Source: Whitworth, W., "Kentucky Fried," The New Yorker Magazine (February 14, 1970) (https://www.newyorker.com/magazine/1970/02/14/kentucky-fried).

a. How did Brown and Massey make their negotiation with Sanders an integrative negotiation?

b. Which of Sanders' interests were satisfied in the negotiation with Brown and Massey?

4. You will be graduating in May with your Bachelor of Business Administration (B.B.A.) degree. You have been interviewing for a series of sales positions with companies located throughout Iowa, Illinois and Nebraska. An Omaha-based insurance company (Good Hands USA) has offered you a job—a sales position

for which you will be compensated based strictly on commissions. The Good Hands USA human resources director told you that most recent graduates being paid on a straight-commission basis make approximately $55,000 per year. You have two weeks to decide whether or not to accept the Good Hands USA offer. Although the straight-commission basis of this offer is not negotiable, the human resources director told you that she would be willing to talk to you about other aspects of the job (e.g., a company car, money for professional development and the company's tuition reimbursement program if you decided to start taking MBA classes).

Accepting a straight commission job worries you since you will have apartment rent and car payments to make after you graduate. Your preference would be for a job that offers some base salary plus commissions based on sales you make to customers. Salary data you have received from your university's career center shows that the average starting salary for recent B.B.A. graduates is $45,000.

This morning you interviewed with a recruiter for a Chicago-based pharmaceutical sales company—Drug Store USA. The Drug Store USA recruiter was very aggressive. She told you, "Look, we have 50 candidates for this job. Although we usually only hire graduates from Chicago-area schools, my boss graduated from your university and we are willing to take a chance on you. I can offer you an entry level sales position with the company. Your base salary will be $25,000 with commissions based on your sales. You have the potential to make about $60,000 per year under this compensation package. Here is the deal though. I can only keep this offer open to you for one day. Base salary is non-negotiable. If I don't hear back from you by noon tomorrow, the job will go to someone else."

You were somewhat taken aback by the Drug Store USA recruiter's aggressive style. Your parents are pushing you to get a job by graduation; however, they have offered to let you live in the basement of their house if you don't have a job in May so that you can continue your job search without worrying about paying for rent. You figure you need a job that will pay at least $45,000 per year so that you can pay your bills. You would also like to work for a company that will give you a chance to be promoted—you would just as soon not change jobs during the first five years after your May graduation—and to work for a company that recognizes the strong work ethic you developed as a university student.

a. What are your interests in these two salary negotiations? What are the employers' (Good Hands USA and Drug Store USA) interests?

b. Do you have a strong BATNA? If not, what steps can you take to improve your BATNA?

c. Are either of these two negotiations an integrative negotiation? Why or why not?

5. One of the techniques that should be included in the toolkit needed for an integrative negotiation is the ability to get in the other negotiator's shoes – "perspective taking." How would you put yourself in the "other person's shoes" in the following situation? You are on a student committee which is responsible for scheduling a keynote speaker at your college's spring awards banquet. The committee's

budget can cover expenses for travel and accommodations for the keynote speaker up to the total amount of $2,500. Students in your college have recommended that the committee ask a famous graduate of your university to be the spring awards banquet keynote speaker. This alumnus of your college (you have discovered through your research) generally charges $5,000 plus travel expenses and accommodations for speaking engagements. She became famous by starting a new technology, "went public" with the company, and ultimately sold her company for millions of dollars to another company. Since selling the company, this alumnus has written a book on leadership and has lectured at several business schools across the country. What do you think you and your committee can offer this alumnus in terms of the spring awards banquet and her visit to your campus, that may convince her to reduce her standard speaking fee so that you can stay within your budget for the event?

Endnotes

1. Fisher, A., & Ury, B. (1981) *Getting to yes.* Boston: Houghton Mifflin.
2. Galinsky, A., Ku, G., & Want, C. (2005). Perspective-taking: Fostering social bonds and facilitating coordination. *Group Processes and Intergroup Relations, 8,* 109–125.
3. Bazerman, M. H., & Neale, M. A. (1992). *Negotiating rationally.* New York: Free Press.
4. Thompson, L. L. (2009). *The mind and heart of the negotiator.* (4th ed.). Upper Saddle River, NJ: Pearson Education.
5. Table adapted from the work of Putnam, L. (2005). Are you asking the right questions? *Negotiation, 8:3,* 7–9.
6. Thompson, L. (1991). Information exchange in negotiation. *Journal of Experimental and Social Psychology, 26,* 528–544.
7. Posavac, E. J., & Carey, R. G. (1989). *Program evaluation: Methods and case studies.* Englewood Cliffs, NJ: Prentice Hall.

5

Planning Your Road Trip: Planning and Preparation for Successful Negotiations

You have been planning to visit a friend who attends another university. This friend visited you at school last semester, and you feel you owe her a return visit. Plus, it would be great to get out of town and away from campus for a few days. You will like to visit your friend during a home football game weekend. Although it would be easier to fly to visit your friend, you will likely have to drive. The trip will take eight hours one way. You would like to arrive at your friend's university around the dinner hour (6:00 P.M.) on Friday and return home in time on Sunday evening to meet with two classmates to work on a class project.

This trip would certainly take some time to plan. You will need to think about how much the trip will cost you in terms of gas for your car, whether you will stay with your friend or will need to find a hotel room, what driving route to take, and the date when your friend's university has a home football game. It would be helpful to find out if any of your other friends would be interested in making the trip (and sharing the cost of gas or a hotel room), whether tickets are available for the football game, and if your car needs any maintenance before taking the trip. Probably the worst thing you could do in this situation is to jump in your car and make the trip to visit your friend without doing any planning at all. Although it is exciting to be spontaneous, this is the type of trip that could be a disaster if not done right.

Good negotiators understand the value of planning. Much like preparing for a short drive to the grocery store is different than preparing to take a cross-country driving trip, the extent to which a negotiator must prepare to negotiate depends on the type of negotiation, the negotiator's alternatives, and her or his relationship with the other negotiator. In this chapter, we will outline a plan for preparation that can be used in a variety of negotiation situations.

CHAPTER OBJECTIVES

- To identify the different stages of a successful negotiation
- To develop a road map to prepare for a successful negotiation
- To understand the importance of a Best Alternative to a Negotiated Agreement (BATNA) in negotiations
- To recognize which negotiation strategies are appropriate to use in different negotiation situations

KEY TERMS

Stages of a successful
    negotiation: preparation,
    rapport-building,
    information-trading, deal-
    making, and closing

Interests (tangible and
    intangible)
Bargaining goals
Rapport
Schmoozing

Mimicry
Role reversal
Authoritative standards and
    objective information

■ ■ ■ ■

The Stages of a Successful Negotiation

Successful negotiations go through a distinct series of stages.[1] The first stage is the **preparation** stage. This stage involves deciding whether there is something to be gained through negotiation, identifying the type of negotiation situation, and developing an appropriate strategy. The second stage is the **rapport-building** stage. During this stage, negotiators attempt to build a personal connection—rapport—so that they feel comfortable discussing different negotiation proposals, sharing information, and working together toward a possible agreement. The third stage is the **information-trading** stage. This stage is marked by an exchange of information between negotiators about their respective proposals. Depending on the type of negotiation—distributive or integrative—the negotiators may emphasize the strength of their positions, discuss the type of leverage they have, or lay out a list of demands (primarily in a distributive negotiation) that must be met for an agreement to occur. The next stage is the **deal-making** stage. The negotiators in this stage actively attempt to find a mix of different proposals that may lead to an agreement. This stage includes problem solving, the brainstorming of ideas, and offering concessions/trade-off proposals. The final stage is the **closing** stage. During this stage, the negotiators make final offers to complete the deal and discuss ways to implement their agreement.

> **TAKE AWAY:** *Negotiations tend to go through a series of distinct stages, although the amount of time spent during each stage may vary depending on the complexity of the issues negotiated, the nature of the negotiators' relationship, and the skill of the individual negotiators.*

Assume you have decided to rent an apartment instead of living in the university residence halls next semester. Your **preparation** will include looking at your budget to decide how much you can spend; thinking about what you are looking for in an apartment—one or two bedrooms, close proximity to campus, the availability of parking for your car, and so forth; identifying

FIGURE 5.1 The Stages of a Successful Negotiation

available apartments in your price range; and finding a possible roommate to help you to pay rent. When you meet with the landlords of the different apartments (or with the representative of a property management company that owns the apartments), you want them to know that you are prepared to negotiate for a fair rent and that you would make a good tenant for their apartment **(rapport-building)**. You will talk about the available apartments and ask questions about parking, the quality of the appliances in the apartments, and the amount of the monthly rent **(information-trading)**. Once you narrow your list of available apartments to the one that best meets your needs, you will start **deal making** with the landlord, using your knowledge of the market rate for apartments to help convince the landlord to rent the apartment to you at a rental rate that is within your price range. You might **close** the deal for your preferred apartment by agreeing to the landlord's rental price if he or she guarantees you a parking spot, agrees to replace the apartment's carpeting, or allows you to sublet the apartment if you are hired for an internship during the school year. If the landlord agrees to your last offer, you will finish the deal by signing a lease.

Stages of a successful negotiation
Preparation, rapport-building, information-trading, deal-making and closing

The Importance of Preparation for Negotiation Success

We all have stories of "failed" negotiations. You may have taken the first offer in a job negotiation and later realized that the employer could have offered you more money. You may have bought a textbook at the bookstore

"Failure to prepare is preparing to fail."

—John Wooden, Legendary UCLA Basketball Coach

only to later find out that the same textbook was available online at a much lower price. You may have agreed to upgrades in a basic cable television package or a cell phone service plan when keeping your current package or plan actually made more economic sense. You may have discovered a cheaper alternative after you booked a flight for a spring break trip. These failed negotiations tend to be explained by our failure to prepare.

Preparation forces a negotiator to determine what he or she needs in order for a negotiation to be successful. If you know what you want to accomplish, you will be less likely to overpay for your negotiated outcome. As an example, your roommate offers to sell you his collection of vintage comic books for $500. Without checking, you have no idea if $500 is a reasonable price or the market value for these comic books. Because he is your roommate, you accept the deal. If the market value turns out to be $300 for these comic books, you have overpaid by $200.

Preparation allows you to have a greater sense of control over a situation that may seem to be unclear and ambiguous. Knowing what you want, and anticipating what the other negotiator may want or need, gives you confidence in your own abilities to reach an agreement. A confident negotiator knows when to stick to a position, when to make concessions, and when to walk away from a deal that does not meet his or her needs.

Preparing to negotiate is like preparing to take an examination. If you don't know how to prepare (or how to study), the amount of preparation time won't matter. In the next section, we provide you with a guide to help you effectively prepare for a negotiation situation.

Dennis Ross was Middle East envoy and chief peace negotiator for Presidents George H.W. Bush and Bill Clinton. His 12 rules of negotiation[2] highlight the importance of preparation:

1. ***Know what you want; know what you can live with.*** "In a high-stakes negotiation, each side may know what it wants in the abstract, but not really have thought through what it may be able to accept. The process of negotiation can alter expectations by transforming the view of the adversary." Negotiators should think "through their bottom lines on the core issues."

2. ***Know everything there is to know about the decision maker(s) on the other side.*** A negotiator must know "who makes decisions and who is able to influence the relevant decision maker or makers" and "have a good picture of the other side's reasons for talking, their principal concerns, and what they want and require from the talks."

3. ***Build a relationship of trust with the key decision maker.*** A relationship of trust can be created by establishing credibility with the other

negotiator—"You must never promise something and not deliver, and you must always deliver *exactly* what you promise"—being "open and revealing," protecting the "confidences" given to you by the other negotiator, and being "prepared at a certain point to deliver something of value to your counterpart that he or she knows is difficult for you to produce."

4. ***Keep in mind the other side's need for an explanation.*** "No matter what the transaction . . . in making a deal each side must be able to explain to itself or others why the agreement was in its interest . . . A negotiator must be thinking about how the other side will explain an important concession even as he/she is pushing for it."

5. ***To gain the hardest concessions, prove you understand what is important to the other side.*** This is Ross' "empathy rule"—a negotiator must demonstrate that he or she knows "what is important to the other side but also why certain concessions are so painful for it" to accept.

6. ***Tough love is also required.*** Where agreement serves both parties' interests, negotiators must understand the "profound, adverse consequence" of not reaching an agreement.

7. ***Employ the good cop–bad cop approach carefully.*** Like the use of many distributive strategies and techniques, "there is often a tendency to view the good and bad cops as contrived or designed to suggest artificial differences or pressures for the purposes of avoiding concessions."

8. ***Understand the value and limitations of deadlines.*** "The higher the stakes in a negotiation, the more a deadline is likely to be necessary to force concessions that each side is ultimately willing to make but reluctant to undertake until they become convinced that there is no choice."

9. ***Take only calculated risks.*** "Knowing when to run risks must be a part of the makeup of any negotiator. And being prepared as a negotiator to make threats at certain critical moments must be accompanied by a readiness to carry out what you threaten."

10. ***Never lie; never bluff.*** "Lies and bluffs will always be exposed, and once he is exposed, a negotiator may never recover his credibility."

11. ***Don't paper over differences.*** ". . . negotiations are about overcoming differences, and the differences cannot be wished away. While it is important to create a context and avoid being provocative, there are moments at which indirection does not work and when differences must be taken on directly, even if this means that a difficult, bitter meeting may be the result."

12. ***Summarize agreements at the end of every meeting.*** ". . . since misunderstandings frequently bedevil negotiations and always set them back, being careful to summarize what has been both understood and not understood on each issue at the end of a meeting is a critical rule of thumb for negotiators."

■ ■ ■ ■

Preparing to Negotiate: Creating Your Road Map

Your GPS navigation system and road maps guide your travels on a driving trip. Effective negotiators take the time to develop a game plan that similarly guides their travels on the negotiation highway. The following questions will help you, the negotiator, develop a negotiation game plan – your road map to a destination of agreement:

- What is it you want or need?
- What do you want to accomplish in this particular negotiation?
- What will happen if you cannot reach an agreement with the other negotiator?
- What type of relationship do you have or do you want to have (i.e., a one-time deal or a longer-term relationship) with the other negotiator?
- What do you think the other negotiator wants or needs?
- What will you do to explain or "sell" your first offer to the other negotiator?
- What strategy best fits this negotiation?

Although the amount of time needed for preparation will depend on the type of negotiation situation, each of these questions must be answered by the negotiator before the negotiation is started. These questions are discussed in greater detail in the following sections.

■ ■ ■ ■

What Is It You Want or Need?

Interests (tangible and intangible) Tangible interests represent things that a negotiator wants or needs that are tangible, and generally easy to identify, such as money, a new job, or a specific price in a sales transaction. Intangible interests, on the other hand, are things a negotiator may want or need which are less obvious, things such as recognition, respect or fair treatment.

You have been training to run your first marathon race. Given the number of miles you have been running each day, you now need a new pair of running shoes. As you walk into a sporting goods store to buy a new pair of running shoes, what is it that you want or need? That seems like a silly question. You are obviously interested in buying a new pair of running shoes. There may, however, be other things on your mind as you enter the store. You may want a particular brand of running shoe. You will likely have a price range. Customer service—how you are treated during the sales transaction—may be important to you. It could be you want the sales clerk to ask you about your training. Perhaps it is important that you find a sales clerk who is as interested in running as you are. Maybe you only have 30 minutes to spend on buying a new pair of shoes, or it could be that you are just "looking at options" before you decide on where to buy your shoes and which pair of shoes to purchase.

Your interests are the underlying reasons for what you want or need for a successful negotiation. **Tangible interests** are generally easy to identify by asking the question, "What do I need?" A manager who is being recruited for a new job may have tangible interests in receiving a salary higher than his or her current salary, a company-provided car, and paid moving expenses. In a business situation, a company may have a tangible interest in paying no more than a set price for web design work or paying all newly hired employees in a particular job classification the same starting salary.

The less visible and sometimes hard-to-detect reasons why we may want something in a negotiation—**intangible interests**—are often key to negotiation success. The use of "why" questions can help identify intangible interests: "Why do I want the store clerk to ask me about my marathon training?" "Why do I want to make more money at this new job compared to what I am making now?" "Why do I want to know about the company's tuition reimbursement program?" or "Why am I interested in an ex pat assignment at the company's European subsidiary company?" Intangible interests include things such as how we are treated in a sales transaction, the need to be valued for what we have accomplished at work, a concern about being treated fairly compared to other people, and recognition for what we know or what we have done.

Going back to your trip to the store to buy running shoes, your tangible interest would be to purchase a pair of top-quality running shoes that are within your budget. That is what you **need**. In this situation, your needs have to be met for you to reach an agreement. Your intangible interests may include being recognized as being more than a casual runner, being respected for what you know about running, and being treated in a courteous way by the store clerk. These interests may be more aspirational—what you would **want** to have in an agreement. Keep in mind that it is up to you to determine the priority of what you both want and need in a negotiation.

> **TAKE AWAY:** *There is a difference between a negotiator's "wants" and "needs." A "want" may be like a negotiator's aspiration level (AL)— where he or she would ideally like to be at the end of the negotiation. A "need," on the other hand, is more similar to a negotiator's bottom line or reservation price (RP). The "need" is more of a "must have" compared to the negotiator's "want."*

Bargaining goals
A negotiator must plan to be successful by identifying specific and desired outcomes in his/her negotiation. These specific outcomes are called bargaining goals and represent outcomes that may exceed what the negotiator may generally expect to achieve in the negotiation.

What Do You Want to Accomplish in This Particular Negotiation?

Determining the reasons for what you need and want—your tangible and intangible interests—gives you a framework for developing bargaining goals. **Bargaining goals** are similar to the destination points you might plan for as part of a vacation. Your interest may be to take some time off from work, relax with friends and family members, stay within your budget, and visit a new place. Stated goals allow you to satisfy those interests. Vacation goals would include spending no more than your budgeted amount for vacation, finding a vacation spot you have not been to before, reserving a vacation house with three bedrooms, booking a direct flight that will minimize your travel time, and reserving a rental car within your budget.

© 2011 corepics. Used under license from Shutterstock, Inc.

Before taking a road trip, careful planning is important. Proper planning is likewise important to negotiation success.

We have found that many negotiation students either set their goals too low or set goals that are too general to be helpful in driving a negotiation toward a successful outcome. For example, if you have not researched the market value for the price of the car you are trying to sell, your asking price may be well under the actual value of your car. Likewise, getting a "fair price" is too general of a goal since it begs the fundamental question about what is a "fair price."

Bargaining goals "should be specific, difficult but achievable, and verifiable."[3] Negotiators need to understand what they want or need and what they can reasonably expect to accomplish in the negotiation.

Assume that you have a job interview with a local company. You are interested in this company because of its national reputation, tuition reimbursement program (you would like to earn an MBA degree sometime in the future), and competitive starting salaries. You are also interested in discussing the company's ex pat program, which allows employees to be assigned to work at the company's European subsidiary company. As a result of working with the university's career services office, you determine that the average starting salary for recent university graduates who have taken jobs with this company is $48,000. Because of your high grades (3.7 GPA on a 4.0 scale) and prior internship experience, you believe that you should receive more than the average starting salary for this company. Starting salaries for last year's graduates in your major (finance)—according to the career services office—is $52,000.

A specific salary goal in your negotiation would be $53,000. Although $53,000 is higher than the average starting salary figures you have for this company, you can justify your salary request based on the average starting salary for finance majors from your university and your own distinguishing abilities and experience. Other specific bargaining goals would be to establish a good relationship (rapport) with the recruiter, obtain a commitment for an ex pat assignment within two years of starting with the company, and talk about your plans to earn an MBA degree and the company's tuition reimbursement program.

What Will Happen If You Cannot Reach an Agreement with the Other Negotiator?

The answer to this question will be your **BATNA.** The BATNA draws a "line in the sand" for a negotiator, a line that should not be crossed during a negotiation. A strong BATNA gives leverage to the negotiator and allows the negotiator to push a little harder than normal to get a deal better than what is available away from the bargaining table. The job candidate with a job offer of $50,000 in his or her back pocket has confidence to ask for more than $50,000 during an interview with another employer. This applicant also knows not to accept anything less than a $50,000 salary offer from the second employer.

A scene from the movie, *Tommy Boy*[4] demonstrates the power of a strong BATNA. The lead character—"Tommy Boy" Callahan—and a colleague (Richard Hayden) sit down to eat at the Cluck Bucket Restaurant. Tommy Boy asks the waitress for an order of chicken wings. The waitress tells Tommy Boy the "kitchen is closed." Tommy Boy convinces the waitress to "throw some wings in the fryer" for him. When Richard asks Tommy Boy why he was so "confident and relaxed" when negotiating with the waitress, Tommy Boy says, "I was just having fun. If we didn't get the wings, so what, we got that meat lover's pizza in the trunk." This strong alternative to negotiating for an order of chicken wings—a pizza in the trunk of his car—gave Tommy Boy the confidence to negotiate in a more aggressive way with the waitress.

By contrast, a weak BATNA tells a negotiator that he or she may have to adopt an accommodating style in the negotiation and offer additional concessions to make a deal. The job candidate with no other job offers who desperately needs a job may have to take the first job offer received. The student who has a ticket to the university homecoming football game but is unable to use it and unable to find a buyer for it may end up giving the ticket away or not using the ticket at all.

A negotiator with a weak BATNA can take steps to improve his or her position. If you are trying to find the lowest-cost copy of your textbook for a class, you shop around. Knowing your options—purchasing the book online or going to the campus bookstore—is helpful when a classmate offers to sell you a copy of the book from the past semester. A business owner in negotiation with a parts supplier may, along these same lines, bid out the work to see if other companies are interested in the work. Generating new alternatives gives the business owner a stronger BATNA to use in the negotiation with its parts supplier.

Identifying new alternatives may convert a negotiator's weak BATNA into a negotiation strength. In 2009, race car driver Danica Patrick reached an agreement to continue racing in the IndyCar Series with Andretti Green Racing (AGR).[5] In the weeks leading up to her decision to continue racing in the IndyCar Series, and to stay with AGR, there were various media reports of Patrick considering leaving the IndyCar Series entirely to drive stock cars in NASCAR races. This "walk away" option—to drive in NASCAR—gave Patrick leverage in her negotiations with AGR and provided her with a strong BATNA.

> **TAKE AWAY:** *A negotiator must be able to identify his or her BATNA before starting a negotiation. A weak BATNA will affect a negotiator's strategy and the approach at the bargaining table. Effective negotiators take steps to improve a weak BATNA by identifying new alternatives.*

What Type of Relationship Do You Have or Do You Want to Have with the Other Negotiator?

The type of relationship you have with the other negotiator will affect your negotiation strategy. As we will discuss later in this chapter, negotiation situations that are "one-time deals," where the future relationship with the other negotiator is not important, generally feature competitive or distributive strategies. Negotiating with a street vendor in another country for a vacation souvenir or negotiating with a ticket scalper for a concert ticket—situations when you are generally trying to pay the least amount of money and have little interest in establishing a long-term relationship with the other negotiator—are examples of these one-time deals that involve competitive/distributive strategies.

On the other hand, if you are negotiating with a friend or family member, you may use a more accommodating or compromising strategy, where you make concessions in recognition of the personal relationship you have with the other negotiator. Think about how you might negotiate with your grandmother who offers to sell you her couch for your apartment. You might accept the first price your grandmother offers. Using the distributive strategies techniques summarized in Chapter 2, which you might use in negotiating with a street vendor or ticket scalper, would hurt the relationship you have with your grandmother.

In situations in which you don't know the other negotiator, or would like to establish a longer-term relationship, building rapport becomes a particularly important part of the negotiation. During your preparation, you will think about how to establish **rapport**—a personal connection—with the other negotiator. Rapport allows a negotiator to feel comfortable sharing information with the other negotiator and in trusting that the other negotiator will implement agreements reached at the bargaining table. As noted by sports agent and attorney Leigh Steinberg (the basis for Tom Cruise's character in the movie, *Jerry McGuire*):

> *One of the first barriers we typically must break through in negotiation is the armor people put up to protect themselves. It's natural to be hesitant to reveal oneself to strangers in almost any setting. It's normal to hide behind roles, titles and carefully guarded words. This wariness is compounded in a negotiating situation, where the tendency is to begin by holding one's cards close to the vest. Anything that can be done to pierce this protective armor and being connected to the other person in a personal way will increase the level of trust and communication that develops between you. As the negotiation unfolds, that trust and communication will become invaluable . . . I would argue that it is not only possible but in most cases necessary for an effective negotiator to approach the other party in a spirit of collaboration. The ability to trust one another, to develop a climate of candor and clarity, will enable both parties to reveal their true agendas. It is only when those agendas are revealed and understood by each side that movement toward an agreement can truly begin.[6]*

Many people equate rapport with "schmoozing." **Schmoozing** in the context of negotiations is an attempt by one negotiator to emphasize similarities (real or contrived) with the other negotiator that can be used for negotiations advantage. There is some logic in the notion that negotiators may have a personal connection with someone who has a similar background.[7] A relationship based on insincere flattery is not, however, the type of relationship needed to build a working relationship. Note we are not talking about a "friendship" between negotiators, since many negotiations are made between people with vastly different personalities and backgrounds. The key aspects of a good working relationship in negotiations are respect and trust. Do you

Rapport
Effective negotiators establish a personal connection with the other negotiator by asking questions, sharing information and building a trusting and sincere working relationship. This personal connection is called rapport and allows both negotiators to share information and trust that negotiated agreements will be implemented and followed by both sides.

Schmoozing
Unlike a personal connection established with the other negotiator (rapport), schmoozing is a tactic used by some negotiators to emphasize similarities (real or pretend) with the other negotiator.

The Fuller Brush Company: Identifying Interests to Build Rapport and Increase Day-to-Day Sales

The Fuller Brush Company built a long-standing business on the door-to-door sale of brushes and house-cleaning products. Fuller Brush Company sales representatives were trained to identify customers' interests to establish rapport, and develop ongoing productive customer relationships. Because household chores can be time consuming, the Fuller Brush Company sales representation would demonstrate to a new customer how the Fuller Brush product line could help the new customer clean the house in far less time – an important customer interest. Testimonials from other "satisfied customers," including positive comments from the new customer's neighbors, would help to persuade the customer to buy Fuller Brush Company products. In other cases, the Fuller Brush Company sales representative might offer a special "introductory" price on a Fuller Brush product, or offer a discounted price on a third Fuller Brush product, if the customer agreed to pay full price for the first two purchased products.

Fuller Brush Company sales representatives knew that earning the first sale with a customer was critical, as it helped the sales representative better understand the customer's needs and interests. The sales representative's personal knowledge of the customer's needs and interests, allowed the sales representative to offer the customer new products that may further benefit the household. When the sales representative showed up at the household, the customer would see the sales representative as "a valuable partner" in the customer's "household enterprise," and not a stranger.

Sources: "The Fuller Brush Story," (https://www.fuller.com/fuller-brush-history); Hipkin, J., "What the Fuller Brush Man can Teach us about Selling," *CustomerThink*, (April 6, 2009) (https://customerthink.com/what_the_fuller_brush_man_can_teach_us_about_selling/).

respect what the other negotiator is telling you, and do you trust him or her to carry out what has been agreed to?

The following exchange demonstrates a failed attempt by a new sales manager to build rapport with a purchasing manager by schmoozing:

> **Sales Manager:** Thanks for taking the time to meet with me today. I was hoping we could review the last two orders you have placed with our company and talk about taking this business relationship to "the next level."

> **Purchasing Manager:** I am not sure what you mean by "the next level." We have done business with your company for the past five years. We are happy with the service you provide but have no need to increase our orders at this time.

> **Sales Manager:** You are right; we should not rush things. How long have you been at the company?

> **Purchasing Manager:** I have worked here for about two years. Before that, I was a pilot in the Navy.

Sales Manager: What type of plane did you fly?

Purchasing Manager: I flew the P-3 Orion.

Sales Manager: How cool; my old boss used to fly for the Navy. Did you go to the Naval Academy?

Purchasing Manager: Yes, I did.

Sales Manager: Hey, I went to West Point. I bet you saw me play football during the Army–Navy football games. I played linebacker.

Purchasing Manager: Look, I really don't have much time today to chitchat or talk about the Army–Navy football games. I played hockey at Navy, so I did not have much time to watch football games.

Sales Manager: Are you kidding me? I love hockey. I grew up in Michigan rooting for the Detroit Red Wings. Do you watch hockey? I bet I could get you some tickets to Red Wings games if you want.

Purchasing Manager: Thanks, but we have a pretty strict gift policy here. I need to get back to work. Good to talk to you. I will let you know if we need anything else from you in the future.

The sales manager in this exchange is likely thinking that the company will increase its sales if he is "buddies" with the purchasing manager. Do you think the purchasing manager sees it that way? The sales manager asked very few questions about the company's future needs or what the purchasing manager would need in order to increase sales. If anything, the sales manager may have caused the purchasing manager to rethink his relationship with the company because of the sales manager's "over the top" attempt to show how much he had in common with the purchasing manager.

Rather than "schmooze," the new sales manager e should have emphasized the reasons why the purchasing manager has been a business partner with the sales representative's company:

Sales Manager: I appreciate your willingness to take some time out of your schedule to meet with me today.

Purchasing Manager: No problem, although I am pretty busy this morning.

Sales Manager: I understand that. I do want you to know that we will continue to give you the service that your company deserves and has come to expect from our company.

Purchasing Manager: That is music to my ears. I worried about having to break in a new sales manager after Charlene Stokes left your company.

Whenever I needed parts, I picked up the phone and gave her a call. I am hoping I can do the same thing with you.

Sales Manager: Charlene was an important part of our sales team. I know she is looking forward to traveling with her family now that she has retired. Going forward, please call or text me any time. My cell number is on my business card [giving the purchasing manager his card]. Say, that was quite an article about your company in the *Wall Street Journal* the other day. I bet expanding into South America will increase the role of your Purchasing Department, won't it?

Purchasing Manager: It sure will. I have no idea how we are going to manage filling these new orders from South America.

Sales Manager: Our company has been working with several customers in Brazil and Argentina. Why don't we set up a time next week when I can give you a call? I can share with you some of the challenges they have had working in South America and what our company has done to help them to be successful.

Purchasing Manager: That would be great. I will check my schedule this afternoon for next week and send you a text about what times work for me.

In this exchange, the purchasing manager's worries about "breaking in" a new sales manager have been addressed by the new sales manager. Rapport is established by the sales manager respecting the purchasing manager's time, doing some research about the company, and identifying a way that he can help the purchasing manager and yet (possibly) expand his own company's sales.

> **TAKE AWAY:** *Rapport means building a working relationship with the other negotiator. It requires an attempt to make a genuine and personal connection. Rapport is different than schmoozing.*

Rapport can be established by showing a genuine interest in the other negotiator and what that person has to say. It involves an "emotional connection"[8] with the other negotiator, so that you can understand their concerns. Famous sports agent Scott Boras attributes his success in representing professional baseball players to the fact that he played minor league baseball and can identify "players' needs, their fears, [and] their anxieties."[9]

The value of meeting the other negotiator face-to-face in terms of building rapport cannot be overstated. While parts of a negotiation can be handled over the telephone, by email or through correspondence, that important first impression should be made face-to-face (even if done virtually). It is, after all, easier to tell someone "no" in an email, text, or letter than to do so in a face-to-face conversation. This point was dramatized in the movie, *We Are Marshall*.[10] Almost every member of the Marshall University football team and its coaching staff died in a 1970 plane crash. *We Are Marshall* chronicles the efforts of the new head coach (Jack Lengyel) and the university president (Donald Dedmon) to field a football team for the 1971 season. President Dedmon had been writing letters (unsuccessfully) to the National Collegiate Athletic Association (NCAA) that would allow first-year students to play on the Marshall football team—at that time, first-year students were not allowed to play varsity football according to NCAA rules. After another rejection by the NCAA, Coach Lengyel asks President Dedmon in a scene of *We Are Marshall* if he is married. When President Dedmon answers yes, Coach Lengyel says, "I am willing to bet you didn't propose over the phone." President Dedmon responds, "No I didn't." Coach Lengyel follows up with, "And I know damn well, she didn't say yes in a letter." The next scene in *We Are Marshall* shows President Dedmon on the steps of the NCAA offices attempting to meet face-to-face with NCAA officials. Ultimately, as a result of this meeting, the NCAA granted Marshall University's request to play first-year players during the 1971 football season.

During your negotiation preparation, you should think about the type of questions you could ask the other negotiator that would allow you to better understand what he or she wants or needs. Offer information to the other negotiator about what you are looking for in the deal and what's important to you. This offer of information is generally met with a reciprocal sharing of information, reflective of the norm of reciprocity discussed in Chapter 3. Also think about how you can get the other negotiator involved (and "saying yes") by talking about the "ground rules" for the negotiation. What issues will you talk about? How much time will you allow for the discussion of the different issues? Where should you meet to negotiate? How long will you have to negotiate? If you reach an agreement, who will write it up? These questions will allow you to reach some initial agreements with the other negotiator, showing the person that the two of you can in fact work together.

Another thing to consider during your preparation is the role body language plays in establishing rapport in a negotiation. Minimal eye contact, a frowning face, and leaning back in your chair with folded arms will not be seen by the other negotiator as a picture of someone who is interested in doing business. As is the case in any social interaction, we look for cues in negotiations how people act in response to things we do and say.[11] A negotiator who, for example, "talks with her hands" and who is very outgoing will respond favorably to a person who "responds in kind" through the use of similar body movements. This is referred to as **mimicry**, and it can be a

Mimicry
Rapport can sometimes be established with the other negotiator by matching ("mimicking") the other negotiator's body language, degree of eye contact or passion about issues discussed during the negotiation.

useful negotiation tactic. When you match certain behavior with the other negotiator, you start to build rapport because you are signaling to that person "I'm interested in what you have to say."

■ ■ ■ ■

What Do You Think the Other Negotiator Wants or Needs?

During preparation for a negotiation, you will be focused on what you need or want and on your planned approach to the negotiation. Skilled negotiators realize that a negotiation involves a certain amount of give and take and that there must be something of value in the deal to make the other negotiator say "yes." Put yourself in the other negotiator's place. What do you have that they might want? How might an agreement with you help them out? The more apparent it is to the other negotiator that you are interested in what he or she wants to accomplish in the negotiation, the more willing the other negotiator will be to try to understand your wants and needs.

Assume that you will be taking a job in New York City and have agreed to rent an apartment with a friend who will also be working in New York City. You will both need to agree on an apartment before you can sign a lease. To do so, you will need to think about what your friend may be looking for in an apartment. Does your friend drive a car? If so, an apartment with reserved parking might be important. If not, the apartment will need to be located close to public transit. Is your roommate on a tight budget? If so, price may be a very important consideration in deciding which apartment to rent. Does your friend enjoy going out or spending time at home when not working? Putting yourself in your friend's place, and thinking about your friend's concerns and needs, allows you to identify common interests as well as areas you might have to compromise.

Role reversal
During preparation for a negotiation, or as a means of identifying new options at the bargaining table, a negotiator may try to see the negotiation from the other negotiator's perspective and anticipate what the other negotiator wants or needs. This technique is called role reversal.

Good sales representatives use this "**role reversal**" technique to understand their customers' buying needs. A clerk in a shoe store may ask customers a series of questions about the type of shoes they wear, their favorite colors and shoe styles, and their price range before showing different shoe choices. When customers walk into the showroom of a car dealership, the sales representative will ask what the customers are looking for in a car, including their price range, favorite colors, past car buying history, and whether or not they have a trade-in. These questions help the sales representative build rapport and, more important, identify the customers' interests. The customer who is looking for a car that can be used to transport her children to and from school, is safe, and has minimal maintenance needs will buy a different car than the single executive who wants to be recognized as a "high roller" based on her choice of vehicle.

© 2011 Kzenon. Used under license from Shutterstock, Inc.

Note how the sales representative from the car dealership is trying to establish rapport with a couple who is interested in buying a car.

What Will You Do to Explain or "Sell" Your First Offer to the Other Negotiator?

Negotiators appreciate other negotiators who are prepared, committed to their bargaining goals, and who can explain the reasons for their proposals. It is one thing to claim that you are looking for a "fair price" for a new television and quite another when you say you are looking to pay "around $600" for a new television because the average retail price for a new television with the features you are looking for is $600.

Using **authoritative standards (and objective information)** such as the *Kelley Blue Book* for car prices, the average price among comparably sized and situated homes in a house seller's neighborhood, or the expert opinion of a jeweler when pricing engagement rings gives credibility to a negotiator's proposals.[12] This type of "objective evidence"[13] is particularly important in price-only negotiations when both negotiators disagree over a "fair" or "market rate price." Other examples of standards that could be used to support a first offer include past agreements with the other negotiators—sometimes referred to as "precedents"—industry standards or more general business standards such as "efficiency" or "profitability."

Authoritative standards and objective information
Authoritative standards and objective information, such as agreed upon market rates, or the opinion of an expert source accepted by both negotiators, can be used by negotiators to better explain or justify their bargaining proposals.

■ ■ ■ ■

What Strategy Best Fits This Negotiation?

In Chapter 2, we used the **dual-concerns model** to identify five different negotiation styles: competing, collaborating, compromise, avoiding, and accommodating. The dual-concerns model identifies negotiation styles based on answers to two questions: (1) How concerned is the negotiator about his or her own outcomes? and (2) How concerned is the negotiator about the other negotiator achieving his or her outcomes? We can use the questions presented by the dual-concerns model to match a negotiation situation with the appropriate style or strategy.

Singular issue transactional negotiations, that is, when a negotiator needs to maximize personal outcomes and has little concern about establishing a long-term relationship with the other negotiator, call for a **competitive or distributive strategy**. Assume that you are ready to graduate and ask your landlord for the full amount of the security deposit on your apartment. Your landlord, however, tells you that the entire amount of your security deposit is going to be withheld to pay for improvements in the apartment—new carpeting, drywall repairs, and a new dishwasher—improvements the landlord says are necessary due to your treatment of the apartment during your residence there. The carpet was in bad shape when you moved into the apartment a year ago, there were water stains on the drywall when you moved in, and the dishwasher never did work quite right, despite your many telephone calls to the landlord. This will likely be a competitive or distributive negotiation with the landlord because you want to receive the entire amount of the security deposit and the landlord is interested in using as much of the security deposit as possible to pay for the repairs to the apartment. You will prepare for this negotiation by identifying reasons that support your position of getting the entire (or as much as possible) amount of the security deposit, anticipating the possible use by the landlord of the distributive tactics identified in Chapter 3, and considering your alternatives (e.g., filing a legal claim against the landlord in small claims court) if you can't reach an agreement.

In situations in which your outcome is not as important as the outcome of the other negotiator—a realtor, for example, who is willing to take a smaller commission payment in order to sell a friend's house—an **accommodations strategy** would be appropriate. A difficulty with the accommodations strategy is that any concession you make in recognition of building a relationship with the other negotiator may become a precedent for future negotiations. The realtor who offers a discounted commission rate to sell a friend's house will likely be asked by the friend for the same discounted commission rate the next time the friend sells a house. The same is true of the sales representative who offers a grocer a discounted product price in exchange for additional shelf space. To avoid creating the expectation that this discounted product price will continue in the future, the sales representative will generally offer the proposal as a "one-time deal," hoping that the success of the discounted product price promotion will help to establish a long-term working relationship with the grocer.

When you have little concern about your outcome or the other negotiator's outcome, an **avoidance strategy** would be the best fit. There are situations when it does not make sense to negotiate. For example, if a sales representative calls asking to sell you a new copier, and you are happy with your current copier and the service you receive from the company that sold you the copier, there is no reason for you to negotiate with the sales representative. You would, therefore, take steps to avoid negotiating with the sales representative in this situation.

A **compromising strategy** is used when a negotiator has some interest in maximizing personal outcome and has some interest in seeing that the other negotiator achieves his or her desired outcomes. Your roommate, for example, suggests that the two of you order a pizza and split the cost. It's late, but you can always eat pizza and there is a local pizzeria just down the street. This might be a quick negotiation, as you say "sure" and you both compromise by each paying half of the cost of the pizza. As another example of using a compromising strategy, say you want to go to Los Angeles for spring break, but your best friend (who will accompany you on the trip) wants to go to South Padre Island. Last year, you both had a good time on a spring break trip to Chicago. Although you both want to go someplace new this year for spring break, a return trip to Chicago might be a compromise if you can't decide between Los Angeles and South Padre Island.

In situations when it is important to maximize both your outcome and that of the other negotiator, a **collaborative**, or **problem-solving**, strategy is appropriate. This strategy would be used in an integrative negotiation of the type discussed in Chapter 4. Negotiating with a friend about which apartment the two of you will rent is a problem-solving/collaborative situation as is a situation in which the executive committee of your student organization is trying to reach agreement on an idea for a fundraising event. In business, two companies that seek to join forces on a joint venture or merger would prepare for collaborative/integrative negotiations. However, using a collaborative or problem-solving strategy will require a significant amount of time both during preparations and during the actual negotiation to identify the different interests and brainstorm options that might lead to a mutually advantageous agreement.

Going back to our spring break example, a problem-solving/collaborative strategy would be necessary to find a spring break location that works for both you and your best friend. Since you can't be in both Los Angeles and South Padre Island at the same time, you will need to explore why you want to go to Los Angeles (there are several art museums there you want to see) and why your best friend wants to go to South Padre Island (the beaches). Once these reasons—the interests—are identified, you would work with your best friend to see if there is a spring break destination that combines the museum scene you are looking for with the beach scene your friend favors. After some Internet research, you will realize that there are several places (we might suggest Miami) that offer what you are both looking for.

> **TAKE AWAY:** *Negotiation strategy is situation specific. A competitive strategy that works well in a one-time deal may not work well in a situation when the negotiators expect to do business with each other in the future. A negotiator must determine the importance of maximizing personal outcomes and the importance of the relationship with the other negotiator when matching appropriate strategy to the specific negotiation situation.*

■ ■ ■ ■   ## CHAPTER SUMMARY

In this chapter, we identified the different stages of a successful negotiation. We discussed the importance of preparing for negotiation success and outlined a road map that negotiators can follow to prepare for a successful outcome. In the next chapters, we will build on our general discussion about negotiation preparation to specifically discuss standards of fairness and ethical issues that arise in negotiations.

Questions/Exercises

1. In this chapter, we have emphasized the importance of preparing to negotiate. Watch the negotiation scene from the movie *Intolerable Cruelty* (2003) between two divorce lawyers. This negotiation scene is available at https://www.youtube.com/watch?v=6PpQk63iIWw. How does the lack of preparation of the husband's divorce lawyer affect the initial negotiation meeting?

2. Negotiations between Ray Kroc, Dick, and Mac McDonald for the business that ultimately became the McDonald Corporation that we are all familiar with today were dramatized in the movie *The Founder* (2016). Analyze the negotiations scene between Kroc and the McDonalds brothers in which Kroc accepts the offer from the McDonald brothers in 1961 to buy their business interests in the McDonald's restaurant for the sum of $2.7 million. How did the McDonalds' brothers determine the basis for their offer to Kroc? How would you describe their interests in the negotiation with Kroc?

3. You are selling cookware door-to-door in Birmingham, Alabama. It is hot. You are not from the South. You stop at what looks to be a well-maintained home and are greeted at the door by someone who looks to be about your age. This person has two small children at the door and looks extremely tired. How do you propose to establish rapport with this person so that you can sell some cookware? What questions would you ask to identify the person's interests?

4. You are negotiating with a landlord to rent a two-bedroom apartment on Johnson Street. The average rental rate for two-bedroom apartments on Johnson Street is $800 per month. You don't want to spend more than $750 per month on your rent. If you can't negotiate to rent this particular two-bedroom apartment, your alternative is to rent a one-room efficiency apartment for $600 per month.

   Note: Assume that the landlord is a close friend of your mother. You want to have a fair negotiation with the landlord, but you don't want to make him mad at you or your father.

   a. What is your RP in the negotiation with the landlord for the two-bedroom apartment?

   b. What is your BATNA? Do you have a strong or weak BATNA?

   c. Using the dual-concerns model discussed in Chapter 2, how would you describe the negotiation situation with the landlord for the two-bedroom apartment on Johnson Street?

5. You are the executive director for a non-profit organization that operates a shelter house for victims of domestic violence—the "Rainbow House." Revenue streams for Rainbow House are based on community donations (40%) and grants from state and local government (60%). Rainbow House has developed a good reputation for its efficient and responsible use of funds.

Residents of Rainbow House are guaranteed shelter for 90 days. After that, they are, with the help of the Rainbow House staff, expected to find their own housing. Most of the residents of Rainbow House come from two local communities: Lakeville and Gantry Town. Due to a downturn in the local economy, the demand for shelter in Rainbow House has increased by 25% over the past year.

The appliances in Rainbow House are scheduled to be replaced in approximately six months. Although the mortgage on Rainbow House was paid in full last year, several members of the board of directors have asked you to start considering ways to finance a new shelter house. The board president has also made it very clear that you are expected to "diversify" the revenue streams for Rainbow House as soon as possible, with an eye toward changing the funding ratio to 70% community donations and 30% state and local governmental grants.

Other board members have suggested that you "build a better relationship" with state and local government officials. At the last board meeting, the newest board member, a CEO for a large manufacturing company, said, "Heads may have to roll if fundraising does not pick up around here."

Last week, Rainbow House received a $100,000 grant from the City of Lakeville. The Lakeville City Council has given Rainbow House $100,000 for each of the last three years. The Lakeville grant is very helpful because it can be used for operational needs, such as buying new appliances for Rainbow House or paying for the increased amount of maintenance (e.g., plumbing, fixing the heat and air conditioning units, etc.) that is required for an older building like Rainbow House.

The annual grant from the Gantry Town Council also came in last week. The amount of the Gantry Town grant was $15,000 and was specifically limited to "programming and training." Your programming and training budget is already more than adequate. It is operational funds Rainbow House really needs.

Gantry Town has never been a big supporter of Rainbow House. Its current $15,000 grant represents a slight increase in the amount of annual grant funding Rainbow House has received from the Gantry Town Council over the past five years. The Gantry Town $15,000 grant is disappointing since (1) two large manufacturing companies have recently relocated to Gantry Town (bringing more people and property tax revenue to Gantry Town); (2) the population of Gantry Town is growing while the population of Lakeville is decreasing; and (3) an increasing number of Rainbow House residents are from Gantry Town. You have two weeks to decide whether or not to accept the Gantry Town grant.

The board president, with the consent of the full board, asked you during last night's board meeting to schedule a meeting with the Gantry Town Mayor to try to "negotiate" a change in the amount of the

Town's annual grant to Rainbow House. As an alternative, the board suggested you convince the mayor to allow Rainbow House to use the $15,000 grant for operational expenses. One board member suggested you "threaten" the mayor with "going to the newspaper to embarrass her about how little Gantry Town gives Rainbow House." You don't think that is such a great idea given the past suggestions of board members about improving relationships with state and local government officials. An additional $15,000 from Gantry Town would, however, help to replace the appliances in Rainbow House.

You know a little about the Gantry Town mayor, as you have coached her son's elementary school soccer team for the past two years. From your view, the mayor seems to be politically ambitious and has been quoted in the *Gantry Town Gazette* newspaper as being interested in running for the state senate.

As luck would have it, you have been able to schedule a meeting with the Gantry Town mayor next Tuesday. Prepare for that meeting. In so doing, identify your:
a. BATNA;
b. interests;
c. bargaining goals; and
d. authoritative standards.

What type of negotiation strategy best fits this negotiation situation?

Endnotes

1. Negotiation books give a variety of labels to the stages of a successful negotiation. In *Bargaining for Advantage: Negotiation Strategies for Reasonable People* (New York: Penguin Group, 2006, p. 119), Shell describes the negotiation process as including four stages: preparation; information exchange; proposing and concession making; and commitment. Carrell and Heavrin use the labels "preparation," "opening session," "bargaining," and "settlement" in *Negotiating Essentials: Theory, Skills, Practices* (Upper Saddle

River, NJ: Pearson Prentice Hall, 2008, p. 31). Lewicki, Barry, and Saunders summarize the different "phase models" in *Negotiation,* (6th ed., New York: McGraw-Hill, 2010, pp. 116–118), along the lines of initiation, problem solving, and resolution.

2. Ross, D. (2007). *Statecraft and how to restore America's standing in the world* (pp. 187–215). New York: Farrar, Straus and Giroux.

3. Lewicki, R. J., Saunders, D. M., and Barry, B. (2011). *Essentials of negotiation* (5th ed., p. 101). New York: McGraw-Hill Irwin.

4. Michaels, L. (Producer) and Segal, P. (Director). (1995). *Tommy boy* [Motion picture]. United States: Paramount Pictures. This particular scene can be accessed on https://www.youtube.com/.

5. "Report: Patrick Re-Signs with AGR." (2010, June 3). espn.com. Retrieved from http://sports.espn.go.com/rpm/racing/indycar/news/story?id=4502149. Interestingly, before retiring from competitive racing in 2018, Patrick ultimately did join a NASCAR team and drove in NASCAR races.

6. Steinberg, L., with D'Orso, M. (1998). *Winning with integrity: Getting what you want without selling your soul* (pp. 133–134, 139). New York: Times Books.

7. Shell refers to this concept on page 142 of *Bargaining for Advantage: Negotiation Strategies for Reasonable People* as the "similarity principle": "We trust others a little more when we see them as familiar or similar to us."

8. Moeller, L., & Christensen-Szalanski, J. (2010). *Making the puzzle pieces fit: How to identify interests and resolve conflict* (2nd ed., pp. 96–97). Dubuque, IA: Kendall Hunt Publishing.

9. O'Keeffe, M. (2008, September 7). A Year After Alex Rodriquez Debacle, Scott Boras Still Rules the Game. NYDailyNews.com. Retrieved from http://www.nydailynews.com/sports/baseball/2008/09/06/2008-09-06_a_year_after_alex_rodriguez_debacle_scot.html, retrieved June 4, 2010.

10. McG (Producer) & McG (Director). (2006). *We are Marshall* [Motion picture]. United States: Warner Brothers. The scene between Coach Lengyel and President Dedmon can be accessed at https://www.youtube.com/.

11. Reardon, K. (2005). *Becoming a skilled negotiator* (p. 85). Hoboken, NJ: John Wiley & Sons.

12. Shell, G. R. (2006). *Bargaining for advantage: Negotiation strategies for reasonable people* (pp. 50–52). New York: Penguin Group.

13. Thompson, L. L. (2009). *The mind and heart of the negotiator* (4th ed., p. 363). Upper Saddle River, NJ: Prentice Hall.

6

Reading the Road Map, Billboard Signs, and Detours: Creating Value in Negotiations

A road map and billboard signs along the highway inform drivers about places to stop during their trip. A GPS may announce, "Recalculating route," if a driver misses a turn. Unexpected detours or "shortcuts" often times become the highlight of a long road trip. Taking a turn from an interstate highway onto a state highway may create opportunities to see local attractions of interest, eat at a small family-run diner, or simply to enjoy different scenery. Learning how to read a road map, paying attention to roadside billboard signs, and trusting the recalculated scenic routes of our GPS can change a long and uninspired road trip into the trip of a lifetime.

Many negotiators reach an agreement, only to later realize that they could have done better. It may be the negotiator settled too quickly, taking the first reasonable proposal offered by the other negotiator. It could be that the negotiator missed the roadside signs or road map notations along their planned negotiation route that would allow them to improve their negotiated outcomes. It may be that the negotiator failed to consider changed conditions in the negotiations that required a new approach—a detour from the initial setting on their GPS—from what they had planned.

Skilled negotiators must be flexible in their approach to negotiations. They understand roadblocks occur during a negotiation and know how to find the back roads that lead to an agreement. They understand that the assumptions, under which an agreement is negotiated, much like road conditions and weather, can change. They understand things may be said at the bargaining table that create opportunities for new proposals and agreements that better meet the interests of both negotiators.

In this chapter, we will provide you with an outline of the steps you can take to better read the road map, find the billboard signs, and reset your GPS so that you can improve the value of your negotiated agreements.

CHAPTER OBJECTIVES

- To identify the type of questions that will lead to a better understanding of the other negotiator's interests
- To understand basic brainstorming rules in order to identify new options that will result in value-added negotiated outcomes
- To use the other negotiator's identified interests to expand the negotiation pie and close the deal

KEY TERMS

Power gap	Concessions	Exploding offer
Ground rules	Brainstorming	Post-settlement settlements
Active listening	Sweetener	Celebrating the deal
Boulwarism	Splitting the difference	

With the exception of your first-year business statistics course, you have done well in your university studies. Fortunately, you met a graduate student who worked in the tutoring center. She helped you understand your business statistics assignments. She also spent extra time with you in preparing for your midterm and final examination. You earned a B in the business statistics course. That was three years ago. Yesterday, you met up again with your business statistics tutor at the local coffee shop. She told you of her plans to open a restaurant and mentioned she had a meeting at the bank next week to negotiate a lease for her new restaurant. As you left the coffee shop, your former business statistics tutor – knowing you are taking a negotiation course - asked if you had any advice for her. You tell her it will be important to think about how a lease agreement for her restaurant space could be seen as a "win" for the bank.

Sports agent David Falk has represented many professional athletes and coaches, including NBA legend Michael Jordan and famed Duke University basketball coach Mike Krzyzewski. When talking about negotiations, Falk references the value of building good working relationships at the bargaining table, "seeing the entire court," and being open to ideas and proposals that will allow both negotiators in a deal to "win":

> *To be a good negotiator . . . good judgment is a critical quality. It's about picking up signals and adjusting your approach . . . In my entire life, I've met very few people who are so persuasive that they could convince me to do something I didn't want to do. What bridges that gap is not verbiage, PowerPoint presentations, brochures or recommendations. It's good will . . . When I was first starting out, I thought my role was to win. I thought negotiations were a zero-sum game with a clear winner and loser. As I got older, I realized that to make a great deal, both sides have to win. They may not win equally but they both have to win.*[1]

Power gap
In most negotiations, neither party can force the other to accept negotiation proposals. This power gap between the negotiators requires that a negotiator convince the other side to accept his or her proposals through the use of proposals that relate to the other negotiator's interests.

As Falk notes, there is a **power gap** between negotiators that cannot be bridged simply by clever argument or words. You cannot force the other negotiator to reach an agreement with you, nor are you obligated to accept the other negotiator's proposals. To overcome this **power gap** with the other negotiator, you must identify what he or she wants or needs (tangible and intangible interests), create a working relationship with the other negotiator, and make proposals that indicate you understand their interests.

Box 6.1 Using Interests to Overcome the Power Gap in Negotiations

Under Armour founder and CEO Kevin Plank faced a daunting task. He identified NFL superstar quarterback Tom Brady as a possible contracted endorser for Under Armour. Brady had been under contract with industry-leader Nike. His apparel contract with Nike expired during the summer of 2010. Plank wanted to feature Brady in Under Armour commercials and ads. With approximately $856 million in annual revenues, Plank knew he could not win a bidding war for Brady with Nike. Plank also knew he could not force Brady to sign a contract with the company. To overcome the power gap present in negotiations with Brady, Plank looked to identify Brady's interests. Brady, a low-round NFL draft pick coming out of the University of Michigan, was able to relate to Under Armour's "underdog" image (compared to Nike). Plank offered Brady an equity interest in the company, something Brady, the unquestioned leader of his (at that time) New England Patriots football team, could identify with and something that would give Brady an income stream when he retired from professional football. Under Armour also gave Brady the chance to become the "face" of the Under Armour brand, a brand that is gaining traction with the teenage market.

Brady's comments to the media announcing that he had signed an endorsement deal with Under Armour reflect the interests that Plank was able to identify and use to generate proposals that clearly connected with Brady:

Under Armour's everything I was looking for. It's cool. It's fun. It's what so many of the kids are wearing, and I like to try to stay cutting edge. I like the company. I think we've got a lot in common. We both want to stay hungry, stay humble . . . At this point in my career, it's got to be about a product I believe in. I felt there wasn't anything better out there. This is such a young company to be where they are. This kind of tells you where the market's at.

Sources: King, P. (2010, November 8). Monday morning QB. Retrieved from http://sportsillustrated.cnn. com/2010/writers/peter_king/11/07/mmqb-nfl-week-9/1. html; and Teitell, B. (2010, November 16). Big gain for Brady, straight from the retailing playbook. Boston Globe. Retrieved from http://www.boston.com/lifestyle/fashion/ articles/2010/11/16/big_market_for_bradys_iconic_status/.

Uncovering the Other Negotiator's Interests

It is frequently difficult to identify what the other negotiator wants or needs. Negotiators see the other negotiator (and his or her proposals) through the filters of their own experience. Words can be imprecise. The comments a negotiator makes about his or her interests may not accurately reflect what the negotiator actually wants or needs. Indeed, the other negotiator may not have thought about his or her interests before the negotiation. Stated positions at the bargaining table—"If we don't get an improved health insurance plan, we will go out on strike" or "If you don't cut your hourly billing rates, we will have to find another accounting firm to do our auditing work"—may hide underlying interests. A negotiator who has generally been involved in distributive bargaining may assume every negotiation is a win-lose transaction aimed at distributing rather than increasing the value of a deal. Quick assumptions may be made based on the negotiator's first offer. A highball or lowball first offer in a salary negotiation may lead the other negotiator to conclude that the negotiation will be strictly based on money and nothing else. Inexperienced negotiators may feel so intimidated by the negotiation process they ignore their own interests and accept the first proposal they receive in order to finish the negotiation as quickly as possible. On the other hand, more experienced negotiators may see a current negotiation as similar to a past negotiation and expect the outcome to be the same in both negotiations, thereby missing out on opportunities for new areas of agreement and the chance to "expand the pie" with the other negotiator.

Ground rules

The rules, by which a negotiation will proceed, as discussed and agreed-upon by both negotiators, are called ground rules.

A negotiator can try to anticipate the other negotiator's interests during the **preparation** stage of the negotiation. Let us return to your conversation with your former business statistics tutor who has developed a business plan for a new restaurant. She has her eye on vacant commercial space near the center of the city's business district, a perfect location for her restaurant. The commercial property (a two-story building) is owned by a bank that acquired the property through foreclosure. The bank is looking to rent the property. Your former business statistics tutor turned entrepreneur can reasonably anticipate that the bank will want a market-rate rental rate for the property. She might even anticipate that the bank would be interested in a long-term lease. Putting herself in the place of the bank (**role reversal**), she can begin to ask herself a series of questions directed at identifying the bank's less obvious interests. What else might the bank be interested in? What concerns might the bank have about renting to an entrepreneur with a new business plan? Is the bank concerned about the type of customers the restaurant will attract? Does bank management worry about how the reputation of the restaurant may reflect on the bank's reputation? Will the bank be concerned about how the restaurant will be staffed or financed? Thinking about the answers to these questions will help your former business statistics tutor develop an understanding of what to expect when meeting with the bank.

> **TAKE AWAY:** *Putting yourself in the other negotiator's shoes will help you see the negotiation from their perspective and will facilitate your ability to make proposals that the other negotiator can say "yes" to.*

Box 6.2 Negotiating about the Negotiation: Agreeing to Ground Rules

Talking about the rules under which negotiations will take place—the **ground rules** of the process—helps establish rapport with the other negotiator, provides structure to the process, and may create momentum for both negotiators to ultimately reach an agreement. Negotiators between the United States, South Vietnam, and North Vietnam famously spent a month during the Paris Peace Talks discussing the size and shape (circular versus rectangle) of the negotiation table. As silly as it may seem to talk for a month about the size and shape of the negotiation table, those discussions set the stage for the end of the Vietnam War.

Specific ground rules will vary depending on the formality and nature of the negotiation. A multi-party negotiation involving several complex issues will require different ground rules than a negotiation between college roommates over an apartment cleaning schedule. At a minimum, parties should discuss (1) where they will meet (each party's "home turf" or a neutral location); (2) the starting and ending times of negotiation sessions; (3) the schedule of negotiation sessions; (4) the format of the negotiation—face-to-face, by email, by telephone, virtual, etc.; and (5) the issues to be discussed.

In more formal negotiations, ground rules may also include things such as the number of negotiators present at the negotiation, whether or not parties can call a caucus during the negotiation sessions to confer with their respective negotiations teams, the manner in which media releases about the negotiations will be handled, and what will happen (e.g., a strike in a union setting, mediation, arbitration, litigation or continued impasse) if the parties are unable to reach an agreement.

The assumptions drawn about the other negotiator's interests through role reversal and preparation must be checked when talking to the negotiator at the bargaining table. This is done by asking questions of the other negotiator. A negotiator's questions trigger participation of the other negotiator in the negotiation process. Taking the time to listen is frequently described by negotiators as the biggest "concession" they can make to the other negotiator. Participation will lead to commitment to the process and to any negotiated outcomes, improving the chances that the deal will be completed and implemented.

Asking Questions

In Chapter 4 we identified types of questions that are generally asked during a negotiation. Different questions will be asked during the different phases of a negotiation. In the **rapport-building** stage, open-ended questions allow a negotiator to better understand the other negotiator's issues and interests. Our restaurant entrepreneur (and your former business statistics tutor) preparing to negotiate with the bank to rent property owned by the bank could, for example, ask the following questions when she meets with the bank officer:

- How long has the bank owned this building?
- What do you see as the best features of this property?
- What is the square footage of the building?
- What type of customer parking is available near the building?
- What qualities are you looking for in a tenant?
- Is the bank renting any other property in the city?
- What issues would you like to talk about?
- What would you like to know about my business plan?
- What concerns do you have about renting this property to be used as a restaurant?

Active listening
This type of listening involves a negotiator reflecting back exactly what they believe the other person said. It serves two important purposes, it lets the other person know you are paying attention to what they say, and it allows them to correct any misunderstandings.

In the **information-trading** stage of the negotiation, the entrepreneur's questions will focus on each side's proposals and attempt to narrow the issues for discussion through the use of clarifying questions. She should expect to hear the word "no" from the bank in response to her questions and proposals. The word "no" from the other negotiator may signal the entrepreneur does not understand the bank's interests, or the bank is not yet ready to reach an agreement. To help demonstrate her understanding of the bank's interests, the entrepreneur can summarize the bank's proposals (paraphrasing what the other negotiator told her about the bank's proposal) in her own words lets the bank know she has been paying attention to what they had to say. Pausing, that is saying nothing after asking questions of the other negotiator, may also allow the bank to provide the entrepreneur with additional information about the bank's concerns and interests. This process of asking questions, listening, and asking follow up or clarifying questions, is an example of **active listening**.

In proceeding through the **information-trading** stage of her negotiation with the bank, our restaurant entrepreneur would ask questions such as the following:

- I understand your last proposal to be X and that the bank is primarily concerned about issue Y. Is that correct?
- Are you thinking about renting out the entire building, or would you consider having more than one tenant in the building?
- Can you explain how you calculated the per square foot rent price included in your proposal?
- You said that the bank is interested in having a long-term lease. What does "long term" mean to the bank?
- Which lease term does the bank prefer, gross or triple net? Why?
- Why do you object to our proposal for a tenant's option to renew the lease?

- How would you calculate the percentage lease term of your proposed renewal provision?
- Can you see why we might object to your proposed maintenance charges in the lease amount when we are proposing to cover the cost of maintaining the property ourselves?

TAKE AWAY: *The more questions you ask and the more actively you listen, the greater the chance you have of finding a mutually acceptable solution.*

The Role of Concessions in Negotiations

During the **deal-making** stage, negotiators ask "if-then" and "what-if" questions in an attempt to find a mix of new ideas and proposals that can lead to an agreement that satisfies as many of the parties' different interests as possible. Our restaurant entrepreneur may, for example, ask the bank officer the following questions during this stage of the negotiation:

- **If I** agree to pay for the improvements in the heating and air conditioning system, could you **then** reduce your proposed monthly rental payment by $100?
- What **if** I agree to a two-year lease term and give you a right to renew the rental rate at the prevailing square footage market rate? Could you **then** agree to renovate the lower floor of the building so that I could expand my catering business?
- **If** you could find another tenant for the second level of the building, could I **then** rent the first-floor at a monthly rate of Z?
- Could we agree on waiving the first two months rent if I agreed to make improvements to the first-floor restroom facilities?

The if-then and what-if questions build on the reciprocity norm. If a negotiator is offered something of value—information about the other negotiator's priorities—he or she may feel a sense of obligation to respond in kind by offering information.

Making concessions also triggers the norm of reciprocity. To some people the give and take aspect of negotiation is unnecessary. Why not, they ask, simply skip making concessions since both negotiators will likely end up reaching an agreement near the midpoint of their first offers? It was this rationale that led General Electric's Vice President Lemuel R. Boulware to create a new strategy for collective bargaining with the company's labor unions following a lengthy union strike in the 1940s. This strategy, later referred to as **Boulwarism**, involved management surveying union employees,

Boulwarism
A negotiation technique in which a negotiator makes an initial "take it or leave it" first and only offer in negotiation. This technique is named after the approach developed by former General Electric Vice President Lemuel Boulware for collective bargaining with General Electric's labor unions.

evaluating market wage rates and the wages and fringe benefits received by employees working for comparable employers, and then making a "fair, firm offer" to the company's labor unions.[2] Management's "fair, firm offer" left little room for negotiation or concessions. This approach was seen by Boulware and General Electric as a better alternative to the "blood and thunder approach" of the parties' past negotiations and a better alternative to the parties' "flea bitten eastern type of cunning and dishonest but pointless haggling."[3]

Boulwarism is described as a strategy in which a party gives the other negotiator a "take it or leave it" first offer. Over time, this strategy has proven to be less than effective, largely because people like to think that they can persuade the other negotiator to move from his or her initial positions. Although not all negotiators like to haggle, the process of trading proposals and reciprocating concessions leaves negotiators with a sense of accomplishment, which creates the momentum needed to negotiate a successful agreement. Noted sports agent Leigh Steinberg described the important role concessions play in a successful negotiation as follows:

I believe that most people covet a sense of progress, of movement. A payer in a negotiation situation wants to feel the satisfaction of having the price drop. The payee wants to see the price go up. In each instance, that sense of movement, that feeling of progress, is sweet in itself, apart from the actual money that is paid or the product or services that have been bought . . . Your willingness and ability to concede a point are critical to the negotiating process. They show the other party that you are earnest about working toward a solution. And small concessions are often the key to making a deal.[4]

Concessions
A concession is a change or modification in a proposal a negotiator has previously made in the negotiation.

Concessions have been described as "the language of cooperation," which "tell the other negotiator in concrete, believable terms that you accept the legitimacy of his or her demands and recognize the necessity of sacrifice on your own part to secure a joint decision."[5] Negotiators "expect a back-and-forth exchange of concessions between parties."[6] There are, however, several rules that a negotiator must keep in mind when considering concessions:

- The normal pattern of concessions in purely distributive (win-lose) bargaining is to make few concessions during the early stage of the negotiation. As the negotiator gets closer to his or her bottom line/resistance point during the negotiation, the concessions should signal that fact by becoming increasingly smaller.
- A negotiator should not make a concession without receiving a comparable concession in return from the other negotiator. This can be accomplished by linking concessions, such as, "I will lower my per unit price by $50, if you can agree to split the cost of shipping."

Box 6.3 Tom Sawyer: Master Negotiator

Mark Twain's book, *Tom Sawyer* chronicles the exploits of Tom Sawyer, a young boy who turns out to be a very good negotiator. Tom's understanding of negotiation tactics and the value of concessions help him to convince another boy (Ben) to pay him for the opportunity of painting a fence Tom was supposed to paint. Tom does this by explaining how painting the fence was a special task, one that not just anyone could do, and that it would take something special for him to give up the opportunity to paint the fence. Tom convinces Ben that painting the fence is not work and asks Ben, "Does a boy get a chance to whitewash a fence every day?" From that point forward, Tom gains a concession from Ben (the apple Ben is eating) without giving up any concessions of his own:

. . . Ben stopped nibbling his apple. Tom swept his brush daintily back and forth—stepped back to note the effect—added a touch here and there—criticized the effect again—Ben watching every move and getting more and more interested, more and more absorbed. Presently he said:

(Ben) *"Say, Tom, let me whitewash a little."*

Tom considered, was about to consent; but he altered his mind: "No—no—I reckon it wouldn't hardly do, Ben. You see Aunt Polly's awful particular about this fence—right here on the street you know—but if it was the back fence I wouldn't mind and she wouldn't. Yes, she's awful particular about this fence;

it's got to be done very careful; I reckon there ain't one boy in a thousand, maybe two thousand, that can do it the way it's got to be done."

(Ben) *"No—is that so? Oh come, now, lemme, just try. Only just a little—I'd let you, if you was me, Tom."*

(Tom) *"Ben, I'd like to . . . but Aunt Polly—well, Jim wanted to do it, but she wouldn't let him; Sid wanted to do it, and she wouldn't let Sid. Now, don't you see how I'm fixed? If you was to tackle this fence and anything was to happen to it—"*

(Ben) *"Oh shucks, I'll be just as careful. Now lemme try. Say—I'll give you the core of my apple."*

(Tom) *"Well, here—No, Ben, now don't. I'm afeard—"*

(Ben) *"I'll give you all of it!"*

Tom repeats this negotiation with several other boys. At the end of the day, Twain writes about the negotiation lesson Tom learned:

He had discovered a great law of human action without knowing it—namely, that in order to make a man or boy covet a thing, it is only necessary to make the thing difficult to attain.

Source: Tom Sawyer Whitewashing the Fence. From Twain, M. (1876). Tom Sawyer (chap. 2). Retrieved from http://www.pbs.org/marktwain/learnmore/writings_tom.html.

- Negotiators should not make equal-sized concessions during any type of negotiation. Equal-sized concessions create the expectation "there is more to be had" and that the negotiator is still a ways from his or her bottom line/RP. Also equal-sized concessions suggest that both parties' opening offers were equally close to their aspiration levels. This will rarely be the case, as some extremely competitive negotiators may start with a figure well above their aspiration level.

- Negotiators should avoid making large concessions (e.g., dropping your price in a sales transaction from an initial price of $50 per unit to $20 per unit) at any point during a negotiation. A large concession made by the negotiator as part of his or her first or second counteroffer suggests the negotiator did not properly prepare or that he or she is a weak negotiator. The other negotiator in that case may respond by playing hardball, refusing to make reasonable concessions and demanding the other negotiator continue to make large concessions in order to reach an agreement. A large concession made as part of the negotiator's final offer may likewise cause the other negotiator to refuse to believe the negotiator is at his or her bottom line/resistance point.
- A negotiator should explain and emphasize the significance of any concession he or she makes. Something gotten too easily or too quickly is often times not appreciated. An example of this is summarized in Box 6.3 "Tom Sawyer: Master Negotiator."

Generating Multiple Possible Options

Brainstorming
Creative negotiations proposals can be identified during the **preparation** stage or during the **deal-making** stage of a negotiation by having negotiators suggest possible ideas without criticizing or evaluating the ideas. This technique is called brainstorming. When the brainstorming is completed, the negotiators indicate their preferred ideas and may work together to rank the ideas that meet as many of their interests as possible.

A challenge many negotiators face during the **deal-making** stage of a negotiation is thinking beyond the obvious solutions to a problem. Many times negotiators focus on the first idea they come up with and do not think beyond those initial ideas. A salary negotiation, for example, may deadlock over the applicant's starting rate of pay. Perhaps the applicant is expecting to make $50,000 per year while the recruiter is limited to offering the applicant $45,000 because of company policy or budgetary constraints. Both negotiators may think that there is no way to break their deadlock. Understanding why the applicant wants a $50,000 starting salary—his or her interests—is important; however, the negotiators need some help in identifying ways to satisfy the applicant's interests.

One way to generate proposals during the **deal-making** stage of negotiations is to use brainstorming techniques. **Brainstorming** is frequently used by a negotiator during the **preparation** stage of a negotiation to identify the different issues to address in the negotiation. At the bargaining table, brainstorming may be used with the negotiator across the table to come up with new proposals that allow the negotiators to break a deadlock or to find ways to increase the value of their agreement.

Brainstorming at the bargaining table should be proposed subject to the following rules:[7]

- A particular time should be set aside for brainstorming. During this period of time, negotiators won't reach any agreements. Their job is to identify as many new "options" as possible.

- Neither negotiator will be bound by any idea that is suggested during brainstorming. Generated ideas are considered possibilities or options, not specific proposals.
- The negotiators are not to criticize any idea generated during the brainstorming, thus avoiding comments like, "That won't work," "That's a crazy idea," or "There's no way my side would agree to that."
- Each idea or option is written down.
- When the negotiators think they are done with the brainstorming, they should give themselves another five to 10 minutes to think of additional ideas, including combining options that have already been identified.
- At the end of the brainstorming, the negotiators indicate their preferred options and try to reach agreement on the options (based on agreed-upon standards) that will allow both sides to best satisfy their interests.

The job applicant and recruiter deadlocked over the applicant's request for a starting salary of $50,000 could use brainstorming to identify different options:

Recruiter: So you are pretty set on a starting salary of $50,000, is that right?

Job Applicant: That's right. I think that's the market rate for someone with my experience. My cost of living will certainly increase by moving here to take this job. Is there anything else you can do?

Recruiter: I can't go any higher than $45,000. We really think you would be a great fit for this company.

Job Applicant: I really like the company, but I need a starting salary of $50,000.

Recruiter: Let's take a step back from our discussion of starting salary. Why don't we take a few minutes to brainstorm, and see if there are some other options we can come up with? You believe you will need $50,000 to cover the higher cost of living here, is that right?

Job Applicant: My rent will be higher here. I will need to upgrade my wardrobe since I will be meeting with clients more often than what I do in my current job.

Recruiter: So, you are concerned about higher rent and paying more for your wardrobe. I guess you may also have some additional transportation costs not to mention entertainment costs—there is a lot going on here with the theater district being close to the office and the two sports teams in town.

Job Applicant: Here's an idea (laughing). Maybe you can buy some new clothes for me or even pay my rent.

Recruiter: That's a thought. Keep going. Other than starting salary, what else would you want or need if we gave you a blank check?

Job Applicant: Okay, an annual bonus would be great, maybe have a salary review after six months, instead of a year.

Recruiter: We have talked about changing the salary review schedule for our high-performing employees.

Job Applicant: I guess I could think about moving on my starting salary request if I knew I could be at $50,000 sometime during my first year with the company. I still have a car payment, though, and parking is crazy in this city, there's the increased cost of rent . . .

Recruiter: We have been talking with a national rental car company about renting cars for our sales staff. If we could get you in that program, the company would pay for the car insurance and the scheduled maintenance.

Job Applicant: I guess if I got a car, I could sell my car and that would save me some money. But what about the cost of housing?

Recruiter: I hadn't really thought about this before, but one of our clients manages several apartment complexes. Maybe I can check with them on making apartment arrangements for our new employees.

As you can see from this example, the use of brainstorming allowed the job applicant and recruiter to start thinking about alternatives that would allow them to satisfy a common interest: having the job applicant work for the company. The recruiter was unable to offer the obvious solution to the deadlock—paying the applicant an additional $5,000 in salary; however, additional discussions identified new possibilities, such as changing the timing of the job applicant's salary review, arranging a car lease for the job applicant, and possibly finding a deal for an apartment with one of the company's clients.

TAKE AWAY: *Just because someone says "no" to you doesn't mean the negotiation is over. Use the "no" to gain a better understanding of what interests must be met in order to turn the "no" in to a "yes.".*

Finding common ground or common interests is a fundamental principle of the "investigative negotiation" approach advocated by Harvard Business School Professors Deepak Malhotra and Max Bazerman.[8] They believe many negotiators wrongly assume they understand the other negotiator's interests and that an investigation of the negotiator's interests will identify new options that will lead to better agreements. Malhotra and Bazerman specifically recommend three ways to obtain information from a negotiator who is not forthcoming about his or her interests:[9]

- ***Share information and encourage reciprocity.*** A negotiator may, for example, share some interests and concerns and ask the other negotiator to do the same. To avoid giving away too much information at first, and to give the other negotiator a reason to reciprocate, information about the negotiator's interests and concerns should be given "a little bit at a time."
- ***Negotiate multiple issues at the same time.*** Rather than negotiate one issue at a time, "identify all the issues up front and put everything on the table at the same time" and "go back and forth between the issues as you make offers and counteroffers."
- ***Make multiple offers at the same time.*** Negotiators like to have options. "[M]ake two offers at the same time that are equally valuable to you but differ on the details of one pair of issues." These two offers will prompt the other negotiator to indicate his or her preferences.

Getting Commitment and Closing the Negotiation

After the **deal-making** stage, negotiators reach the **closing** stage of their negotiation. At this stage, the negotiators attempt to reach agreement by exchanging and modifying their last offers. The questions asked at this stage aim to determine whether there is any more room for movement and to raise issues about the parties' alternatives if they cannot reach an agreement. Our restaurant entrepreneur seeking to rent commercial property from the bank will be asking questions of the bank officer that confirm whether the bank is at or near its bottom line/resistance point and that signal what the bank has to lose if it does not rent the property to the entrepreneur:

- Is that your final offer?
- I understand that you have offered what you are authorized to offer. Can you contact the bank management to see if they have any more flexibility?
- What will it take for us to finish this agreement today?
- We have made a lot of progress in our negotiation. I would hate to have us walk away today without an agreement. Wouldn't you agree? We are so close.

Exploding offer
An exploding offer is a proposal made during the **closing** stage of a negotiation that has a specific time limit for acceptance. This proposal will not be available to the other negotiator once the stated time period expires.

Sweetener
A sweetener is a small proposal or concession that is made during the **closing** stage of negotiation to persuade the other negotiator to agree to a final offer.

- I really like this property and think we have a solid business plan. If we can't reach an agreement, I will have to look at some other properties for my restaurant.

During the **closing** stage both negotiators will present their last and best final offer. A negotiator may need a slight nudge to accept the other negotiator's final offer. An **exploding offer**—"I will give you until 5:00 P.M. today to accept our last offer; after that, the offer is off the table and we will end negotiations"—uses a deadline to create a sense of urgency that may motivate the other negotiator to reach an agreement. Some negotiators offer a small concession at the end of the negotiation as a way to persuade the other negotiator to accept their final offer. This "**sweetener**" is usually a low-cost item to the negotiator but gives the other negotiator the sense that he or she received the last concession and thus is "the winner" of the negotiation. In the commercial lease negotiation between the restaurant entrepreneur and the bank, the entrepreneur could sweeten her final offer by agreeing to cater the bank's holiday party.

Box 6.4 The "Twists and Turns" of Closing the Deal

Things occur during the closing stage of a negotiation that frequently are nott expected. John W. Henry of New England Sports Venture (NESV) discovered the "twists and turns" of closing a deal to purchase the Liverpool Football Club of the English Premier League in the fall of 2010. Henry, the principal owner of the Boston Red Sox baseball team, thought he had a purchase-and-sale deal in place on October 8, 2010, to purchase the Liverpool Club for $476 million. Within days of reaching what Henry thought was a binding agreement, the owners of the Liverpool Club filed a lawsuit trying to block the deal. This sudden change of events caused Henry to make several trips back and forth between Boston and England. Legal actions were filed in the United States and in England. Deadlines loomed. If the deal was not completed soon, the Liverpool Football Club would be placed in bankruptcy. Henry and his lawyers worked around

the clock. Learning that the Liverpool Club owners had dropped their lawsuit to block the deal, Henry discovered one of the banks that was owed money by the Liverpool Club was requesting an additional $10 million to finalize the deal. Henry told his lawyers, "This is crazy. I'm not going to give them another dime." He threatened to walk away from the deal. The bank backed down from its $10 million demand. The deal went through. On October 15, 2010, Henry and NESV became owners of the Liverpool Football Club. As Henry remarked, the closing stage of this deal was full of "twists and turns."

Source: Grossfeld, S. (2010, October 21). Tough way to get your kicks: Henry's purchase of Liverpool FC was fraught with legal complications before the goal was finally reached. Boston Globe. Retrieved from http://www.boston.com/sports/soccer/articles/2010/10/21/tough_way_to_get_your_kicks/.

Perhaps the most frequently used closing technique is **splitting the difference** between the parties' last offers. Splitting the difference is quick, easy to do, and seems inherently fair. If Ansel is offering to sell his house for $250,000 and Shumin's last purchase offer was $230,000, a compromise price of $240,000 (the midpoint of the parties' last offers) would seem to be a fair outcome. A negotiator should not, however, offer to split the difference unless he or she is confident the parties are at their bottom lines/reservation point and the distance between the last offers is not extreme. For example, assume that you make a reasonable first offer, one that is not far off from your bottom line/reservation point, to buy an autographed photograph of movie star George Clooney. You think the market value of this photograph is approximately $80 and are willing to spend up to $75 for the photograph. Your first offer for the photograph is $65. The seller offers the photograph to you at a price of $120. You counter with an offer to buy the photograph for $70. The seller responds by offering you the photograph for the price of $110. When you say, "no deal," the seller suggests you both just split the difference. Although you really like this particular photograph, is it a wise move for you to split the difference and buy the photograph for $90? The answer is no. Ninety dollars exceeds what you consider the market value of the photograph to be; plus, splitting the difference provides more of a gain to the seller because she gave you an extreme opening offer ($40 over the market value) as contrasted with your more reasonable opening offer ($15 under the market rate).

Sometimes the last resort in an attempt to close a deal is for a negotiator to demonstrate what the other negotiator has to lose if they cannot reach an agreement. This approach requires a good understanding of the negotiators' BATNAs and their leverage. We will review different types of negotiation leverage and power in the next chapter.

Splitting the difference
A popular closing technique during negotiations is to have both negotiators to agree to accept on the mid-point between their last proposals to reach an agreement.

Box 6.5 "Never Split the Difference"

Former Federal Bureau of Investigation (FBI) hostage negotiator Chris Voss wrote a book (with colleague Tahl Raz) titled *Never Split the Difference: Negotiating as if your Life Depended on it (New York: HarperCollins, 2016)*. Acknowledging that "splitting the difference" is a standard closing technique in negotiations, Voss emphasizes that "splitting the difference" is inappropriate and difficult to implement in hostage negotiations due to the stakes involved in the negotiation – the life and wellbeing of the hostages, the extreme demands of the hostage takers, and the significant amount of ransom money at play. Instead, Voss advocates a negotiations approach built on establishing an understanding of the other negotiator's interests by asking questions, engaging in active listening, and identifying what the other negotiator is feeling (their emotions) – something he refers to as "tactical empathy."

Get It in Writing

A final, but important, step of any negotiation is for the negotiators to summarize their agreement. This means not only talking about the terms of their understood agreements but also to putting their agreement in writing. Negotiators should take notes during each negotiation session and make special notes on issues that the parties agree to throughout the process. These specific agreements on the issues addressed by the negotiators will ultimately provide the framework for the parties' final agreement.

A final agreement should be reduced to writing before the negotiators leave the bargaining table. "Writing up" an agreement, whether it involves lawyers drafting the language of a contract, a supervisor emailing two employees after working out a changed work schedule, or two college roommates writing their agreed-upon apartment cleaning schedule on the refrigerator whiteboard, helps the negotiators avoid misunderstandings. In their haste to finish a negotiation, an inexperienced negotiator might assume an agreement has been reached on issues that are still open or in dispute. While the negotiators will want to wrap up their agreement quickly, they must fight the human tendency to "get things over with" and carefully review what they both believe was agreed to.

Negotiators should aim to create an agreement that is "durable," that is, an agreement the parties will comply with. Answering the following questions when writing up the agreement will help ensure the agreement is durable:

- Who is covered by the agreement?
- What are the parties expected to do under the agreement?
- When will the parties carry out their agreed-upon obligations?
- How will they enforce the agreement?

© 2011 artur gabrysiak. Used under license from Shutterstock, Inc.

It is important to work out any disagreements over the details of an agreement before the negotiators leave the bargaining table.

The Post-Settlement Settlement

There are times when negotiators feel they have reached the best agreement possible given time or other constraints (like the lack of complete information). If the negotiators have built trust throughout the negotiation (trust issues in negotiation will be discussed in Chapter 8) and they believe more time or information sharing or discovery might have led to a better agreement, they may agree to a post-settlement settlement. A **post-settlement settlement** is an agreement that if one or both parties can find an outcome that is better for at least one, and no worse for the other, both parties will agree to move to the new settlement. This concept is based on the assumption that parties have negotiated in good faith up to the point of the initial settlement but each negotiator agrees that with more time and effort a better settlement might be found.

Perhaps an example will help here. Imagine that you are involved in negotiating your employment contract with the Human Resources Director at your soon to be new place of employment. You have agreed on all the issues: salary, bonus, moving expenses, job title, vacation days, and location. You aren't completely happy with the location (Dallas), as you would rather be in the Denver office, where you could live closer to your family. At this point of the negotiation, only the Dallas position is open, so you have agreed to go there. If, however, you have agreed to a post-settlement settlement with the Human Resources Director and she knows your location preference is Denver, it is possible that she can get back to you before you move and let you know if there is an opening in the Denver office.

A post-settlement settlement basically says: "I'll accept and honor what we have agreed to, but if something better comes along (new information that we don't have at the time of the initial settlement) and it is better for me and makes no difference to you, then we will both agree to the new settlement." In this case, it is a win-win because you are happy to be located in your preferred city, and the Human Resources Director knows she will have a new employee who is likely to stay in the position because it is located in the preferred city.

Note, however, that if the Denver opening doesn't materialize, you still have your initial settlement that you will honor. And, it works both ways. Some people wince at the suggestion of a post-settlement settlement, but we argue that this is because they are mired in distributive thinking. That is, they assume if one option is better for the other party, then it must be worse for them. This type of logic ignores the fact that there is often common ground (i.e., parties are not diametrically opposed on every issue) or that one party may be indifferent about some issues, so they can agree to be flexible if it makes the deal better for the other party.

Of course, post-settlement settlements usually have to occur in an agreed-upon time frame. Otherwise, it is possible that one party may try to continue

Post-settlement settlements
if negotiators have negotiated in good faith and feel they have done the best they could given the information they had, they may agree that if either party can suggest another settlement that is better for at least one of the parties and no worse for either, that they will agree to the new settlement. For this process to be effective, negotiators have had to build trust; also it is important to put a limit on the time for suggesting new settlement options.

negotiation long after the negotiation is over. So, in the previous example, the parties may have agreed that if the Denver position opened up in the months between signing the contract and the actual moving date, then both parties would agree to the Denver location. If the Denver location opened up after your move to Dallas, then that would be a new negotiation.

■ ■ ■ ■

Celebrate the Deal

Celebrating the deal

Once an agreement is reached, both negotiators should congratulate each other and celebrate the fact that they were able to negotiate an agreement.

Once a deal is reached and the agreement written up, the negotiators need to **celebrate** their agreement. "Celebrating" the deal may occur by way of a simple handshake, having a celebratory drink, or doing something more formal, such as a media release or joint news conference. One of the authors represented a school district in collective bargaining negotiations with its teachers. The school district and the teachers' union always celebrated their negotiated collective bargaining agreements by having a potluck dinner with various types of gelatin salads for dessert.

Reaching an agreement is hard work, and acknowledging the parties' success in doing so is important for three reasons. First, it recognizes the parties have established an effective working relationship, and a relationship that can continue into the future. Second, maintaining the good feelings from reaching a deal will help the parties commit to carry out their respective obligations under the agreement and work together to resolve any disagreements that may arise from implementing the deal. Lastly, if the negotiators have done all they could to identify their interests in the negotiation, there should be none of the "should haves" or "could haves" that haunt many ineffective negotiators once an agreement is reached.

■ ■ ■ ■

CHAPTER SUMMARY

The objective in negotiations is to reach an agreement that satisfies as many of the negotiators' interests as possible. Identifying interests—yours as well as those of the other negotiator—is difficult. Many negotiators accept the first offer that is remotely close to their bottom line/RP. They leave money on the table and fail to recognize opportunities that will add value to their negotiated agreements. In this chapter we have reviewed the type of questions negotiators can ask during the different stages of a negotiation to identify interests and discussed ways to generate additional value-added options available to both negotiators.. We have also discussed the ways negotiators can close a deal and the necessary steps they should take once an agreement is reached to make sure both have a clear understanding of what they agreed to when the negotiation is complete.

Questions/Exercises

1. What is active listening, and how is it related to building rapport in a negotiation?
2. What signals is a negotiator sending if her proposals in a price-only negotiation reflect the following pattern of concessions? Explain each pattern of concessions.
   a. $1,000 (first offer), $750 (second offer), $500 (third offer), and $250 (fourth offer)
   b. $1,000 (first offer), $900 (second offer), $700 (third offer), and $300 (fourth offer)
   c. $1,000 (first offer), $800 (second offer), $700 (third offer), and $650 (fourth offer)
   d. $1,000 (first offer), $500 (second offer), $500 (third offer), and $500 (fourth offer)
   e. $1,000 (first offer), $900 (second offer), $850 (third offer), and $500 (fourth offer)
3. A well-known brainstorming exercise involves identifying different uses for the common paper clip. Identify as many uses of a paper clip as you can. With the help of two or three friends, use brainstorming techniques to identify as many new uses of a paper clip that you can. Compare the ideas generated by your brainstorming group with the initial list of uses of a paper clip that you identified. How are they different?
4. If a person says "no" to your first offer, what should be your next step be in the negotiation?
5. In February 2014, country-western music superstar Garth Brooks announced he would play two concerts at Croke Park (the largest sporting stadium in Ireland, with a seating capacity of 83,000 fans)

in Dublin, Ireland. Tickets for the two concerts sold out quickly, and Brooks announced he would play an additional three concerts at Croke Park. Approximately 400,000 tickets were sold for Brooks' five concerts. These concerts were planned to be held in the evening and scheduled for five consecutive days.

The addition of three concerts at Croke Park angered residents living around the stadium. The Dublin City Council refused to issue license to the concert promoters to hold all five of the proposed concerts. During negotiations between Brooks, the local residents and the Dublin City Council, representatives of the Council and Brooks himself were reported to have made the following comments:

The "scale, magnitude and number" of concerts, with an expected attendance of in excess of 80,000 people per night over five consecutive nights, three of them being week nights, was "unprecedented" for Croke Park Stadium, the council said.

In response to the decision, Brooks had said he would play five concerts or none.

"To choose which shows to do and which shows not to do, would be like asking to choose one child over another. However this plays out, Ireland has my heart and always will," he said.

Eventually negotiations failed and Brooks announced all five concerts would be cancelled. The economic impact of holding the five concerts in Dublin was estimated to be approximately $68 million.

Based on the comments made by representatives of the Dublin City Council and Brooks, what do you believe their interests to be in this negotiation? What questions would you ask Brooks to better determine his interest in playing "all five or none" of his concerts in Dublin?

Sources: Flaherty, R., "All Five Garth Brooks Dublin Concerts Cancelled," *Irish Times* (July 8, 2014) (https://www.irishtimes.com/news/ireland/irish-news/all-five-garth-brooks-dublin-concerts-cancelled-1.1859348); McDonald, Soraya Nadia, "Garth Brooks Cancels Dublin Shows after Flap with Local Council, Triggering a Record Number of Ticketmaster Refunds," *Washington Post* (July 15, 2014) (https://www.washingtonpost.com/news/morning-mix/wp/2014/07/15/garth-brooks-cancels-dublin-shows-after-flap-with-local-council-most-refunds-ever-for-ticketmaster/)

Endnotes

1. Falk, D. (2009). *The bald truth: Secrets of success from the locker room to the boardroom* (pp. 160, 186–187, 286). New York: Pocket Books.
2. Walton, R. E., & McKersie, R. B. (1965). *A behavioral theory of labor negotiations: An analysis of social interaction system* (pp. 360–365). New York: McGraw-Hill.
3. *NLRB v. General Electric Company,* 418 F. 2d 736 (2nd Cir. 1969).
4. Steinberg, L., with D'Orso, M. (1998). *Winning with integrity: Getting what you want without selling your soul* (pp. 151, 153). New York: Times Books.
5. Shell, G. R. (2006). *Bargaining for advantage: Negotiation strategies for reasonable people* (2nd ed., p. 164). New York: Penguin Books.
6. Thompson, L. L. (2009). *The mind and heart of the negotiator* (4th ed., p. 51). Upper Saddle River, NJ: Prentice Hall.
7. Fisher, R., Patton, B., & Ury, W. (1991). *Getting to yes* (2nd ed., p. 61). New York: Penguin Books; Mnookin, R., Peppet, S., & Tulumello, S. (2000). *Beyond winning: Negotiating to create value in deals and disputes* (pp. 37–39). Cambridge, MA: Belknap/Harvard University Press.
8. Malhotra, D., & Bazerman, M. H. (2007, September). Investigative negotiation. *Harvard Business Review,* pp. 72–78.
9. Malhotra, D., & Bazerman, M. H. (2007, September). Investigative negotiation. *Harvard Business Review,* p. 77.

7

What If You Are Driving a Scooter and They Are in a Semi-Truck?: Power, Leverage, and Influence in Negotiation

You are on a leisurely afternoon ride on your newly acquired midnight blue Vespa (an Italian motor scooter), and you hear the roar of a semi-truck approaching behind you. It is a two-lane county road without a shoulder, and you are traveling at the 50 mph speed limit, yet the truck is bearing down and the driver is honking his horn. You are feeling bullied. You are obviously no match for a test of wills with the semi, so you move over as far as you can to the right and he roars past buffeting you with diesel fumes. You are furious and shaking, but what else could you could have done? You were powerless in this situation.

We have all experienced situations where we feel powerless. It might be because we are the smallest vehicle on the road, but there are numerous other situations that can leave us feeling this way; perhaps the other person controls all the resources we need or has more clout or knowledge than we do; or maybe they have a group of toadies in tow and you are alone. When it comes to negotiation, we never want to find ourselves feeling powerless, because if we do, we fear being crushed and, worse, humiliated. In this chapter we will examine the different kinds of power and differentiate power from leverage. We will learn ways to garner power and use leverage to our advantage. Furthermore, we will discover how to be more persuasive and influential in situations where we might previously have felt powerless.

CHAPTER OBJECTIVES

- To understand the sources of power that can influence negotiations
- To identify what power we have and evaluate whether it is useful to use it
- To understand the difference between power and leverage
- To learn how to use leverage to our advantage
- To learn to evaluate interests versus rights versus power approaches to resolving disputes
- To understand the power of persuasion and influence in negotiation

KEY TERMS

Compliance	Referent power	Foot-in-the-door
Expert power	Leverage	Door-in-the-face
Reward power	Normative leverage	Boundary spanners
Coercive power	Transaction costs	Call to action
Legitimate power	Moment of power	Sources of power

CHAPTER CASE

MLB Negotiations During 2020 Covid 19 Crisis

Power in negotiation can come from multiple sources and not all of them may be obvious at first glance. It is worthwhile to consider the sources of power in negotiation and your approach to negotiation even if primarily focused on interests.

Major League Baseball (MLB) is a billion dollar industry, that like many others, has been severely impacted by the Covid 19 pandemic. No one involved will escape the negative economic impact and revenue will likely be a fraction of what it was pre-pandemic. Negotiations lasting over a month were aimed at safely salvaging a partial season (60 compared to 162 games) for 2020.

The case illustrates several aspects of power that will be detailed in this chapter. From one angle we see a demonstration of how interests, rights, and power are often nested and all may be at play during a single negotiation. For example, the fact that negotiations took place between the Major League Baseball Players Association (MLBPA), the owners and Commissioner of Major League Baseball illustrates an attempt at an interest based approach where input was sought from all relevant parties. Rights came into play as the interest based approach stalled, lawyers got involved, and we saw a reliance on outlined organizational policies and laws. In this case, ultimately power and rights were relied on to determine the outcome when Commissioner Rob Manfred mandated a 60 game season.

We can also view these negotiations from the perspective of French and Raven's different types of power. Commissioner Manfred exercised his legitimate power afforded to him by his position to impose a decision. The baseball team owners held both reward and coercive power as they control the pay players receive (reward) and pay here is tied to the number of games played (coercive). Players and their union the MLBPA wanted a longer season with more games and owners wanted to pay players less than the previously agreed upon per game amount. Expert power influenced the outcome in terms of health experts who contributed to designing safety protocols and lawyers who represented the players and the terms of their contracts. And finally, there were attempts at garnering referent power as players took to social media during negotiations to gain fan support and additional influence.

This case highlights many aspects of power we will discuss in more detail in this chapter.

Source:
"MLB 2020 season: Timeline of how testy negotiations led to Rob Manfred mandating a 60-game schedule

MLB commissioner Rob Manfred imposed a 2020 season"

Retrieved from: https://www.cbssports.com/mlb/news/mlb-2020-season-timeline-of-how-testy-negotiations-led-to-rob-manfred-mandating-a-60-game-schedule/

By R.J. Anderson, Katherine Acquavella, Matt Snyder, Dayn Perry & Mike Axisa

In most situations in which we find ourselves, it is fairly obvious who is in charge. Certainly in organizations and companies there is usually a power hierarchy; but even in social situations, one person may be in control, whether formally elected to a position of power or simply because that person is able to control the minds and hearts of the group through persuasion.

As we approach a negotiation, one of the first questions we may ask ourselves is, "What power do I have to bring the other negotiator to my side?" To the extent that we believe we have more power than they do, we may have more confidence in our ability to succeed in the negotiation. On the flip side, if we realize that the other side holds most of the power, we do not expect to do very well and may even choose to withdraw from the negotiation entirely, if possible. It is important to remember, however, that power is usually relative. Very few people have absolute power over another. If one were all-powerful, one would not need to negotiate at all; one would simply take from the other what was wanted or force the other to comply.

For example, if your boss asks you to come in to finish an important project on the weekend, you may feel powerless to say "no." After all, she is the boss. Yet the very fact your boss asks rather than gives you an ultimatum suggests that you have something that the boss values, be it your time, your talent, or your unique set of skills or abilities. Thus, you are not powerless in this situation; you may still feel compelled to come in to work on the weekend, but you may be able to negotiate the time you will come in, or even better, negotiate some time off during the week in return for working on the weekend.

> **TAKE AWAY:** *If you have something the other person wants or needs, you are not powerless in the negotiation.*

The primary reason people want power is to gain **compliance** from others. Many years ago, social psychologists French and Raven[1] classified five major types of power that influence social relationships: expert power, reward power, coercive power, legitimate power, and referent power. We discuss each in the following sections and expand on the ways in which they are relevant to negotiations.

Compliance
getting another person to do what you want them to do.

■ ■ ■ ■

Expert Power: Power Based on Information

We tend to defer to those who have more information about a subject than we do. Experts can control situations where they hold unique information, particularly if it is required for solving a problem or achieving required results. Imagine that you lose your Internet connection while working on an important assignment that is due the next day. Much as you hate to, you dial your Internet provider's number and spend the next hour on the phone talking to a technician halfway around the world, doing whatever that person suggests

Expert power
the power that another negotiator may have over you if they are an expert in an area you know nothing about.

in order to get the Internet connection restored. Even though this individual is not known to you personally, and you will never interact together again, at this moment you are completely dependent on his or her expertise to solve the problem. The technician holds all the power in the situation.

The implication for negotiators is that whenever possible, they need to do their homework so they are the ones with expertise. Of course, one cannot be an expert in every situation, but at a minimum, a good negotiator needs to be knowledgeable about the issues being negotiated. Otherwise, they are at the mercy of the "expert."

Let's return to our much maligned car salesperson. Like it or not, he or she is likely to be more expert not only in knowledge about the condition and value of the vehicles on the lot but also in the process of negotiating. After all, the salesperson negotiates the sale of a car several times a day, and most people may do it only a few times in their lifetime. Fortunately, there is a multitude of good information online that can increase your expertise in terms of understanding the true value of a vehicle you want to purchase. You may never reach the same level of expertise in negotiating for a car, but armed with good information you will not be powerless. Remember also that you should have another **source of power**: your BATNA. Having a good alternative will increase your power in any negotiation, even if you are not the expert.

Sources of power
one way to force compliance is to have power over another person. There are many sources of power; several are listed below.

© 2011 Kzenon. Used under license from Shutterstock, Inc.

Reward Power: The Carrot

■ ■ ■ ■

When we control rewards that are valued by others, we have **reward power**. That is, we can gain compliance from the other person by dangling the carrot as an incentive. There are benefits and burdens to having reward power. It may be satisfying to get others to do what you want by offering rewards to bring them to your side. On the other hand, this form of power comes at a cost. First, you must monitor the other's behavior to ensure compliance, and second, you must constantly give out rewards to ensure future compliance. If your end goal is to get the other to embrace your point of view or internalize your values, you are not likely to achieve this goal with reward power. Without the reward, there is no incentive for the other person to do so.

Reward power
a way to force compliance by controlling rewards.

Parents often struggle with the decision to reward or punish in order to gain compliance from their children. Offering cookies or cash in return for something the children should do anyway, like cleaning their rooms, does little to instill the value of cleanliness in the children. Rather, the children are cleaning only to receive the reward, and the parent will have to continue doling out rewards to receive the desired behavior.

There are times that all of us will comply with requests in order to receive a reward. And the person who has the resources to dole them out often has the power to control behavior. But beware: *Gaining compliance through rewards is a short-term solution. When the reward is gone, so also will be the compliance.*

Coercive Power: The Stick

■ ■ ■ ■

Just as we can get others to comply through rewards, we can also gain compliance with the threat of punishment. Needless to say, this form of power is one we would not like used against us and, truth be told, probably would not enjoy using ourselves, masochists aside! Although threats (the stick) and promises (the carrot) can both be used to gain compliance, the person using them has the additional burden of monitoring the other's behavior in order to ensure compliance. If people are moving your way due to a threat you make, it stands to reason that as soon as the threat is removed, the behavior will stop. Thus, you would have to remain vigilant in monitoring behavior.

Coercive power
a way to force compliance by being able to punish the other if they don't act in the desired manner.

Threats differ from promises in terms of the information they provide to the receiver of the message.[2] Threats provide more explicit information because they tell the receivers exactly what will happen to them if they do not move in the desired direction. Promises tell the receivers what they will receive if they move in the desired direction, but they are mute about what will occur if they don't. Thus, threats tend to be more effective in the short term. For threats to continue to be effective, they must be delivered if the desired behavior does not occur. Otherwise, threats will be ineffective and be seen as "cheap talk."

Negotiators who use coercive power must accept that it will be effective only if they make good on their word, and they must also accept the hostility that will result if they do so. Later in this chapter we will discuss the transaction costs of using power in negotiations.

■ ■ ■ ■

Legitimate Power: Power That Comes with the Position

Legitimate power
power that comes with the position you hold in an organization or society.

As children, we accepted that our parents had legitimate power over us, as teenagers we may have tested that legitimacy, and as adults we no longer see our parents as holding legitimate power over us. We may still comply with their wishes, but it is more likely to be out of love and respect rather than a sense that they hold legitimate power over us.

In work settings we accept that our boss and those further up the hierarchy hold legitimate power in the organization. We therefore abide by the rules they set and question their power at our own peril. Those whose power is legitimized by the position they hold can make demands without expecting reciprocity.

At times one may be vested with authority from someone higher in the organization to negotiate on his or her behalf. As such, we may receive the deference that we wouldn't normally receive. However, this special treatment will disappear quickly if we do not have the authority to actually make the decision or do the deal.

■ ■ ■ ■

Referent Power: Having the Power of the Crowd behind You

Referent power
the power of the crowd. One way to accrue power is to find like-minded others and join together to increase your power.

One can be said to have referent power if others respect you for your ability to get things done or for your past successes in helping disputing parties reach consensus. Unlike power that comes from the top, referent power rises from bottom like cream in a bottle of milk. One with referent power may not hold a position of legitimate power; rather the power that accrues to this person comes from others, hence the power of the crowd.

We can all think of charismatic individuals we know who seem to emerge from the crowd as leaders. They are almost always effective communicators. But more important, they have a way of connecting with others in a meaningful way. They listen, and they gain our trust. These are the individuals who can count on our help when they need it.

For each of us, it is a useful exercise to take stock of our supporters. In situations where we don't hold any of the other types of power, we may still be able to influence others because of the referent power we have over them or their constituents. It helps to know how and where to direct your appeals for support. In summary, when thinking about and planning for negotiations it is important to identify what sources of power you may have. Remember also that if you are using power only to gain compliance that it runs counter to both our working definition of negotiation which is a <u>process</u> that helps people work together to achieve goals and the integrative approach discussed in Chapter 4. It is worth considering the sources of power and where you may have some leverage prior to negotiating.

> "Negotiations and making deals is a function of knowing when you have the leverage, when you can push the envelope a little and when you don't have the leverage and so have to perhaps take less than you'd like to achieve and graciously walk away knowing you did the best job you could under the circumstances."
>
> —Sports Agent David Falk. (2009). *The bald truth: Secrets of success from the locker room to the boardroom* (p. 251). New York: Pocket Books.

Power versus Leverage

G. Richard Shell[3] differentiates power from **leverage**. More specifically, he argues that the two differ in two important ways: power is *positional* and *static,* whereas leverage is *situational* and *dynamic.* That is, leverage can change as situations change. An example or two should help you understand the difference.

In a negotiation context, if you have something the other party needs, then you have leverage. If you and you alone can fulfill that need, then the other party is at your mercy. Perhaps your roommate is writing a term paper and her hard drive crashes. It is late on a Sunday evening, there is a blizzard outside, and she has no transportation to get to a computer elsewhere. You are using your laptop, but you are just playing a video game. Your roommate begs you to let her use your laptop. You have something she needs, and she is likely to do anything you ask in return for the use of your computer. You have the leverage in this situation. Whether you choose to use it will depend on the nature of your relationship with your roommate. If you are also good friends, you might loan the computer for the evening and expect nothing in return; however, if your relationship with her is simply transactional, you may demand reciprocity or even a fee for using the computer.

Another situation where negotiators have leverage is if they have good alternatives. Having a good BATNA allows you to hold out for something better, even if the person you are negotiating with has more positional power. For example, you may be negotiating with the head of human resources over an employment offer. This person certainly has more legitimate power, but if you have good outside offers, you will have leverage in the situation.

You may also have leverage if you have time on your side and the other negotiator is in a big hurry. There are countless stories of naïve U.S. negotiators going to Japan in the early 1970s to negotiate technology transfers or for microchips. The first thing the Japanese negotiators would do was find out when the U.S. negotiators return trip was scheduled. Then they would spend several days wining and dining the U.S. negotiators, taking them to

Leverage
unlike power, which tends to be static and positional, leverage is dynamic and situational. Leverage increases to the extent you have what they need. Your BATNA can also provide you with leverage.

Box 7.1 Referent Power and Leverage: The Case of Republic Windows and Doors

Employees at Republic Windows and Doors, a Chicago-based manufacturer of vinyl replacement windows, arrived at work in December 2008 only to find the plant closed. The company announced that it was declaring bankruptcy because the company's primary lender, Bank of America, had canceled its line of credit. The company also announced that employees would not receive any severance pay or their accrued vacation time and that their health insurance coverage would be terminated within days.

The employees seemed to have no power whatsoever. They did, however, take steps to improve their leverage with the company. The employees first took matters into their own hands by organizing a sit-in of the factory. They contacted the media and various political figures, creating a coalition of supporters, to let the public know about the company's actions (they tapped into their referent power). The employees then worked with their labor union to threaten the filing of a lawsuit claiming a violation of the federal plant closing law (the WARN Act). After the employees had occupied the plant for six days, the company agreed to pay the employees 60 days of severance pay and their earned vacation pay.

Source: Luo, M., & Cullotta, K. A. (2008, December 13). Even workers surprised by success of factory sit-in. New York Times. Retrieved from http://www.nytimes.com/2008/12/13/us/13factory.html?_r=1.

play golf and to Karaoke bars at night. Finally, on the final day they would begin seriously negotiating. Because the Japanese had time on their side and the U.S. negotiators were anxious to close the deal before departing, the U.S. negotiators made many unnecessary concessions. The Japanese team had leverage because they had something the U.S. team did not—time.

We can also accrue leverage if we can create the perception in the other person that he or she simply cannot meet his or her goals without us. This does not have to involve deception; it simply means that you understand the other side's needs so well that you can create a unique offer that is not available anywhere else. Sometimes we need to create our own leverage.

Normative leverage
a type of leverage that plays on the other's norms and values. If you make an offer that is consistent with the other person's norms and values, it will be difficult for them to say no to your offer.

Like power, leverage can be either positive or negative. However, the best type of leverage is **normative**. If you can create an offer that is consistent with the other side's existing norms and values, this will bring that person to your side without the need to use threats, promises, or monitoring.

For example, if you are working with a structural engineer in building a new home and you have concerns that the engineer may try to cut corners to save costs, you might subtly mention that you hired him because you noticed the ring on the small finger of his hand, which signals his pledge to uphold ethical standards in engineering. That reminder should serve to make his code of engineering ethics salient, and normative influence will guide his behavior.[4] Other professional organizations, such as those for accountants (AICPA), lawyers (the American Bar Association), and doctors (the Hippocratic Oath) serve similar functions. Never underestimate the power of normative leverage.

TAKE AWAY: *If you appeal to the other's norms, standards, and values that are consistent with the behavior you desire, you will have leverage in the negotiation.*

Interests, Rights, and Power

In Chapter 4 we discussed interest-based negotiations and the value of focusing on joint gain. Ury, Brett, and Goldberg[5] consider interests as one of three approaches used in resolving disputes, the others being rights and power. They argue that when attempting to resolve disputes, people first assess their power; if they can resolve the dispute using power alone, they may choose to use this approach. If one doesn't have the power to resolve the dispute, or if one chooses not to use a power-based approach because of the possible damage to relationships, then one may consider a rights-based approach. A rights-based approach seeks to find norms, precedent, standards of law, or fairness that could support one's position. To truly enforce one's rights, one may have to resort to the legal system, which can be both costly and time-consuming. An interest-based approach is more likely to meet the needs of both parties as well as preserve the relationship. Those who have applied this model of dispute resolution[6] argue that all three approaches exist simultaneously and that interests are nested within a rights and power framework (Figure 7.1). To

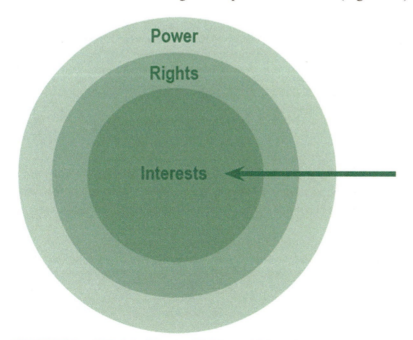

FIGURE 7.1   A Model of Power, Rights, and Interests

Box 7.2 The Use of Normative Leverage in Labor Relations

Collective bargaining between management and labor unions provides many examples of the use of different types of leverage. Positive leverage can be seen when management offers unionized workers pay increases or improved benefit plans. Negative leverage can be seen when a labor union threatens to go on strike or management threatens to lock the employees out of the plant unless they accept management's last offer. A 2010 strike between management at the Mott's Apple Juice plant in upstate New York and the company's unionized workforce was driven by what both sides saw as their normative leverage.

Mott's Apple Juice is a brand owned by the Dr Pepper Snapple Group, a corporation that reported a 2009 net income of $555 million. The company claimed in negotiations that its employees were overpaid compared to other production employees in the area and demanded that the union accept a $1.50 per hour wage cut along with other fringe benefit cuts. Its leverage was based on the norm that Mott's employees should take a wage cut because of the area's high unemployment rate and "local" wage rates—Mott's employees reportedly were being paid an average of $21 per hour while the average wage rate of other food industry production workers in the area was

$14. The union rejected the proposed wage and fringe benefit cuts because of the company's profitability. Its leverage was based on the norm that significant wage and benefit cuts are appropriate only if a company is losing money or such concessions are the only alternative short of moving the plant to an area with cheaper labor rates. As stated by the local union president: "Corporate America is making tons of money—this company is a good example of that. So why do they want to drive down our wages and hurt our community? This whole economy is driven by consumer spending, so how are we supposed to keep the economy going when they take away money from the people who are doing the spending?"

The union ended the 16-week strike by accepting a wage freeze (but not the company's proposed $1.50 per hour wage cut) and changes in the company's pension contributions for production workers.

Sources: Greenhouse, S. (2010, August 17). In Mott's strike, more than pay at stake. New York Times. Retrieved from http://www.nytimes.com/2010/08/18/business/18motts.html; and Greenhouse, S. (2010, September 13). Ending strike, Mott's plant union accepts deal. New York Times. Retrieved from http://www.nytimes.com/2010/09/14/business/14mott.html?_r=1.

get to interests, disputants have to work their way through determining who has the power and who has the rights. Even if one chooses to negotiate at the interest-based level, one does so fully understanding the rights and power he or she has.

TAKE AWAY: *You do not lose your rights or power just because you use an interest-based approach. If you are feeling exploited while using an interest-based approach, you can always go back to using rights or power.*

When considering which of three approaches to use, one should evaluate the "goodness" of the three approaches by using the following four criteria:

1. **Transaction costs** of using the approach
   - Time, money, energy expended in disputing
2. Satisfaction with the outcomes
   - How well were the interests met?
   - How fair was the outcome?
   - How fair was the process?
3. Effect on the relationship
4. Likelihood of reoccurrence

Transaction costs the costs associated with using a power- versus rights- versus interest-based approach to negotiation.

A **power-based approach** can be cost-efficient if the outcome is forced on the other; however, only the one with the power is likely to be satisfied with the outcome. The powerless party is not likely to have his or her interests met or feel the outcome or the process is fair. No one likes an outcome forced upon them, so power-based approaches tend to damage relationships. The dispute is likely to recur as those low in power may retreat from the situation to regroup and find allies to amass their own power to fight another day. Thus, conflict spirals are likely to occur when power-based approaches are used.

A **rights-based approach** can be costly if it means using the legal system to enforce one's rights. Moreover, trials or judgments often take considerable time to be rendered. With a rights-based approach, usually only one side "wins"; the other is not likely to feel that his or her interests are met or that the outcome is fair. On the other hand, to the extent that one trusts the legal system, even the party who loses may feel the process itself is fair. As to the relationship, most of us don't continue relationships with those who take us to court, although in a business context it may be possible. A legal decision may reduce the likelihood of the dispute recurring, but parties can always appeal and the dispute could drag on.

A rights based approach also applies to using relevant industry standards and organizational policies and procedures. Any time you rely on using accepted and legitimate rules or guidelines beyond just the legal system you are using a rights based approach to dispute resolution.

An **interests-based approach** also incurs transaction costs, mostly in terms of time. To understand the other's interests, one has to spend time preparing for the negotiation and analyzing the needs and wants of the other side. This approach is much more likely to leave both parties satisfied with the outcomes because both should have their interests met and feel that the process and outcomes are fair. An interests-based approach should improve the relationship between parties and reduce the likelihood of the dispute recurring.

■ ■ ■ ■

Influence

In many ways, much of what we are trying to do in negotiation is influence others to come to our side or to see our perspective. Perhaps somewhat surprisingly, to be persuasive we also have to be open to persuasion ourselves. Roger Fisher, one of the authors of the seminal book on negotiation, *Getting to Yes*,[7] makes this point in a video training a negotiator to use principled negotiation. Why is this so? It is largely due to the *norm of reciprocity* that we have discussed previously. To get people to see things our way, we have to show a willingness to see things their way as well. Once we understand their needs, we can formulate what Fisher calls "a yesable proposal." In constructing such a proposal we make an offer that meets our own needs and incorporates as much as possible the needs of the other side. Not surprisingly, the other person will be much more persuaded by such a proposal than by one that didn't take his or her interests into account.

> **TAKE AWAY:** *To persuade others, you must be open to persuasion yourself.*

The noted social psychologist Robert Cialdini has devoted much of his research career to understanding and explaining influence tactics. We discuss his six principles of influence[8] next.

Reciprocity: Be the First to Give

Reciprocity is a universal norm. In negotiation, in particular, it plays a key role. If someone does you a favor, you *owe* that person a favor in return. If someone makes a concession to you, you feel a strong pressure to respond in kind. Interestingly, Cialdini argues that you should be the first to give favors or concessions. When you walk into a room, rather than considering what others can do for you, you should be thinking instead, "Who can I genuinely help here? Are there services I can render? Information I can share? Concessions I can make?" To the naïve negotiator this approach may seem counterintuitive, foolish actually. But the truth is the norm of reciprocity is so strong that whenever you help others, they will feel indebted to you. And you can call in those debts when you need them, because those feeling indebted to you will be more than happy to comply, as the weight of obligation to repay is heavy. Try it. It works!

Moment of power according to Cialdini, this moment is right after someone says "thank you" to you. It is your opportunity to take credit for what you did, and remind the other that they would do the same for you. This evokes the norm of reciprocity.

On the other hand, others may not feel beholden to you if you dismiss what you did for them as "nothing." How often have you done something for someone, and when they said, "Thank you," you replied, "Oh, it was nothing." Cialdini argues that when someone says, "Thank you," to you, it is your **moment of power**. If you dismiss it, you lose the power the norm of reciprocity provides. Rather, you should acknowledge that yes, you did perform a service or do a favor and follow that acknowledgment with the statement, "And I know if the tables were turned, you would do the same for me." Now you receive credit for what you have done and can call in that credit when you need it. Even responding with "You're welcome," rather than "it was nothing" or "no problem" acknowledges that you gave or did something.

> **TAKE AWAY:** *Don't fumble away what is rightly yours. Take credit for your good deeds, and they will be returned to you in kind or in another currency. Consider being the first to give.*

Scarcity: The Rule of the Rare

People want what they can't have. Anytime you can convince someone that what you are offering is in scarce supply, be it knowledge, unique information, or a one-of-a-kind item, you will be able to demand a higher price for it than you normally would. Tickets for the 2011 college BCS national championship game were extremely scarce, and National Public Radio announced on the day of the game that tickets were being sold by third-party vendors (hawkers) at prices exceeding $2,000 per ticket.[9] One can think of similar examples. Parents will pay almost any price for a scarce item desired by their child right before Christmas. At the peak of their popularity in the 1980s parents across the United States flocked to stores to try to obtain one of the Cabbage Patch Kids for their children, with fights occasionally erupting between parents over the hard-to-find dolls. The same was true for Wii systems in the mid-2000s. Monster Dolls were going for $100 in December 2010, but in January 2011 they were selling online for only $25. In marketing we often see the use of the scarcity principle in limited time deals or limited editions of products. NBA teams scrambled in the summer of 2010 to make whatever deals they thought necessary to convince superstar player LeBron James, a unique player with unique talent, to sign with their team. Universities that admit more students than they have beds in the residence halls for may encounter higher-than-normal prices when negotiating with local landlords to rent apartments for the students because of the scarcity of available space and the immediate need of finding places for the students to stay.

Many negotiators use the scarcity effect in offering deals with tight time deadlines. An "exploding offer," for example, when a job candidate must accept the job within the next 24 hours or otherwise lose a signing bonus or the job offer itself, creates a sense of urgency and sends the message that this is a unique and scarce opportunity. Sales representatives who use pressure closing techniques—"If you don't take this deal now, you will be missing out on the deal of a lifetime" or "You had better grab this property now before someone else does"—likewise use the scarcity effect to convince customers to take their proposed deals.

People can be unscrupulous in situations where scarce items are in high demand. To wit, the black market for body organs, inside trader information about upcoming mergers, and so on, thrive. But one does not have to be un-ethical to take advantage of the scarcity principle; there are many situations where what you have to offer is truly scarce, and if so, you should capitalize on this advantage.

Authority: Showing Knowing

People respect those in authority; if you are in a position of authority, you should use it to your strategic advantage. If you have professional creden-tials, you should display them on your business cards and hang your licenses and diplomas where they can be seen in your office. If you have special train-ing or industry knowledge that will aid you in being more influential with a constituency, make sure they are aware of it. We are often too modest about what we know or what we bring to the negotiating table.[10]

Unless you have a lengthy resume or someone has given you a strong and flowery introduction, it is up to you to establish your authority with an audience or individual you are trying to persuade. Give examples of past suc-cesses, especially those that demonstrate your trustworthiness.

Commitment: The Starting Point

As discussed earlier in the section on normative leverage, one of the best ways to persuade is to first get commitment to your cause, idea, sugges-tion, and so forth, and then present an option or offer that is consistent with that previous commitment. People want to demonstrate consistency in their preferences. An astute negotiator can capitalize on this desire. A technique that demonstrates using commitment is referred to as the "**foot-in-the-door**" technique[11] based on the concept of a door-to-door salesperson. The salesper-son (you in this case) first gets the other to commit to a cause that is hard not to support, such as, "Do you agree that we must do all that we can to protect the earth for future generations?" How can someone disagree with such a broad goal? Then the salesperson whips out a box full of "green" products that if the homeowner buys and uses will help protect the earth. To demon-strate consistency the homeowner can justify the purchase. You also can use this principle to your advantage in negotiation.

Cialdini has done research using a technique that is the direct opposite of foot-in-the-door. He calls it the "**door-in-the-face**" technique.[12] The idea is that you first make a request that is very large and likely to be rejected, such as, "Would you become a big brother or big sister to an underprivileged

Foot-in-the-door
a persuasion technique where you get someone to say "yes" to a small request, and then later ask them for a larger request that is consistent with the small request you made earlier. This technique relies on normative leverage.

Door-in-the-face
a persuasion tech-nique where you ask someone for a very large request—one they are likely to say "no" to. Then after they say no you come back with a smaller request (what you hoped to receive all along) and they are more likely to say "yes" to it that if you had not asked for the larger request first.

child for three years?" After the person rejects this request (i.e., slams the door in the face of the requester), rather than walk away the person knocks on the door again and follows with a smaller request (the one he had hoped to get commitment to all along), such as, "Well, if you can't do that, would you be willing to escort a group of underprivileged children on a day trip to the zoo?" Cialdini found that significantly more people said yes to the last request (the zoo trip) if it followed a larger request that was rejected, than when the request for the zoo trip was made alone. The door-in-the-face technique is very similar to a negotiation tactic we have already discussed—having a high aspiration and opening offer. We may begin a negotiation by asking for something we don't really expect to receive, but when we show a willingness to make concessions that are closer to what we are willing to accept, we increase the probability of getting a "yes" to that smaller request than if we had begun the negotiation by asking for it in the first place.

> **TAKE AWAY:** *Give people a chance to say "yes" to you by using the consistency principle; and if they say "no" to you, you can concede in the negotiation and ask for what you really wanted in the first place.*

Liking: Making Friends to Influence People

We are more likely to say yes to people who like us and who *are* like us. Thus, before engaging in an influence attempt, it is useful to identify any similarities you may have with the other person. Do you belong to the same clubs? Do you have friends in common? Do you support the same sports teams? Anytime we can find common ground with another, even if it is on an issue not at all related to the current discussion, we have a better chance of influencing that person than if we have no similarities. You do not have to be disingenuous in searching for similarities with another; it is amazing how much we can find in common with a complete stranger.[13]

People are more likely to like us if we compliment them, and we should search for areas where those compliments can be genuine. False flattery is usually transparent and not an effective strategy to pursue.

You should also exploit your social networks when seeking common ground. To the extent that you belong to a number of different social networks you will be more influential. The sociologist Ron Burt[14] has demonstrated that those individuals who can connect various social networks to one another—he calls them **boundary spanners**—have the opportunity to be very influential, simply because they serve as a link between people who might not otherwise be connected. They have the opportunity to gather unique and useful information. We all know individuals like this, and they tend to be the "kingpins" in their social networks.

Boundary spanners individuals who are extremely influential because they have social ties that span many different social networks.

Consensus: People Proof, People Power

We can be more influential if we can show that we are not alone in advocating what we want the other person to do. If there are lots of other people doing it, then the assumption is, it must be the right thing to do. This is why testimonials of similar others can be effective in influencing behavior. Clearly marketing people understand this phenomenon. Cialdini provides the following example of invoking the power of consensus as a cue for the desired behavior. Telemarketers use a "**call to action**" line at the end of their presentations. It often goes something like this, "Operators are waiting, please call now." When this call to action was changed to, "If operators are busy, please call back," calls went through the roof. Notice the difference between the two calls. The first implies that operators are simply sitting around waiting for your call; the fact that they are not busy (waiting) suggests that no one else is calling in. The second call to action evokes a busy place where calls are coming in so fast that they can't answer them all; in other words, it evokes the power of consensus. If everyone is doing it, it must be good.

Call to action
when persuading someone this is the moment when you ask them to respond. In infomercials it is when they ask you to "pick up the phone."

■ ■ ■ ■

CHAPTER SUMMARY

In this chapter we have focused on the ways we can get people to say yes to us. We discussed the different kinds of power that may be available to us, and we differentiated power from leverage. We may not always be powerful, but we can often find leverage in a situation, even if it is simply invoking our BATNA. The chapter also covered interests, rights, and power as three different approaches to resolving disputes, and we considered transaction costs, satisfaction with the outcomes, the effect on relationships, and the likelihood of the dispute reoccurring as ways of evaluating the three approaches. We ended the chapter with a discussion of Cialdini's six principles of influence.

Questions/Exercises

1. Think of an upcoming negotiation you have. Which two of Cialdini's influence tactics will you use and what advantage will they give you?

2. Interests, rights and power can be thought of as being nested and each provides different advantages and disadvantages when applied to dispute resolution. Explain the advantages and disadvantages of each approach.

3. You have a cellphone contract with a national cellular company. Your plan gives you 450 minutes per month with rollover minutes that extend and stay for 12 months, a plan that costs you approximately $59 a month. It also includes unlimited texting; data use is not unlimited and is billed based on use ($0.01 for every megabyte sent). The other day during a 10-minute break in your night class, you

checked your Facebook account using the data feature on yourcell phone; however, in your haste—after all, you had to get back to class—you forgot to sign off of the Internetand Facebook. You realized your mistake when the class finished, 1 hour and 30 minutes later. The significance of your mistake became apparent when you received your bill for $347.83. The bill is due next week. You have never been late with your bill. Of your bill, $286.51 is attributed to your Internet use. You don't have enough money in your checking account to pay for your bill. You can't ask your parents for help, because they recently paid for $500 worth of repairs to your car. Plus, your mother has been "on your case" the past few months about how you need to be better "managing your money." Your only hope is to negotiate a deal with the company. How do you plan to do that? What power or leverage do you have?

Note: It will cost $250 to break your contract. You still have nine months on your contract. Your average monthly phone bill is around $63.

Be specific in how you will approach the company and how you will respond if they start by saying, "No."

4. You are halfway through your apartment lease. To help pay for your apartment lease, you advertised for a roommate. You found a roommate on Craigslist. You thought your new roommate would work out fine because he had a full-time job (or so you thought) and worked nights (7:00 P.M.–7:00 A.M.). A few months ago,

your roommate lost his job. Now all he does is sit on your couch, watch your television, use your pots and pans, and mess up the kitchen. The past two months your roommate has been late with his share of the rent, meaning that you have had to pay for the entire month's rent and then attempt to collect your roommate's share from him. Only your name is on the apartment lease. You really want to work out a deal with your roommate so that he pays his share of the rent on time each month. The trouble is, every time you set up a time to talk to your roommate, he finds a reason to "blow you off." You are getting mad. Things have to change with your roommate. You, however, have no idea as to how to make your roommate agree to pay his share of the rent on time. What do you do? What is your power or leverage? What leverage or power does your roommate have? When deciding how to deal with the issue, keep in mind the transactions costs, satisfaction with the outcome, effect on the relationship, and likelihood of the problem recurring.

5. You are president of your student organization. You want to convince the undergraduate dean to "bend the rules" to allow your group to have a function in the college that will have music when classes are in session. In thinking about how to approach the dean, first analyze the types of power that each of you have, and then consider the leverage that you may have. Finally, what types of influence attempts can you try that may influence the dean to say "yes" to your request.

Endnotes

1. French, J. R. P., & Raven, B. (1959). The basis of social power. In D. Cartwright (Ed.), *Studies in social power*. Ann Arbor, MI: Institute for Social Research.

2. Pruitt, D., & Rubin, J. (1986). *Social conflict: Escalation, stalemate and settlement*. New York: Random House.

3. Shell, R. (2006). *Bargaining for advantage* (2nd ed.). Penguin Books.New York

4. One of the authors was teaching an executive MBA course and a Canadian-trained engineer showed her a ring he wore that was to remind him of his professional code of conduct. Graduating engineers participate in a ceremony where Iron Rings are given to those engineers who choose to "obligate themselves to the highest professionalism and humility of their profession. It is a symbol that reflects the moral, ethical, and emotional commitment made by the engineer who wears the ring." See http://en.wikipedia.org/wiki/Iron_Ring.

5. Ury, W. I., Brett, J. M., & Goldberg, S. B. (1988). *Getting disputes resolved*. San Francisco: Jossey-Bass.

6. Lyle, A. L., Brett, J. M., & Shapiro, D. I. (1999). The strategic use of interests, rights and power to resolve disputes. *Negotiation Journal, 15*, 31–51.

7. Fisher, R., & Ury, W. (1981). *Getting to yes: Negotiating agreement without giving in.* Penguin Books.New York.

8. Cialdini, R. (2001). *The power of persuasion* [DVD]. Presented at Stanford breakfast briefings, Mill Valley, CA: Kantola Productions.

9. The Auburn/Oregon game played on January 7, 2011. Auburn won 22–19, scoring a field goal in the last two seconds of regulation time.

10. After years of teaching in the Midwest, we have observed that modesty seems to be particularly true of Midwesterners. It takes some convincing at times to get students to take credit for their accomplishments. We are not promoting boisterous bragging, but not taking credit for what you deserve is like leaving good money on the table.

11. Beaman, A. L., Cole, N., Preston, M., Glentz, B., & Steblay, N. M. (1983). Fifteen years of the foot-in-the-door research: A meta-analysis. *Personality and Social Psychology* [Bulletin]. *9*, 181–215.

12. Cialdini, R. B. (1975). Reciprocal concessions procedure for inducing compliance: The door-in-the-face technique. *Journal of Personality and Social Psychology, 31*, 206–215.

13. The play "Six Degrees of Separation," by John Guare (1990) Viking Books, suggests that using our social networks any person using a "friend of a friend chain" can be connected to another person anywhere in the world in six steps or fewer.

14. Burt, R. S. (1992). *The social structure of competition*. Cambridge, MA: Harvard Press.

What If They Don't Obey the Rules of the Road?: Trust, Ethics, and Reputation in Negotiation

When you pull out onto the road you make some basic assumptions about your own and others' driving behavior: first, that you will drive on the right side of the road (if you are in North America), and second, that everyone else will too. Moreover, you expect that others will obey traffic laws: they will stop at stop signs, won't run red lights, and so on. Furthermore, you trust that others on the road are licensed drivers, are sober, won't text and drive, and will be responsible drivers. We also trust that law enforcement officers will catch those who don't obey traffic laws and that repeat offenders will lose their right to drive. Imagine what driving would be like if there were no rules of the road. Pure chaos would result.

In negotiation, there are no universal rules, nor is there a recognized authority that enforces proper negotiation behavior. Rather, we rely on social norms and implicit rules to govern and guide negotiation behavior. Each party to a negotiation has the ability to walk away if they feel that the other negotiator is not acting in a trustworthy manner, is using unethical tactics, or is not acting in good faith. Furthermore, we can punish the unethical negotiator by sullying his or her reputation. In this chapter we discuss the roles that trust, ethics, and reputation play in the negotiation process.

CHAPTER OBJECTIVES

- To understand the role of trust in negotiation
- To learn how to build trust in negotiations
- To learn how to protect yourself from others' untrustworthy behavior
- To understand the role of ethics in negotiation
- To understand your own personal ethical standards
- To learn how to create a solid negotiation reputation

KEY TERMS

Deception	Ethics of purpose	Relation-based trust
Essential competition	Identity-based trust	Selective disclosure
Ethics of consequence	Institutional-based trust	Trust dilemmas
Ethics of principle	Knowledge-based trust	

CHAPTER CASE

In 2009 the *Chicago Tribune* broke the story of a secret admissions program at the University of Illinois. Called "Category 1" internally, this secret program admitted 800 students to the university between 2005 and 2009, after they had been recommended by state lawmakers, university trustees, and other high-power individuals. On average, these applicants were admitted at higher rates than others, even though they were less qualified. Fallout from this story led to the resignation of the president of the university, B. Joseph White, after it was revealed that he intervened to get a relative of a political fundraiser admitted to the school. The university created a firewall to protect the admissions process from outsiders' influence.[1]

■ ■ ■ ■

Trust

We describe negotiation as an interdependent process because parties cannot achieve their goals without the other. When one is dependent on another, one of the first questions that comes to mind is, "Can I trust this person?" We are concerned because trust and risk are intimately associated. Trusting someone means you are taking the risk that you will not be exploited. Whether one answers "yes," "no," or "I don't know" to this question will largely determine how the negotiation process will unfold.

When Trust Is Present

Relation-based trust when you have a strong pre-existing relationship with the other person you can predict their trustworthy behavior with accuracy. In this type of relationship you can freely share information and assume the other will not exploit you.

Trust is likely to be present if:

1. You have a positive relationship with the other that has developed over time and you know the person to be reliable and trustworthy. We call this **relation-based trust**, and it is probably the best predictor of future trustworthy behavior.
2. You or someone you know has had prior interactions with the other person and the person has shown himself or herself to be trustworthy. This is often referred to as **knowledge-based trust**, and although it may not be as reliable as relation-based trust, it can still provide a solid basis for a trustworthy interaction.

3. You share a common identity with the other person. Perhaps the person is from your hometown, goes to the same church, or belongs to the same business fraternity that you do. This **identity-based trust** is based less on personal experience with the other individual and more on trust in the identity you share with them.

4. The institution or organization the person represents has structures or policies in place that require their members to behave in a trustworthy manner. Referred to as **institutional-based trust,** this trust, like identity-based trust, is founded on faith that the person negotiating on behalf of his or her organization will behave in ways the organization desires.[2]

Research shows that when there is a basis for trusting the other negotiator, more information will be shared, which, in turn, increases the likelihood of reaching an integrative outcome. Acting in a cooperative manner elicits similar cooperative behavior from others.[3] Moreover, when there is mutual trust and goodwill, negotiators do not have to waste time playing negotiation jujitsu[4] and trying to protect themselves from exploitation. They can get to the heart of the matter with little risk.

When Trust Is Absent

If you have reason to believe the person across the negotiations table from you cannot be trusted, you will likely hold your cards close to your chest and be reluctant to share critical information.[5] Integrative potential is unlikely to be recognized, never mind achieved. Rather, the negotiation will take on a more distributive tone, with each party claiming as much value as possible with little or no effort to create value first. Not surprisingly, given the choice, most people would choose to not engage in negotiation at all if they deem the other person to be untrustworthy.

When the Trustworthiness of the Other Is Unknown

If you have no prior information about the trustworthiness of the other person, you should approach the negotiation with caution. You might begin testing the person's trustworthiness by first setting expectations and seeing if they are met. For example, you might use if-then statements such as, "I'm willing to tell you some of my interests in doing a deal with you, if you will do the same." Then you might share a small piece of non-critical information and see if the other person reciprocates in information sharing, which builds off of the reciprocity norm. If the person does reciprocate, you can build on this foundation gradually, keeping careful track of trustworthy and untrustworthy behaviors. This type of trust is referred to as *calculus-based trust*, because the negotiator is doing internal and external bookkeeping to calculate whether the other can be trusted.

Knowledge-based trust
the type of trust that develops when you know the other person and have had some prior interactions with them such that you can be confident in predicting their behavior.

Identity-based trust
trust in another person that is based on a shared identity—like same religion or same sorority. You do not actually know or have personal experience with the individual, but you trust them due to your shared dentity.

Institutional-based trust
the type of trust you have in someone because you know the institution or organization they represent has structures or policies in place that require their members to act in trust-worthy ways.

Deception
giving information that implicitly encourages people to draw false conclusions.

Assessing Situations

Astute negotiators recognize that certain situations can provide incentives for others to act in untrustworthy ways. Many situations have a mixed-motive structure, in that both the incentive to cooperate and to compete exist simultaneously. **Trust dilemmas** arise in situations where there are incentives for both parties to compete (defect) in the short run, even though over time, both would be better off by cooperating. It is important to recognize such situations because they can tempt even the most honest and trustworthy individuals to exploit the other if the short-term payoffs are sufficiently high. Box 8.1 details ways to deal with the trust dilemmas that arise in mixed-motive situations.

Individual Differences in the Propensity to Trust

Up to this point in the chapter, we have focused on the different types of trust one can have in another and on ways to increase the other's trustworthy behavior. It is important to note, however, that individuals differ in their overall propensity to trust.[6] They can be said to fall into one of three camps. First are those extremely cautious and risk-averse individuals who take the following stance: "I do not trust anyone until they give me a reason to." These are the individuals who will not allow themselves to be exploited and, as such, will not give you the benefit of the doubt. You have to prove your trustworthiness first.

Trust dilemmas are mixed-motive situations where there are short-term incentives to compete. To move the other person toward thinking long-term you must focus on the future of the relationship, increase communication, focus on joint outcomes and institute accountability.

Box 8.1 General Strategies for Promoting Trust

1. **Enlarge the shadow of the future.**
   Move the focus from the short term to the long term. Focus on building a long-term relationship that leads to mutual dependence.

2. **Change the payoff structure to eliminate the conflict between self-interest and mutual interest.**
   Establish side payments through contracts or create other incentives to cooperate.

3. **Increase communication.**
   Talk to one another frequently to communicate your intention to act cooperatively. Silence raises suspicion.

4. **Persuade the other party to focus on joint outcomes.**
   Take the focus away from your own gain and help the other see the value of striving toward mutual gains.

5. **Institute accountability.**
   Make cooperators and competitors identifiable. Increase the importance of reputation in the decision to trust.

In the second camp are those who endorse the following code: "I trust everyone until they give me a reason not to." Some would characterize these people as wearing rose-colored glasses; they have a genuine belief in the goodness of people. This belief can lead people to be overly trusting, perhaps taking risks they should not. Yet demonstrated trust in others can lead to a self-fulfilling prophecy—it is possible these individuals will elicit more trustworthy behavior from others than will those in the "trust no one" camp. Given a choice, most of us would prefer to interact with these folks than with those in camp one who would treat us all like we are untrustworthy.

The third camp might be dubbed "the realists," as their philosophy is, "Trust, but verify." This value system captures the good will of the "trust everyone" camp without exposing the trustor to undue risk. This is the value system we endorse. Even with people we know well (relation-based trust is high), it is not a bad idea to check in from time to time to make sure our trust is not misplaced.

Trust Repair

Once you have established a reputation for being trustworthy, you should do everything in your power to maintain it. Research has demonstrated that breaches of trust are very difficult to repair.[7] The saying "once burned, twice shy" applies here. You have to work much harder to repair trust once it is broken than you do to gain trust in the first place.

A number of research studies have addressed the issue of repairing or restoring trust.[8–11] We highlight in Box. 8.2 the main takeaways from this research.[12]

Box 8.2 Repairing Broken Trust in Negotiation

- Set up a face-to-face meeting with the other negotiator.
- Put the focus on the relationship instead of on who is right or who is wrong.
- Apologize to the other negotiator.
- Let the other negotiator vent about why he or she is upset or frustrated.
- Do not get defensive when talking to the other negotiator, even if you believe the person is misinformed or wrong.

- Ask for clarifying information.
- Formulate a plan; ask the other negotiator what he or she thinks is fair or what they need.
- Think about ways to prevent a future problem.
- Do a relationship checkup after working things out.

■ ■ ■ ■

Ethics

When a breach of trust occurs, the issue of ethics is also likely to raise its head. When we discover that someone has cheated or lied to us in a negotiation, not only do we feel betrayed, we are also likely to judge the other negotiator as unethical. Ethics can be a sticky subject to raise in the negotiation classroom because people can differ considerably in their judgments of what is and is not ethical. Our ethical principles are based on our own moral values. These values are imparted to us early as children by our parents, and they continue to develop with the influence of friends, teachers, co-workers, and bosses. Over time, we develop our own ethical standards.

When discussing ethics as they relate to negotiation, it is often helpful to pose ethical dilemmas and ask students in the negotiation classroom what they would do. Not surprisingly, most students judge behaviors such as inflicting outright harm to another individual as highly unethical. They also see many traditional competitive bargaining tactics (stating a higher reservation price than what you are actually willing to accept or inflating your aspiration level) as perfectly acceptable and ethical. Behaviors that most agree are clearly ethical or clearly unethical are not the interesting ones; rather, it is the behaviors that fall into the gray areas in-between where ethical issues arise. If you are using a negotiation tactic that you deem ethical (overstating the value of your BATNA, for example) and the other negotiator learns the real value of your alternative, that person is likely to judge your bargaining behavior as unethical. Likewise, if the other negotiator holds a very high ethical standard (i.e., is an absolutist), he or she may judge behaviors that most see as ethical (e.g., inflating your target price) as unethical.

TAKE AWAY: *You cannot assume everyone shares the same ethical standards; learn as much as you can about the person across the table from you, including his or her ethical standards, both before and during your negotiation.*

Next, we discuss ethical theories, then turn to the issue of what makes people engage in unethical conduct, and the consequences of doing so. Finally, we pose some questions to help you consider your own ethical standard.

Ethical Theories

There have been volumes written on ethics, going back to the time of Aristotle, and a thorough discussion of ethics goes beyond the scope of this text. Most of these theories evaluate the means people use to reach the ends they desire. For simplicity, we narrow the field to three basic ethical systems or principles where actors are either absolutists, relativists, or pragmatists

Aristotelian ethics are often referred to as **ethics of purpose**. Aristotle (384–322 B.C.) viewed people as basically good and argued that they will use a good means to reach a good end. This is an *absolutist* approach—people good, means good, ends good.

Immanuel Kant (1724–1804), a German philosopher, championed rationality as the ethical standard, sometimes referred to as **ethics of principle**. Kant assumed that people are rational; they will do the right thing to pursue rational means. Kantian ethics are *relativist* in that rationality is grounded in the culture and cultures can differ in what they endorse as rational means and rational ends. The Golden Rule, "do unto others as you would have them do to you," is consistent with Kantian philosophy.

John Stuart Mill (1806–1873), an English philosopher, is most associated with the third theory called **ethics of consequences**. This is a utilitarian or *pragmatic* approach to ethics. It assumes that people carefully consider the pros and cons of any action and who will be affected by the action. Then one chooses the action that produces an outcome that does the least harm and the most good. This philosophy assumes that people can judge what is a good end and that they can justify the means they use to reach that end (as long as it minimizes harm).

What philosophical school or principles do you endorse? Consider the following question: "Is it ethical to misrepresent your intended use of a piece of property you are buying, because you know that the owner might not want to sell if he or she knew what you were going to do with it?" If you answer "yes" to this question, then we can assume you do not subscribe to the ethics of purpose or the ethics of principle approaches. Rather, you are more likely a pragmatist and endorse ethics of consequences—assuming, of course, that you think the intended use will be good for the property and the community, even if it means cutting down specimen trees.

Ethics of purpose is an absolutist approach to ethics that views people as basically good and suggests they will use a good means to reach a good end.

Ethics of principle a relativist approach to ethics that is grounded in the prevalent culture. It assumes that people are rational and will do the right thing to produce an outcome that is consistent with the culture. A "do unto others" approach.

Ethics of consequence a utilitarian or pragmatic approach to ethics. It assumes the individual will choose the action that produces an outcome that does the least harm and the most good.

Calvin and Hobbes © 1995 Watterson. Dist. By Universal Uclick. Reprinted with permission. All rights reserved.

■ ■ ■ ■

What Motivates People to Act Unethically?

Many corporate failures in the late 1990s and the 2000s (Enron, WorldCom, Tyco, to name some of the more notable) led to thousands of people losing their jobs, their savings, and their retirement pensions. The downfall of many of these organizations was due to fraudulent accounting practices, and not due to just a few loners, like Bernie Madoff. Rather, the fraudulent practices became part of the corporate culture and were widespread. It makes one ponder how so many could do so wrong.

Greed and the Profit Motive

Certainly the pressure for stockholders of public companies to do well may have played a role in these failures. Yet, it would be hard to argue that the profit motive itself is unethical. Many people and organizations make reasonable profits without resorting to unethical tactics. One practice that has changed over the years is that publicaly held companies forecast their expected profits for each quarter. Stock prices are known to drop precipitously when companies don't meet their projections, even if they are in fact doing quite well. Thus, there is a situational incentive for companies to not report shortfalls or to "make the numbers come out right." What might have been a one-time "correction" over time became routine and institutionalized, dragging everyone down to the lowest common denominator.

Unfortunately, when unethical tactics work, they give the person using them more leverage in the situation and often a more successful outcome. So, it becomes easier and easier to justify the use of the tactic, which, in turn, increases the likelihood of using it again. Justifications such as, "It was harmless," "It was unavoidable," "It avoided negative consequences," or "It was appropriate given the situation" can lead people down the slippery slope.[13] As a negotiator for yourself, or for your company, you don't want to find yourself going down that slippery slope.

Essential competition
the type of competition where there can only be one winner. In business it can be when there is a very small niche market and there is not room for two competitors, thus it is essential that one must "win." Some will be tempted to use unethical tactics when there is essential competition.

Competition, the Desire to Win

Some negotiators will do whatever it takes to "win." And there is little doubt that extremely competitive situations may bring out the worst in people. Still, we know it is possible to be both competitive and honest, so competition alone cannot account for unethical conduct.

It is important to differentiate between incidental and **essential competition**. If you are selling t-shirts outside the football stadium on game day and someone else is also selling t-shirts at another entrance, you are experiencing incidental competition. That is, there are enough fans to go around, and both you and the other t-shirt seller can make a good profit on game day.

> ## Box 8.3 Forms That Unethical Behavior May Take in Negotiation Settings
>
> 1. Selective disclosure and/or exaggeration
>   - Overemphasizing good points, failing to expose the bad
>   - This is legal, but it can hurt relationships.
> 2. Misrepresentation
>   - Of aspiration levels, reservation prices
> 3. Deception
>   - Giving information that implicitly encourages people to draw false conclusions
>
> 4. False threats
>   - Threatening to induce fear, with no intention of following through with the threat
> 5. False promises
>   - Not following through with a promise can be promissory fraud
> 6. Falsification
>   - Out-and-out lies
> 7. Inflicting direct and intentional harm

Essential competition, on the other hand, occurs when there is a limited market for a product or service and there is not room for multiple players in the market. When people feel that it is a zero-sum situation, where there can be only one winner, then the temptation to use unethical tactics may be stronger.

Justice or Redressing Unjust Behavior

Not surprisingly, when people feel that they have been unjustly treated by another, they may feel that retribution is appropriate. Although most people would argue that they would never initiate the unethical behavior, if they feel someone "did it to them," they would feel justified in returning the favor, so to speak.

In Box 8.3 we address the various forms that unethical behavior in negotiations can take beginning with the milder (or less questionable) tactics and finishing with those most agree are unethical.

How to Avoid Being "Taken" by Unethical Tactics

Ask Questions

If you believe someone is lying or being deceitful, you need to take control of the negotiation process by asking questions. Ask again and again. Ask in different ways. Keep probing. Are the answers consistent? Are there warning signals? If someone seems to be dodging the questions you ask, you have reason to be concerned.

Check Your Assumptions

We always go into negotiations with some assumptions about the other person or what that person is promising. Perhaps you assume that the person you are dealing with has the authority to do the deal. Perhaps you assume that the house you are buying includes all appliances and window dressings. You should never proceed as if those assumptions are true. It is your obligation in the negotiation to verify your assumptions.

Don't Get Caught up in Ingratiation or Flattery

A wily negotiator will tell you exactly what you want to hear. Make sure you are not taken in by this tactic. Accept the compliment, and then follow with an objective response. When someone flatters your good taste in interior design, thank the person and tell him or her the price you charge for your services.

Check Their Reputation

People's reputations usually precede them. Ask others who have dealt with this person or firm what the experience was like. Do they have a reputation for good faith negotiations? There are websites you can review to learn about customer complaints. This should be part of your preparation, especially if it is a high stakes negotiation.

■ ■ ■ ■

How to Avoid Ethical Traps

There may come a time in your professional career where you are asked to do something that violates your personal ethical standards. Maybe your boss has asked that you don't fully disclose some aspect of a sale you are trying to make. Perhaps your boss has just heard from the manufacturer that a structural weakness has been discovered in the materials you are using. What should you do?

First, you should have your own personal standard; that is, you should know your ethical bottom line. If someone asks you to do something that violates this standard, you'll feel more comfortable saying "no" if you can explain why. Second, you should be aware of situations where it is difficult to uphold your standard. If you find yourself in these situations, you may be forced to make split-second ethical decisions. You should be prepared to answer the question you don't want to answer, such as, "Have any structural flaws been found in the materials used for the product?" The best advice we can give is that if you are constantly finding yourself in these situations, you may need to seriously reconsider if you are in the right business. Third, at a minimum you should understand and accept the implications of not following your standards. Will it hurt your reputation? Can you live with that?

> ### Box 8.4 Questions to Ask to Determine If Your Actions Are Consistent with Your Personal Ethical Standard
>
> 1. Will it hurt my reputation?
> 2. Is it legal?
>   - If you can't answer yes to this question, you may be in trouble. There are many things that are perfectly legal but could still be deemed unethical by others.
> 3. What would someone I highly value think of the behavior?
>   - This is sometimes called the mom test. Could you tell your mother what you did?
> 4. Shoes test
>   - If you were in the other person's shoes and this tactic was being used against you, would you still think it was ethical?
> 5. Newspaper test
>   - Could you live with yourself if what you did was in the headlines tomorrow?
> 6. Mirror test
>   - This is the penultimate question. Can you live with yourself?

What Should Your Personal Ethical Standards Be?

As we mentioned at the beginning of the ethics discussion, no one can tell you what your negotiation ethics should be. If you look at Box 8.3, some of you would draw the line after **selective disclosure**, some before. Others might be comfortable with all the tactics up to inflicting harm. Regardless of where your line in the sand is, it is up to you to know where it is. Box 8.4 highlights some questions you can ask yourself to determine where your ethical standards are.

Selective disclosure
in negotiation, this means you don't disclose all your information, rather you share only that information that it is in your best interest to share.

Reputation

As you build your strengths and skills as a negotiator, you will also develop a reputation. One of the things we observe in the negotiation classroom is that reputations develop early, they tend to persist even in the absence of data to support them, and they are hard to change once established. One of the authors always tells students on the first day of role-playing that they can "do anything they want" as far as strategies and tactics are concerned but that they "are responsible for everything they do." That is, the instructor cannot control the perceptions that others may have of their negotiation behavior, and they alone are responsible for the reputation they gain.

Developing a reputation is somewhat of a self-fulfilling prophecy. If you develop a reputation as a "tough guy," then those who are planning to negotiate with you prepare with your tough guy reputation in mind. Hence, they are more likely to decide to use a competitive strategy to combat the strategy they are expecting from you. You notice that they are taking a particularly competitive stance and decide to match it with your own, even though you had planned to be more collaborative. The next thing you know you are in a conflict spiral and your reputation for being a competitor is reinforced.

Another reason for reputations persisting is that people have a tendency to process only data that support their theories or beliefs and discount information that does not. Thus, two of your goals should be to develop an early reputation for being honest, trustworthy, and fair and to protect that reputation at all costs.

You should not leave your reputation to chance. Part of being a good negotiator is managing others' perceptions of you. If you care passionately about an issue and it is very important to you, you need to convey to the other party that you are standing firm on this issue but that you are willing to be flexible on other issues. You want the other negotiator to come away from an interaction with you believing you are "firm but fair" rather than "tough and inflexible." It is up to you to leave the other party with the right impression. However, it doesn't hurt to check if you have by asking for feedback. Seeking feedback communicates to the other party that you care what he or she thinks. It also provides you with the opportunity to correct any misperceptions.

When you are negotiating as part of a group or team, you are still responsible for what you do as a team member. Sometimes, due to diffusion of responsibility, people let things slide and are not as careful as they should be in terms of what they say and do as a team member. Although groups and teams can effectively negotiate, it is important to assign roles and responsibilities to team members. One of the downsides of negotiating as a group or team is that a "them versus us" attitude prevails, which can lead to extremely competitive behavior. If you join in, you can be labeled as "one of them"—and your behavior is a lot more visible as part of a team, so your reputation can spread like wildfire in such situations.

One of the authors recalls two different classroom occasions where reputations were damaged beyond repair; both were instances where people were negotiating as part of a team. In one negotiation, modeled after a prisoner's dilemma situation, the negotiators for each team agreed to leave a pile of "earnest money" by the door that each agreed would lead to collaborative, rather than defecting, behavior in the dilemma game. As the end game drew near, one group stole the money and kept it. The three members of that team were never treated the same way in class again. Although they tried to argue that "it was just a game," others clearly didn't see it that way.

The other example took place in a coalition bargaining exercise where each of the three teams could potentially be shut out of the agreement. As coalitions are inherently unstable, it is often the case that one party can be shut out. In this case the team that was shut out believed they brought more to the table than the other teams did and they played hardball early on in the negotiation, never believing that they could be shut out of the deal. But they were. The other two teams were willing to split a smaller pie and receive less than they could have received in a three-party deal just to punish those playing hardball. To make matters worse, one player of the shut out team stormed out of the classroom, leaving behind two people who he had promised a ride home on a snowy night (one of whom was on an opposing team). As this was the last classroom exercise of the term, there was no opportunity for the hardball player to save face.

Revisiting the Chapter Case

The case at the beginning of the chapter might leave you with the impression that it was a few "really bad apples" that led to the unfair admission of unqualified students. However, as Max Bazerman and Anne Tenbrunsel argue in their book, *Blind Spots: Why We Fail to Do What's Right and What to Do About It,*[14] many people who others perceive as acting unethically don't believe this of themselves. That is, when interviewed by the *Tribune,* some lawmakers who had advocated for certain people simply saw that as part of their job and felt it was completely appropriate. Before being too judgmental, Bazerman and Tenbrunsel suggest that we should examine our own behavior and see if we have ever asked for or done special favors for a friend or relative. Of course we have. The ethical issue arises when the commodity is scarce (slots in a First-year class) and when more qualified people are left out. It is even more of an issue if the left out people are "not like us," that is, if the favoritism slants toward people who "are like us" in race, ethnicity, religion, and so on.

CHAPTER SUMMARY

We began this chapter with a discussion of trust and the important role it plays in negotiation. We considered different types of trust and differences in individuals' propensity to trust. We presented three different ethical perspectives that determine how people judge what is and what is not ethical behavior in negotiation. We discussed ways to determine your own ethical negotiating standard. The chapter concluded with a discussion of your reputation as a negotiator and how important it is to guard your reputation because it is difficult to change a negative reputation once it has been established.

Questions/Exercises

1. You are negotiating with someone for the first time over an issue that is very important to you. It is important to you that you come across as trustworthy, and it is also important that the person you will be negotiating with can be trusted.
   a. Name three things you could do to show the other negotiator that you are a trustworthy person.
   b. Name three things you can do to ensure the other person is trustworthy.
2. Explain the differences between the 4 types of trust. Think of an example of each type of trust by thinking of 4 people you know each of whom exemplifies one of the different types of trust.:
   a. Calculus-based trust
   b. Relational trust
   c. Identity-based trust
   d. Institutional-based trust

3. You are involved in a negotiation for the sale of your couch. A sales representative at the local furniture store told you the other day that the market value for this type of couch is between $300 and $500. The potential buyer asks if you have any other offers for the couch—you don't. How will you answer this question? What does your answer suggest about your negotiation ethics? Which ethical theory best describes your response and why?
4. How can you best deal with a negotiator who is known for using "unethical" tactics?
5. Suppose you used an unethical tactic in a negotiation and the other negotiator found out. How could you go about rebuilding trust with that person? How could you try to restore your reputation?

Endnotes

1. Program on Negotiation. (2011, April). Our ethical "blind spots" in negotiation. *Negotiation, 14,* 1–4.
2. Rousseau, D. M., Sitkin, S. B., Burt, R. S., & Camerer, C. (1998). Not so different after all: A cross-discipline view of trust. *Academy of Management Review, 23,* 393–404.
3. Kramer, R. (1994). The sinister attribution error: Paranoid cognition and collective distrust in organizations. *Motivation and Emotions, 18,* 199–203.
4. Fisher R., Ury, W., & Patton, B. (1991). *Getting to yes: Negotiating agreement without giving in* (2nd ed.). New York: Penguin.
5. Butler, J. K. (1991). Toward understanding and measuring conditions of trust: Evolution of a conditions of trust inventory. *Journal of Management, 17,* 643–653.

6. Rotter, J. B. (1967). A new scale for the measurement of interpersonal trust. *Journal of Personality, 35,* 651–665
7. Robinson, S. L. (1993). Trust and breach of the psychological contract. *Administrative Science Quarterly, 41,* 574–599.
8. Boles, T. L., Croson, R. T. A., & Murnighan, J. K. (2000). Deception and retribution in repeated ultimatum bargaining. *Organizational Behavior and Human Decision Processes, 83,* 235–259.
9. Bottom, W. P., Gibson, K., Daniels, S., & Murnighan, J. K.. (2002). When talk is not cheap: Substantive penance and expressions of intent in the reestablishment of cooperation. *Organizational Science, 13,* 497–513.
10. Schweitzer, M. E, Hershey, J. C., & Bradlow, E. T. (2006). Promises and lies: Restoring

violated trust. *Organizational Behavior and Human Decision Processes, 101,* 1–19.

11. Tomlinson, E., Dineen, B., & Lewicki, R. (2004). The road to reconciliation: Antecedents of victim willingness to reconcile following a broken promise. *Journal of Management, 30,* 165–187.

12. Thompson, L. L. (2009). *The mind and heart of the negotiator* (4th ed.). Upper Saddle River, NJ: Pearson Prentice Hall.

13. Lewicki, R. J., Saunders, D. M., & Barry, B. (2011). *Essentials of negotiation* (5th ed.). New York: McGraw-Hill Irwin.

14. Bazerman, M. H., & Tenbrunsel, A. (2011). *Blind spots: Why we fail to do what's right and what to do about it.* Princeton, NJ: Princeton University Press.

9

Objects in the Mirror May Be Closer than They Appear: Perceptions, Biases, and Communication in Negotiation

When driving, our visual field is constantly being bombarded with information that we must process and react to so that we don't end up in a ditch at the side of the road. Imagine that the car in front of you on the freeway has had the left turn indicator on for some time but there doesn't appear to be a car in front of it; is the driver planning to pull out, or has he simply forgotten to turn the indicator off? You are likely to decide the latter is true, but what if the vehicle in front of you is a truck and you can't see if there is something in front of him? Based on your past experience, you may decide that the truck is planning on pulling out because, in general, truck drivers are less likely to carelessly leave an indicator on, and they also have a better view of what is up ahead than you do. You may use a heuristic like, "Truck drivers are better drivers than most other people on the road," to make a decision about what the turn signal means. Heuristics are decision shortcuts that usually serve us well when we have to make fast judgments, but they can sometimes be wrong. When we apply them repeatedly, we may develop a bias in judgment. Biased information processing can cause us to interpret information incorrectly because we tend to filter out or ignore information that suggests things may be otherwise. That is, the truck in front of you may have left his turn indicator on by mistake after all; if you don't correct for the biased perception that truck drivers don't make mistakes, you may be behind that truck for a long time.

Think of a biased perception as trying to see through a dirty or cracked windshield and correcting that bias as getting a fresh perspective by using the washer fluid in your windshield wipers. In this chapter we address how our perceptions color the way we process information and how biased information processing can affect judgments and behavior in negotiation. We also discuss the role that effective communication plays in correcting those biases.

149

CHAPTER OBJECTIVES

- To appreciate the ways perception serves as a lens that colors and filters the way information is processed
- To understand how cognitive biases and heuristics can affect negotiation judgment and behavior
- To learn how to improve communication in the negotiation process

KEY TERMS

Active listening

Anchoring and adjustment

Availability heuristic

Communication channels

Endowment effect

Fixed pie perception

Framing effects

Halo effect (and horns effect)

Irrational escalation of
   commitment

Loss aversion

Overconfidence

Preference reversals

Prospect theory

Reactive devaluation

Representativeness heuristic

Selective attention

Stereotyping

CHAPTER CASE

In observing students in negotiation classes over the years, we have always found it interesting that even though the roles they receive to enact in class are randomly distributed, once they are assigned that role, they tend to interpret information related to their own side in a self-serving way. This *self-serving role bias* isn't limited to undergraduate or MBA students. James Sebenius, a Harvard professor, reports executives are equally susceptible to the bias.[1] Researchers gave a large group of executives financial and industry information about one company negotiating to acquire another. The executives were randomly assigned to the negotiating roles of buyer or seller; the information provided to each side was identical. After time for analysis, all the participants were asked for their private assessment of the target company's fair value (not how they might portray that value in the bargaining process). Those assigned the role of seller gave median valuations more than twice those given by the executives assigned to the buyer's role. These valuation gulfs had no basis in fact; they were driven entirely by random role assignments.

Sebenius suggests that even comparatively modest role biases can blow up potential deals. For example, if a plaintiff believes he has a 70% chance of winning $1 million judgment, while the defense thinks the plaintiff has only a 50% chance of winning, in settlement talks, the plaintiff's expected BATNA for a court battle (to get $700,000 minus legal fees) will exceed the defendant's assessment of his exposure (to pay $500,000 plus fees). Even without risk aversion, the divergent assessments would block any out-of-court settlement. This cognitive role bias helps explain why companies like Microsoft took such a confrontational approach in its struggle with the U.S. Department of Justice several years ago. The company appeared overoptimistic about its chances in court. Likewise, Arthur Andersen exhibited overconfidence in its arbitration prospects over the terms of separation from Andersen Consulting (now Accenture). Getting too committed to your point of view—"believing your own line"—is an extremely common bias that Sebenius calls "failing to correct for skewed vision."

Perceptions

All That Glitters Is Not Gold

There are individuals who see only the good in situations and people. They wear rose-colored glasses and can put a positive spin on almost anything. Although they might be somewhat delusional, they are probably a lot more pleasant people to be around than those who view only the dark side of situations and people. Our perceptions color everything we see. They are affected by our upbringing, our culture, our values, and our current state of mind, to name but a few.

Our perceptions are the lenses through which we make sense of the world. And because the world is a busy complex place, we cannot always attend to everything around us. We have to filter out the noise to pick up a clear signal. This process is referred to as **selective attention**, and it keeps us from being bombarded by all the stimuli around us.

Although selective attention helps us be more efficient in processing information, it can also lead us astray. In the previous chapter, we discussed how we attend more to information that confirms what we already know and how this process can lead us to ignore information that might be important. So it is with selective attention. In the following sections, we discuss some of the errors that can result in negotiation due to selective attention.

The Dark Side of Selective Attention

One of the brain's functions is to categorize people as friend or foe. This basic biological function probably developed in the days of the Neanderthals when snap decisions had to be made as to whether the other animal in the jungle was going to eat you or share food with you. The brain is very good at putting people, objects, and so forth, into meaningful categories. We form prototypes in our brain that represent different categories, and when we have to make a quick judgment about a person or a situation, we compare the features of the object we are attending to with the different prototypes we have stored in memory. If a sufficient number of key features match the prototype, we categorize the person or situation as an X or a Y. These stored categories also have a label attached to them, such as "good" or "bad" or "friend" or "foe." This categorization process takes place almost automatically, with little conscious thought.

The process just described can explain stereotyping. If we have a negative stereotype about a group of people, we can quickly make a negative judgment about someone simply because we perceive them as a member of the stereotyped group. Although useful for categorizing, prototypes or stereotypes are not good for predicting how a specific person drawn from that group might behave. For example, you may be a Midwesterner, and you know there

Selective attention the tendency to focus only on information in our environment that is consistent with what we already believe or know. This can lead to biased information processing where decision makers ignore information that is inconsistent with prior beliefs and only attend to self-confirming evidence.

is a stereotype about Midwesterners that suggests they are farmers who grow corn and raise pigs. And many Midwesterners do fit this stereotype. But you happen to be a city person, are well educated, and enjoy the fine arts, none of which are an obvious fit with the Midwestern stereotype. If someone you are about to negotiate with knew only one thing about you before the negotiation, namely, that you are a Midwesterner, that person would assume you fit the stereotype—and how wrong he or she would be.

Another phenomenon of categorizing people into groups is known as in-group favoritism and out-group denigration. We have a tendency to believe that people like us (the in-group) share our good qualities and that those not like us (the out-group) do not. In resource allocation tasks, people give more resources to in-group members than to out-group members, even if both worked equally hard on a task.

Halo effect (and horns effect)
this effect occurs when we only know one good (bad) thing about another person and then generalize this information to other attributes of the person without good reason. If someone is nice (mean) you may also assume they are smart (stupid).

An additional perceptual error in judgment is called the "**halo effect**" (or alternatively the "**horns effect**"). If we know only one attribute about a person and it is positive, we may generalize this to other attributes of the person without good reason. If someone is friendly toward you, you may also assume this person will be cooperative and make more concessions in the negotiation. Alternatively, if someone is standoffish, you may assume the person will be a competitive negotiator. We are more likely to be influenced by "halo" or "horn" generalizations if we know little else about the person. And, these perceptions tend to persist even when there is little objective information to support them.[2]

In negotiation contexts, these perceptual distortions can lead to costly errors in judgment. When negotiating with in-group members, we may trust them more than we should and learn too late that the trust was unfounded. On the other hand, we may be stingy when it comes to sharing sufficient information with out-group members and thus fail to realize the gains that might have been achieved if we had been more trusting.

Framing Effects in Negotiation

Framing effects
these effects occur when a situation is described in terms of what you stand to gain versus what you stand to lose. People are much more sensitive to and influenced by loss frames, and they are more risk-seeking in the domain of losses.

Frames can be thought of as the windows through which we perceive the outside world, including other negotiators, their offers, their behaviors, and their intentions. Put simply, framing affects our point of reference and determines whether we see the glass as half full or half empty. Consider the following situations:

Situation A
Imagine a very kind person gives you $200. Then she tells you that you must choose between the following two options:

Option 1: She will give you an additional $100.

OR

Option 2: She will toss a fair coin; if it comes up heads, she will give you an additional $200, but if it comes up tails, she will give you nothing more (you will still have the original $200).

Which option would you take? Write down either Option 1 or Option 2.

Situation B

Now consider the following scenario:

Imagine a very kind person gives you $400. Then she tells you that you must choose between the following two options:

Option 1: You must give her back $100.

OR

Option 2: She will toss a fair coin; if it comes up heads, you will have to give her back $200, but if it comes up tails, you will not have to give back anything (you get to keep the $400).

Which option would you take? Write down either Option 1 or Option 2.

Now let us consider your choices. Did you choose Option 1 for both Situations A and B? Did you choose Option 2 for both Situations A and B? If you did choose the same option both times, you can be said to have a consistent preference structure and are not affected by these **framing effects**. However, if you are like many people, you chose Option 1 in Situation A and Option 2 in Situation B and have demonstrated what is known as a **preference reversal**.[3] That is, if the choice problem is framed as a choice between a sure gain or a 50/50 chance of no further gain, most people go for the sure thing, Option 1 in Situation A. When the choice problem is framed as a choice between a sure loss and a 50/50 chance of no further loss, most people prefer the gamble. That is, they want to avoid the sure loss of $100 in Option 1 of Situation B. So why is this called a preference reversal and considered to be non-rational? Because, if you look at the two situations more closely they are asking essentially the same question, which is: *Do you prefer getting $300 for sure or do you prefer taking a gamble where there is a 50% chance of ending up with $200 and a 50% chance of ending up with $400?*

But people don't immediately see the problem this way; rather, they are influenced by whether the situations are framed as a choice among gains or a choice among losses. Faced with losses, people tend to be risk averse. They would rather gamble and hope they lose nothing rather than accept a sure loss of $100. This is called **loss aversion**.

Loss aversion assumes that people are more sensitive to losses than they are to gains of the same size. To understand this phenomenon better, consider Figure 9.1. This figure shows a subjective utility curve plotted on two

Preference reversals are related to framing effects in that people will give responses that are intransitive depending on how the question is framed. That is, they will reverse their preference as a function of whether the question is posed in terms of possible gains or possible losses.

Loss aversion people are much more sensitive to losses than they are to gains of the same size. Loss aversion can be explained by the subjective utility curve in Prospect Theory.

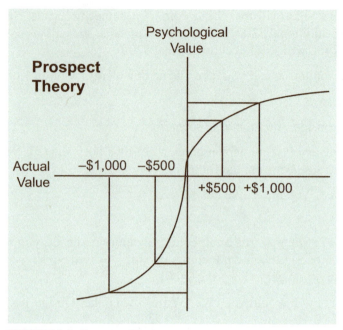

FIGURE 9.1 Prospect Theory

Prospect theory
a subjective utility theory that shows individuals' psychological value for money is not linear. Most people have a utility curve that is concave in the domain of gains and convex in the domain of losses, and the slope is steeper in the domain of losses, which can account for loss aversion.

dimensions. One is the actual value of money (in this case), and the other is the psychological value for money. What we see immediately is that our preference for money (and other goods) is not linear, as an economist would suggest it should be. Rather we see an S-shaped curve (considered from a neutral reference point) that is concave in the domain of gains and convex in the domain of losses. Moreover, the slope of the curve is steeper in the domain of losses than in the domain of gains, which can explain loss aversion. In the example depicted in Figure 9.1, we can say that psychologically losing $500 feels twice as bad as winning $500 feels good. The theory that explains this phenomenon is **prospect theory**,[4] a theory that won its authors the Nobel Prize in Economics in 2002.

So, you may be asking yourself, what does prospect theory have to do with negotiation? Imagine that someone "frames" his or her offer in terms of what you stand to gain by considering the arguments; that is, the person tries to persuade you by telling you all the good things that will happen to you if you move in his or her direction. Now consider your reaction if the offer is framed in terms of what you would lose if you don't move in the other person's direction. Research has shown that the loss frame is much more persuasive.[5]

■ ■ ■ ■

Heuristics and Biases That Affect Negotiation Process and Outcomes

There is a massive literature on cognitive biases that affect human judgment and decision making. Max Bazerman[6] has written a book on managerial decision making that illustrates many of these, as does his earlier work with Margaret Neale.[7] We focus in the following sections on a subset of these biases (in alphabetical order) that have specific implications for negotiation.

Anchoring

Suppose someone asked you to estimate the distance to the moon. You probably have no idea of how far away it is. Suppose, however, that they asked you to estimate if it is closer or farther than 1 million miles away. You would probably decide it is closer than 1 million miles and might estimate it is something closer to 750,000 miles. Now suppose this question is asked of someone else, but the person is asked if the moon is closer or farther than 250,000 miles away; the person says, "farther," and estimates that is about 350,000 miles away. You would both be wrong, the actual distance is about 238,857 miles. However, the number of miles you estimated was influenced by the "anchor" in the question; those who get the million mile anchor estimated the distance to the moon to be up to 400,000 miles farther away than those given the 250,000-mile anchor. Anchors can influence judgments in situations where the person doesn't have a very good idea of the actual value. The person may have a sense that the real value is more or less than the anchor, and will adjust his or her estimate away from the anchor, but not sufficiently. If you were an astronomer, you would likely know how far away the moon is and the anchor wouldn't influence your estimate.

Anchoring can play the same role in negotiation, especially if it is used as a first offer and the other person doesn't have a good understanding of the market value of the item under negotiation. Someone may set a very high value for an antique that is for sale, and even though you may not pay what is being asked, you will still be likely to be swayed by the asking price, especially if you have no way to assess its value. On the other hand, if you were at an auction the day before and saw the prices that others' paid for similar pieces, you would be less likely to be swayed by the opening price.

Anchoring and adjustment
a decision bias where in uncertain situations people will be influenced by an "anchor" to make their decision, and even if they know the anchor may not be accurate, they do not adjust away from the anchor sufficiently.

TAKE AWAY: *Anchors can work for you or against you. If you don't know the market, do not be swayed by the other's opening offer. If you do know the market, then it would be to your advantage to make the first offer and set the anchor in your favor.*

Availability Bias

Availability bias
this bias occurs when people overestimate the frequency of an event or occurrence based on how easily they can recall instances of the event.

The **availability bias** occurs when people are asked to estimate the frequency or likely causes of an event or occurrence and their judgment is influenced by how available in memory these occurrences are. Instances that come readily to mind are overestimated relative to instances that are hard to retrieve from memory. For example, if you were asked to estimate the number of women who are currently leaders of their countries in terms of positions holding executive power, you may have a hard time recalling any female presidents or prime ministers and give a number as low as 1 or 2 (in fact, in early 2020, there were 16 countries with women leaders).[8]

This biased recall can affect negotiations as well. Suppose you are trying to negotiate a lower amount for the cleaning deposit on your apartment lease. You have just talked to two friends who gloated that they were able to get their deposits lowered by $50. Having this information available in memory is likely to make you overestimate the likelihood that you too can negotiate a lower price. That is, their stories are more memorable to you than are the 30 other friends of yours who tried to negotiate a lower price, but failed. They maintained the status quo, which isn't nearly as memorable as a change that improves the status quo.

The Endowment Effect

Briefly this effect is as follows: "If an item is mine, I think it is more valuable than you do, even if you want it." A series of experiments have demonstrated this effect by showing the differences between "willingness to pay" and "willingness to accept" as a function of whether or not the item is yours.[9] In the studies, students who were not given a coffee mug rated the value of the mug at about $3, and said they would be willing to pay up to $3 to get the mug. Another group of students were given the mugs first, and then asked the least they would be willing to accept for the mug. The average amount they stated was $7. The mugs were exactly the same. Once something is yours it takes on extra value in your eyes.

Endowment effect
this is an effect whereby the value of an object can change as a function of whether or not it belongs to you. People tend to "endow" things and ideas that are their own with added value over the same object or idea generated by another person.

In negotiation this effect can keep people from achieving good deals. We see effects of the **endowment effect** most often in real estate, where sellers believe their house is worth more than one just like it next door, simply because it is theirs.

Fixed Pie Perception

This negotiation bias is the tendency to view all negotiations as distributive, zero-sum, where someone must win and someone must lose, even when integrative potential exists. People with this perception are unwilling or unable to create value by sharing information and making mutually beneficial trade-offs. Even when there are multiple issues, they will insist on negotiating each separately and treating each as a distributive negotiation. Students in negotiation classes are usually cured of this perception in the first few weeks when they see how making trade-offs among issues truly can "expand the pie." But until someone has this experience, it is often very difficult to persuade him or her otherwise.

Irrational Escalation of Commitment

Bidding wars are a good example of this bias. When people are bidding only to win, they may find winning to be a hollow victory if they end up paying more for the item than it was worth. We also observe this bias when people have invested a considerable amount of time, money, and effort into a business that is clearly failing. Investors will often continue to "throw good money after bad" rather than admit failure. As negotiators, it is important to reassess goals from time to time. Just because a goal made sense at one point in time, situations and economies can change; therefore, it is important that your goals and objectives make sense given the changing reality. Clinging to goals when evidence suggests they are no longer achievable is a form of **irrational escalation of commitment**.

Overconfidence

Being confident is an important attribute for a negotiator. Yet, there is a fine line between being confident and being overconfident. **Overconfidence** is somewhat like the endowment effect: people have a tendency to believe that once they make a judgment or decision about something then it must be right. To illustrate this tendency to be overconfident, Bazerman[10] gave managers 10 questions that they were unlikely to know the answers to (such as, What was Walmart's total revenue in 2006?) and asked them to estimate the answer and set a range around their answer that they were 98% confident would include the real answer. If you know that you don't know the answer, then the correct confidence interval should be something between zero and infinity. But people don't put between zero and infinity, rather they tend to set a much smaller confidence interval around their answer. When the correct answer for the 10 questions is given, the participants could take credit for having the question right only if it fell within their 98% confidence interval. On average, less than 2% of people get all 10 answers correct, with most getting 2 or fewer answers correct. If they were accurate in setting their confidence intervals, they should have had 9.8/10 answers correct! By the way, Walmart's revenue in 2006 was $351,139,000,000.

In negotiation, overconfidence can lead to a lack of flexibility because a negotiator who believes he or she is always right will be reluctant to listen to the positions and interests of others.

Irrational escalation of commitment this bias occurs when people get into bidding wars and end up paying more for something than it is worth. Additionally, people may honor sunk costs and continue to throw "good money after bad" even when the evidence suggests it is a losing cause.

Overconfidence once individuals have generated an answer to a question that has been posed, they are more confident than they should be that their answer is correct. This is especially true when they are asked to make estimates about something that they are aware they really don't know the answer to.

TAKE AWAY: *Be aware of the tendency to be overconfident; when negotiating, you should be sure you can support the arguments you make with objective criteria.*

Reactive devaluation
is the tendency to undervalue the concessions that other negotiators make.

Representativeness heuristic
a decision heuristic where judgments about persons or events are made based on how well the person or event fits into a prototypical or stereotypical category. If enough features of the person or event fit the category, we tend to overgeneralize and assume all the characteristics of the category fit the person.

"Stereotypes are devices for saving a biased person the trouble of learning."

—Author anonymous

Reactive Devaluation (or Reactance)

This process is devaluing the contributions of others' contributions to the negotiation. In particular, it is the tendency to undervalue the concessions that others make. We may believe, "If they gave up on that issue, it must not have been important to them." The flip side of this bias is also the remarkable tendency we have to overvalue our own contributions and concessions. Like in the endowment effect, we reason that the things we concede in a negotiation are more important and more meaningful concessions than those made by others.

Representativeness Heuristic (and Bias)

When making judgments about an individual (or object or event), people tend to look for traits an individual may have that correspond with their previously formed stereotypes. If enough features match, we are quick to put people in that category and ignore disconfirming evidence that suggests they do not belong in that category. The representativeness heuristic can cause us to cling to outdated and downright wrong beliefs. For example, if someone you just met reminds you very much of your sister's ex-boyfriend, who you absolutely despise, you may stereotype this person as a loser and a cheat. Needless to say, if you do so, you are unlikely to have a positive negotiation experience with this person, largely because you won't listen to him or believe anything he has to say. The process of stereotyping is based on the **representativeness heuristic** that leads to discounting base rate information, which is a much more reliable source than categorizing someone based on a few features.

Are We Doomed?

The preceding discussion of heuristics and biases has probably left you wondering how people are able to negotiate or maneuver through life at all, given the many cognitive biases we are susceptible to. The truth is that sometimes these heuristic shortcuts can serve us quite well, particularly if we don't have time to thoroughly prepare. But we need to recognize that they can also steer us terribly wrong. The first step to avoid making them is understanding them and recognizing when you find yourself (or someone else) falling prey to them. That is half the battle. Sometimes it helps to negotiate with a partner and ask that person to be particularly observant and point out to you if you are not negotiating rationally.

Communication

Communication is the essence of negotiation; without it there can be no negotiation. Those who can communicate their good case well stand a better chance of achieving their goals than those who cannot. Communication is not only what is said and how it is said but what isn't said and why. Next we discuss what is typically communicated in negotiation and the different modes (or channels) of communication

> "The single biggest problem in communication is the illusion that it has taken place."
>
> —George Bernard Shaw

and the advantages and disadvantages of each. We also consider the role of non-verbal behaviors, how to read others' non-verbal behaviors, and how to manage your own.

What Is Communicated in Negotiations?

Typically, negotiations begin with an effort to build rapport. Negotiators may engage in small talk to ease nerves and to set a positive tone for the negotiation. They may also talk about the process they will use: Will they take breaks? Will others be involved? How will they ensure that parties negotiate in good faith? Research has shown that the tone and communication patterns set early (within the first five minutes) in the negotiation do affect the outcomes that parties eventually agree to.[11]

Most of the communication effort in negotiation centers around offers and counteroffers, with each party doing his or her best to persuade the other of the viability of his or her arguments. In integrative situations the communication may center more on information sharing about interests and priorities in order to create value for both sides. In certain situations negotiators may choose to communicate about their alternatives to a negotiated agreement. This can be perceived as a threat, but it can also communicate urgency for movement in the negotiation.

Roger Fisher, a professor emeritus from Harvard Law School and a founder of the Program on Negotiation, said in a training video that there are two parts to communication in negotiation; one part is talking, and the other part is listening. The most important part is listening.[12] Nothing could be truer. Negotiators are often so busy formulating their next argument while the other negotiator is speaking that they are not really listening to what is being said. If we don't listen well important information that may be key to achieving a mutually beneficial outcome can be overlooked or missed altogether.

The best kind of listening is *active listening,* which is repeating back to the other what you heard him or her say. This type of listening achieves several communication goals. First, it acknowledges that you heard what the other person said. Second, it gives the person the opportunity to correct any misunderstandings you may have about what was said. Third, it sets a positive tone for the negotiation by showing respect for the other negotiator. And finally, it sets an expectation of reciprocity that the other person will also actively listen to what you have to say.

Non-Verbal Communication

Silence is golden. Sometimes not saying anything can be a very successful negotiation communication tactic. People are uncomfortable with silence and often will say anything to get past the pregnant pause. Try following what you consider to be an extreme or outrageous offer made by the other with stony silence, and you may find that the other person fills that space with a concession. This is a communication tool negotiators should employ more often, and alternatively, they should not make unilateral concessions when the other side uses silence. Rather than giving up information yourself, try following the silence with a question.

Most other non-verbal communication has to do with body language. Standing erect and making eye contact when the other is speaking are signs of respect and show that you are earnest about the negotiation; they also signal honesty. Slouching in a chair with your feet up on the coffee table communicates your lack of interest and lack of respect for the other person. Smiling may indicate openness and willingness to work collaboratively, whereas arms folded across your chest may indicate close-mindedness and an expectation of competitive behavior. We need to be careful in interpreting non-verbal behavior, however; the person crossing their arms may be open-minded and cooperative and is simply cold.

What is most revealing about non-verbal behavior is in the extent to which it corresponds with what is being said verbally. Gestures, for example, need to be considered within the context of what is being said. If someone pushes away from the table while verbally communicating, "This negotiation is over," there is no confusion about the non-verbal message. If the person pushes away from the table while sharing interests with you, the message sent by the gesture is less clear because it doesn't correspond with what is being said. Perhaps the person is pushing away from the table to go up to the whiteboard to write down his or her interests. We need to pay attention to non-verbal behaviors and the cues they may send, but we would be foolish to make important decisions based on them, especially if we do not know the other person very well. It is easier to interpret non-verbal behavior when we know the other negotiator quite well because we know what the gestures signal.

> **TAKE AWAY:** *To get your message across clearly, make sure your non-verbal behaviors are sending the same message as your verbal communications.*

Channels of Communication

Changes in technology have increased the ways negotiation can occur. It is now possible to negotiate with anyone anywhere in the world without leaving your chair. The typical, and stilled preferred, way to negotiate is in a face-to-face interaction. However, in today's global economy, face-to-face interactions are not always possible. Negotiators can negotiate over the phone, over email, using text messaging and chat, and other forms of online communication including interactive video conferencing.

Communication channels differ in the *richness* of what is communicated. Face-to-face interactions are the richest because they reveal a plethora of information: tone of voice, gestures, and other non-verbal behaviors, such as eye contact, facial expressions, body language, and so on. Video conferencing negotiations that allow you to see and hear the other person on the screen can capture much of the same information, although images can be blurry and usually only facial expressions can be observed, making them less rich than face-to-face interactions. Telephone communications capture tone of voice, but that's all. Email and text messages rely completely on the ability of the negotiators to express themselves well with the written word. They also may not occur in real time, in that minutes, hours, or even days can pass before a reply is received. Table 9.1 illustrates the various communication channels and their potential effects on negotiation performance.

Communication channels
the different ways in which people can communicate and therefore negotiate. These channels include face-to-face, phone, email, text or chat, and video conferencing. Communication channels vary in the richness of what can be communicated.

> **TAKE AWAY:** *Use face-to-face negotiations whenever you can. If this is not possible, you should select a process that you are most comfortable with, while being fully aware of its possible implications. Email negotiations preceded by and ending with a phone call can cement the deal.*

TABLE 9.1 The Richness, Synchronicity, Pros and Cons, and Effects on Negotiator Performance of Different Communication Mediums

Communication Medium	Richness	In Real Time/Place?	Pros of Using the Medium	Cons of Using the Medium	Effect on Negotiation Performance[13, 14]
Face-to-face	Extremely rich Full of information.	Same time Same place Synchronous	Efficient Can read tone and body language. Easier to establish rapport.	Real-time pressure to respond immediately. Frustration and negative reactions visible to others.	The majority of research data are from face-to-face negotiations, so almost all we know about negotiation performance comes from face-to-face.
Online Video Conference	Very rich Some delays Captures tone and facial expressions, but little body language.	Same time Different place Synchronous	Free Efficient Can negotiate anywhere in the world.	Camera quality may not be good Voice can break up. Connections can be lost.	Little data exist, but these interactions should be more similar to face-to-face negotiations than those done through email.
Phone	Moderately rich Captures the message and tone only.	Same time Different place	Efficient Can negotiate anywhere in the world.	Connections can be lost, especially in international negotiations. May take several calls to complete. International calls can be expensive.	Less rapport is built.
Email	Less rich Captures message only.	Different time (asynchronous) Different place	Captures everything that is said. Gives you time to reflect before responding. Recipient can't see you sweat.	Takes more time. Some may not respond for extended periods. Train of thought can be lost. May make incorrect attributions about the other when they don't respond.	Less rapport and trust are built. Produces more counter normative social behavior. There is more room for misunderstanding. Email negotiators do make more multi-issue offers than face-to-face negotiators. Personal disclosures can reduce impasse.
Text or chat	Least rich Short messages only.	Different time (asynchronous) Different place	Generally quicker response to texts than to emails.	Limits on the number of words that can be sent at one time.	Little, if any, rapport is built. No existing research exists on negotiating through text messaging.

CHAPTER SUMMARY

In this chapter we discussed the ways in which our perception colors and filters the information that we take in and how that can influence judgments we make about others. We also considered how **framing effects** can cause us to reverse our preferences as a function of whether options are presented as potential gains or losses. A number of cognitive biases and heuristics were discussed to demonstrate how they have the potential to affect negotiation behavior negatively. We discussed what, how, and why information is communicated in negotiation. And finally, we discussed the pros and cons of using the various types of communication channels for negotiations.

Questions/Exercises

1. Imagine that you are a graduate student who recently moved apartments to be closer to campus and to reduce your rent. You like your apartment well enough, but last week the landlord's twenty-one year old son and two of his friends moved in across the hall. Since they moved in you have heard nothing but constant door slamming and swearing in the stairwell. You have nothing against people partying and having a good time, but you are in the middle of preparing for your major exams so it is important to you that you are able to study and sleep in your apartment without being interrupted by yelling and door slamming. A couple of days ago you asked the landlord's son if he and his friends could please not yell and swear in the stairwell. He apologized and promised they would keep it down. Unfortunately, he seems to have forgotten all about his promise as it is 12:00 A.M. on a Thursday night and he and his roommates are standing outside your bedroom window smoking and laughing and talking loud enough to keep you awake. How might stereotypes affect your attempt to persuade the landlord's son and his friends to quiet down?

2. Why should a negotiator generally explain the significance of what he or she is giving up when making a concession?

3. You are planning on graduating from the university next month and starting a new job in Seattle, Washington. Upon graduation, you will have access to a small ($5,000) trust fund set up for you by a favorite uncle. You hope to save as much of the $5,000 as possible. You do, however, plan on spending some of the money to help pay your expenses associated with the cost of riding in a summer bike race (RAGBRAI—The Register's Annual Great Bike Race Across Iowa) in Iowa.

    Your current bicycle, a Trek 800, is about five years old and is generally considered to be a "mountain bike." You would need to buy new "road" tires (at a total cost of approximately $120) to ride your bike on the RAGBRAI route. Because you are concerned that "serious" bike riders may laugh at you when they see you riding RAGRAI on a mountain bike, you have thought about using part of your trust fund money to buy a new road bicycle.

You have heard that your freshman-year roommate works in the bicycle department at the local bicycle shop. You have also heard that bicycle prices at the shop are "negotiable." The shop's current advertisement features a Trek road bike that caught your eye. It has a list price of $1,759.99. You would like to spend no more than $1,500 for a new road bike.

Your freshman-year roommate is working at the bicycle shop this afternoon. Although you have not talked to your freshman-year roommate in the past two years, you plan on trying to negotiate with your freshman-year roommate to buy the Trek road bike. What specific cognitive biases would most likely impact your negotiation?

4. Explain the difference between synchronous and asynchronous communication and which do you think is most useful for getting your message across in a negotiation?

5. The other negotiator says to you "I can't pay that much, the price you are asking is much too high." How would you respond if you were engaging in active listening?

Endnotes

1. Sebenius, J. K. (2001). The negotiator's secret: More than merely effective. *Working Knowledge* [Newsletter]. Harvard Business School. Cambridge, MA.

2. Cooper, W. (1981). Ubiquitous halo. *Psychological Bulletin, 90*, 218–244.

3. Goldstein, W. M., & Einhorn, H. J. (1987). Expression theory and the preference reversal phenomena. *Psychological Review, 94*, 236–254.

4. Kahneman, D., & Tversky, A. (1979). Prospect theory: An analysis of decision under risk. *Econometrica, 47*, 263–291.

5. Cialdini, R. B. (1993). *Influence: Science and practice*. New York: Harper Collins.

6. Bazerman, M. H., & Moore, D. A. (2010). *Judgment in managerial decision making* (7th ed.). Wiley. Hoboken, NJ

7. Bazerman, M. H., & Neale, M. A. (1992). *Negotiation rationally*. New York: Free Press.

8. Encyclopædia Britannica, & Various sources, & Council of Women World Leaders. (June 2, 2020). Number of countries where the highest position of executive power was held by a woman, in each year from 1960 to 2020* [Graph]. In Statista. Retrieved June 28, 2020, from https://www-statista-com.proxy.lib.uiowa.edu/statistics/1058345/countries-with-women-highest-position-executive-power-since-1960/

9. Kahneman, D., Knetsch, J. L., & Thaler, R. H. (1990). Experimental tests of the endowment effect and the Coase Theorem. *Journal of Political Economy, 98*, 1325–1348.

10. Bazerman, M. H., & Moore, D. A. (2010). *Judgment in managerial decision making* (7th ed.). Wiley: Hoboken, NJ

11. Curhan, J. R., & Pentland, A. (2007). Thin slides of negotiation: Predicting outcomes from conversational dynamics within the first 5 minutes. *Journal of Applied Psychology, 92*, 802–811.

12. Fisher, R. (1985). The HackerStar negotiation. *Harvard Negotiation Project*. Morgan Guaranty Trust Company.

13. Thompson, L. L., & Nadler, J. (2002). Negotiating via information technology: Theory and application. *Journal of Social Issues, 58*, 109–124.

14. Thompson, L. L. (2009). *The mind and heart of the negotiator* (4th ed.). Upper Saddle River, NJ: Prentice Hall.

10

Understanding What It Is Like to Drive on the Other Side of the Road: Gender and Cultural Differences in Negotiation

Just when you thought you knew everything you needed to know to be an excellent driver, you find yourself on vacation in New Zealand (lucky you). You have reserved a car at the rental agency at the airport. You find the car, and when you go to get in, you realize the steering wheel is on the wrong side of the car! Not only that, but this car has a manual transmission and you'll need to shift with your left hand. When you ask the person next to you in the lot where the trunk release is, he looks at you as if he has no idea what you are talking about. You tell him you need to put your luggage in the trunk, "Oh," he laughs, "you mean the boot," and he shows you how to open it. He also refers to the front on the car as the "bonnet." Here you thought your vacation would be uncomplicated because you are in an English-speaking country, but New Zealanders seem to have a different name for everything. As you are pulling out into traffic, what should be a yield sign says, "Give Way." "Well, it can't be that hard," you think. "I'll just drive on the left, and everything will be fine." But no sooner have you pulled out on the road than you realize you need to make a right-hand turn. "Oh no!" It is not immediately obvious how you should do this, as there are several lanes of traffic.

Welcome to navigation in the wider world. As in driving, so it is with negotiating in a different country and culture. You don't have to forget everything you've learned, but you do need to learn much more to be an effective negotiator in the global arena. In this chapter we address how differences in gender and in culture can affect negotiation process, strategy, and outcomes.

CHAPTER OBJECTIVES

- To understand gender differences in negotiation
- To learn to appreciate cultural influences on negotiation
- To prepare yourself to be a truly global negotiator

165

KEY TERMS

Cultural sensitivity	GLOBE study	Polychronic time (P-time)
Ethnocentrism	Egalitarianism	Emotionalism
Power distance	Hierarchy	Top-down and bottom-up
Uncertainty avoidance	High- and low-context cultures	agreements
Individualism	Direct and indirect	Guanxi
Collectivism	communications	Foreign Corrupt Practices Act
Long-term orientation	Monochronic time (M-time)	

CHAPTER CASE

One of this book's authors is a past president of the International Association of Conflict Management (IACM). This is an international organization of academics and practitioners in the field of negotiation and conflict management. IACM holds an annual conference, alternating years between the United States and other countries. One of the roles of the president-elect is to find the site for the next annual meeting and to negotiate the necessary contracts with hotels, service providers, and so forth. Seville, Spain, was selected for the next conference, partly because the author could speak a little Spanish, but mostly because IACM members who worked at the university in Seville were willing to serve as local arrangement chairs. Having someone on the ground is critical, as many details must be worked out in advance for a large conference. The former president told the author that although the local arrangements chair does the legwork, it is up to the president to negotiate the hotel and venue contracts. The author arrived in Spain about 10 months before the conference date to look over sites recommended by the local arrangements chair, and selected a recommended site. The local arrangements chair said she would be glad to do the negotiating on the author's behalf, but based on advice from the previous president, the author felt responsible for doing the actual negotiations. The local arrangements chair agreed to accompany the author and gave assurances the general manager of the hotel could speak English. The negotiation began with four people at the table, the local arrangements chair (LA), the author (AU) the general manager of the hotel (GM) and his point person (PP). The contract negotiations went something like this:

AU: What a beautiful hotel. We are very much looking forward to having our conference here.

GM: Bueno, bueno.

AU: Can you tell me what the room rate will be if we guarantee 300 attendees and 200 rooms?

GM: Would you like to have a glass of wine?

AU: No, thank you, now about those rooms . . .

PP: Come out and see the gardens. Have you seen the patios?

AU: I admired them coming in. Could we talk about the room rates? Or can you tell me if you will comp rooms for the officers of our organization if we guarantee a certain number of rooms?

GM: You must come and see our elegant dining and buffet rooms.

AU: Okay, but I'd really like to discuss the contract.

GM to local arrangements chair (LA): [long conversation in Spanish not understandable to AU.]

LA to GM and PP: [long conversation in Spanish not understandable to AU.]

AU to all: Could we speak in English, please?

GM and LA: Oh sorry; we forgot. Would you like to see the dining areas now?

AU: No, I'd like to talk about the room rates, the comp rooms, and the receptions we will hold here.

LA to AU: I think you should look at all the facilities first.

GM to LA: [long conversation in Spanish]

LA to GM and PP: [long conversation in Spanish]

AU: [Silence and dumbfounded. Don't they know that the reason I am here is to negotiate the contract? Didn't they agree to speak in English?]

Lessons Learned

- Don't rush the pre-negotiation process; it is rude to talk about the contract without establishing a relationship first.

- Even if people agree to conduct a meeting in English, if the native language of everyone else at the table is something other than English, they are going to speak to each other in their native language and you will be left out of the conversation.
- The author likely made the local arrangements chair lose face by insisting on doing the negotiations.
- In hindsight, the author realized that the president of the organization was viewed as a figurehead and the real work gets done locally and often behind the scenes

Eventual Outcome

A very general agreement was arrived at; nothing was signed. Excellent Spanish wine was served and the author and the hotel general manager shook hands. After the author left Spain, the local arrangements chair worked out all the details of the contract and put on a fabulous conference complete with flamenco dancers and a live band. The author received a very lovely complimentary room.

Gender Differences in Negotiation

You may be wondering why gender differences are included in a chapter on cultural differences in negotiation. If you consider that an important goal of a negotiator is to learn as much as possible about what to expect from the person across the negotiation table, then it would seem that you would want to know if half the population negotiates differently than you do. There are some basic differences between men and women in negotiation process and outcomes, and yet research shows there are not as many differences as one might believe. We address those areas where differences might be expected, where they are found, and why.

Why We Would Expect Gender Differences in Negotiation

If we think of societal expectations of men and women in the 19th and 20th centuries, it is clear that roles for men and women were more clearly differentiated than they are today. Traditional male skills and values would be consistent with aspects of distributive bargaining: being competitive, hierarchical, rational, and unemotional with a focus on winning. Female values would be more consistent with an integrative negotiation style: cooperative, equalitarian, intuitive, and empathetic, with a focus on maintaining relationships. Even if these differences in skills and values may no longer accurately reflect the roles of men and women today, traditional expectations often remain.

Let's do a thought experiment. Imagine you were preparing to negotiate with someone the same gender as you, then at the last minute you learned you were going to be negotiating with someone of the opposite gender. Would that affect your strategy or expectations of the other negotiator's strategy? For many people, it would. In teaching negotiation classes over the years, we have witnessed the different ways people react when they learn with whom they are going to be negotiating. When men learn they are going to be negotiating with another man, they make direct eye contact, possibly shake hands, and go off to negotiate. When women learn they are negotiating with another woman, they smile, nod at each other, and leave the class room in a relaxed manner. However, with mixed dyads, it is quite different. Women appear to be concerned and sometimes passive as they approach the negotiation, whereas men seem to be quite confident and comfortable. The more important question, however, is do they actually negotiate differently, and does one gender receive better outcomes than the other?

Research Findings on Gender and Negotiation

Over the past two decades there has been considerable research attention on the topic. In zero-sum situations, like buyer-seller negotiations, it is generally true that men are able to claim more value than women.[1,2] However, investigations into "why" indicate it is not that men are taking advantage of women, but rather that women do not set their aspirations as high as men do and thus do not expect or ask for as much as men do.

Linda Babcock and her colleagues have done a series of experiments to investigate why women don't ask for more.[3] She had men and women play a game of Boggle (a game in which the players compete to find as many words as possible from a scrambled group of letters) and told them they would be paid between $3 and $10 for their participation. When participants left the experiment, one by one, they were offered $3 and were paid $10 only if they asked for $10. Women and men were equally likely to complain about not being paid more, but the experimenters paid more only if participants specifically asked for a certain dollar amount. Nine times as many men as women asked for $10. This is a startling difference.

Trying to understand why women are less likely to initiate negotiations, the experimenters wondered if was because women and men are treated differently when they attempt to negotiate. In two experiments, participants evaluated written accounts of job candidates who did or did not initiate negotiations for higher compensation. In their ratings, evaluators penalized female candidates more than male candidates for initiating such negotiations. When participants evaluated recordings of candidates who accepted compensation offers or initiated negotiations, male evaluators penalized female candidates more than male candidates for initiating negotiations; female evaluators penalized all candidates for initiating negotiations.[4] These findings suggest that one factor that contributes to women's hesitancy to initiate negotiations is that they fear they will be seen in a negative light by both men and women for doing so. The *Non Sequitur* comic strip provides a poignant example of how identical behavior by men and women are judged differently.

Other gender researchers have investigated if the way negotiations are framed influences women's propensity to initiate negotiations.[5] Using the same Boggle experiment, they found when the situation was framed as "an opportunity for negotiation," women initiated negotiations with the experimenter much less than men; however, when it was framed as "an opportunity to ask for more," there were no differences between women and men in their willingness to ask.

Another interesting difference in what women will ask for in negotiation has been shown to depend on whether they are negotiating for themselves or for another. An experimental study showed that when women were told they would be negotiating for another person, they set higher pre-negotiation targets and had higher initial offers than when they were preparing to negotiate for themselves. When expecting to negotiate on another's behalf, women asked for 22% more per hour for someone other than themselves.[6]

Situations can also influence whether there are gender differences in negotiation. One is the extent to which the situation is ambiguous or unambiguous in terms of whether there is a clear zone of potential for agreement. Using a very large sample (nearly 2,000 people), researchers found in highly ambiguous situations, men had more optimistic goals and made higher initial offers than women and also negotiated significantly higher

**NON SEQUITUR
BY WILEY**

payoffs. Yet, when the situation was unambiguous (that is, there was a clear zone of potential agreement), women and men did not differ in their goals, first offers, or outcomes.[7]

What can we take away from the research on gender and negotiation? It appears that in purely distributive situations, men do better than women primarily because women do not set targets as high as men do. Women appear to be sensitive to the way situations are framed (negotiating for self versus negotiating on behalf of another; opportunities to negotiate versus opportunities to ask) and to the extent that there is ambiguity in the negotiation. One should not generalize these findings too broadly; certainly not all men set high targets, and some men also struggle with ambiguous situations. We might expect that as more women continue to move into upper management and leadership positions, gender differences in negotiation will diminish accordingly.

Culture and Negotiation

Nearly everything discussed in this book up to this point has been based on Western (and primarily North American) culture. As the world has become smaller in terms of the ability of individuals to cross borders and oceans easily, and the availability of technology makes it possible to be in touch with anyone anywhere in the world with the push of a few buttons, it is no longer enough to know how to negotiate only in the United States or Canada. The study of global negotiations merits more than part of a chapter in a textbook, and indeed entire courses are taught on the subject. Still, we would be remiss if we didn't address the topic at all. In this chapter we provide an overview of the major research findings and, equally important, the practical knowledge imparted by business people who negotiate globally.

Cultural sensitivity
the extent to which individuals are aware of the cultural norms, and belief systems of the individuals with whom they are interacting.

To be a successful global negotiator, you must begin by understanding and gaining an appreciation of cultural differences. **Cultural sensitivity** means understanding why people from different cultures do things differently and learning to appreciate those differences rather than seeing them as roadblocks to successful negotiations. Many people think of culture as being synonymous with nations or countries (the German culture, the Chinese culture, etc.), but culture is a broader concept than nations or countries. Culture is a characteristic of social groups and the norms and values that they share that set them apart from other social groups. Within any country there may be many different cultures, and many cultures span national boundaries. Cultural values are reflected in the clothes people wear, the roles assigned to men and women, the way families interact, attitudes toward work, and many other aspects of daily life.

Ethnocentrism
the tendency to believe that one's own culture, belief system, ideas, etc. are centrally important and correct and all other groups are measured in relation to one's own

There is a tendency for all people to be somewhat ethnocentric in their views. **Ethnocentrism** is the belief that your culture, your religion, or your views are the "right" ones and that those who do not share your perspective are somehow "deviant." To the extent that we are mired in ethnocentrism, we will fail to truly appreciate other cultures. In the case of the hotel negotiations at the beginning of this chapter, one of the authors was ethnocentric in believing the contract would be negotiated as it would be negotiated in the United States.

Hofstede's Cultural Dimensions

Hofstede collected data from IBM employees from all over the world.[8] From this large sample, she identified five basic dimensions that can differentiate cultures: (1) power distance, (2) uncertainty avoidance, (3), individualism-collectivism, (4) masculinity-femininity, and (5) long-term orientation. We discuss each briefly.

Power distance refers to the extent to which there is equality or inequality among the people in a country's societies. And perhaps more important, it is the extent to which people accept the distribution of power in the society. Countries with high power distance have most of the decision-making authority at the top and hierarchies are the norm. There may be large status differences among people in the society, and people accept their "place" in the society. Leaders in high power distance cultures are not to be questioned or challenged. Countries and cultures low on power distance are more egalitarian, with distributive decision making. Leaders are respected, but they can be challenged or removed from power if necessary. Figure 10.1 shows how Japan and the United States differ on the five dimensions. They are more similar on power distance than one might expect, but differences are attenuated on the other dimensions. Countries that score extremely low on power distance are Austria, Denmark, New Zealand, Israel, and Ireland. Those on the high extreme include Malaysia, Philippines, Panama, Mexico, and Venezuela.

One *implication of power distance for negotiation* is that in high power distance cultures, negotiators may not have the authority to close the deal and may need to get a superior's approval before making a commitment. This could slow the negotiation process considerably or stall it altogether. In low power distance cultures, individuals prefer distributed decision making, shared authority, and power.

Uncertainty avoidance refers to the level of comfort the society's members have with unstructured situations. Cultures high on uncertainty avoidance tend to be more structured, rule-bound, and controlling in an effort to reduce uncertainty. Countries low on this dimension tend to be more tolerant of diverse perspectives, are less troubled by ambiguity, are more willing to take risks, and are more accepting of changes to the status quo. Countries scoring high on this dimension include Singapore, Denmark, Sweden, Hong

Uncertainty avoidance one of Hofstede's cultural dimensions—the level of comfort a society's members have with unstructured situations. Those high on this construct are more rule-bound and controlling, whereas those low are more tolerant of diverse perspectives and less troubled by ambiguity.

Kong, and Jamaica. Countries low on uncertainty avoidance are Greece, Belgium, Portugal, Poland, and Uruguay.

The *implication of uncertainty avoidance for negotiation* is that those high on uncertainty avoidance may be less trusting and less likely to share information than those from cultures low on this dimension.

Individualism—Collectivism
one of Hofstede's dimensions—individualists value independence, free will and individual rights. Collectivists value close ties between individuals and an individual's identity is tied to the group.

Individualism-collectivism is the dimension that describes the degree to which the society is organized around the individual or the group. Individualistic societies value independence and protect individual rights. Children are raised to think and act for themselves. Collectivist societies value close ties between individuals, and an individual's identity is tied to the group(s) to which they belong. People are responsible for in-group members. This dimension, perhaps more than any of the others, differentiates societies and has received considerable research attention. The United States scores the highest on this dimension, along with Australia, Great Britain, Holland, Canada, and New Zealand (note that with the exception of Holland, all are English-speaking countries). Countries high in collectivism include Pakistan, Taiwan, Indonesia, Costa Rica, and Columbia.

The *implications of individualism-collectivism* for negotiation are many. Negotiators from collectivistic societies value building strong relationships with the other negotiator(s) before the negotiation begins, and they will not rush the negotiation process. They also strive for consensus, which means that any individual is not likely to be able to make a decision alone. Individualistic societies value the competency and ability of an individual to represent their group or organization. They also see individuals as interchangeable; if one person leaves the company for another job, someone equally qualified can take his or her place. This can lead to problems when negotiating with collectivists who value the long-established relationship between individuals and don't see them as substitutable. The relationship will have to be rebuilt with the new negotiator. Collectivists tend to look at the big picture, whereas individualists are mired in details. Collectivists value relationships; individualists value signed contracts. Thus, the essence of the deal is characterized very differently between individualists and collectivists.

Masculinity-femininity is the dimension that measures the degree that the culture values and reinforces traditional masculine traits such as assertiveness. Masculine cultures value achievement and control and tend to have higher gender differentiation then feminine cultures, which are more nurturing and have higher gender equality. In masculine cultures, males tend to hold most upper-level positions in society and government. In feminine cultures, service, quality of life, and the environment are highly valued.[9] Countries ranked high on masculinity are Austria, Hungry, Venezuela, and Italy. Countries high on femininity include Sweden, Norway, Holland, Denmark, and Costa Rica.

The *implications of masculinity-femininity for negotiation* are that women may have more difficulty getting respect and being treated as equals in countries high in masculinity. It is important to note that Hofstede's data were collected in the 1980s, and in the past 30 years many countries, such as Japan and China, are much more accustomed to seeing women across the negotiating table.

Long-term orientation is the fifth dimension identified by Hofstede. It refers to the extent to which the Confucian values of honoring tradition and hard work are embraced. Cultures high on this dimension look toward the future and do not expect immediate gratification for their efforts. Those low on this dimension are more concerned with immediate rewards, saving face, and looking good in the eyes of others. Those who have a short-term orientation are more open to change. Countries high on long-term orientation are China, Hong Kong, Singapore, Japan, and South Korea. Countries low on long-term orientation include Canada, the United Kingdom, the United States, Pakistan, and the Philippines.

The *implications of long-term orientation for negotiation* are that cultures high on this dimension do not rush the negotiation process and often view negotiations as a series of continuing events in the context of a long-term relationship. Short-term deals have little or no value. Negotiators from countries low on long-term orientation are likely to view negotiation as an isolated episode in business deal making, and the primary focus is on getting the deal done as quickly as possible.

> **Long-term orientation**
> one of Hofstede's dimensions. Those high on this dimension value tradition and hard work and do not expect immediate rewards. Those low on this dimension seek immediate gratification and are concerned with looking good to others

Other Cultural Perspectives

The **GLOBE** (Global Leadership and Organizational Behavior Effectiveness) **study**[10] examined the effect of cultural variables on business practices. It included a large sample (17,000) of middle managers from 62 countries. These countries were grouped into nine regional clusters: Latin Europe, Germanic Europe, Anglo, Eastern Europe, Confucian Asia, Latin American, Southern Asia, Sub-Sahara Africa, and the Middle East, based on how they shared cultural dimensions on each society's aspirations. The **GLOBE study** ranked cultures on nine dimensions: (1) performance orientation, (2) in-group collectivism, (3) institutional collectivism, (4) power distance, (5) uncertainty avoidance, (6) future orientation, (7) gender egalitarianism, (8) assertiveness, and (9) humane orientation. Six of these dimensions are rooted in Hofstede's dimensions, with performance orientation and power distance remaining the same; in-group and institutional collectivism distinguishes between families and institutions. Assertiveness and gender egalitarianism replace Hofstede's masculinity-femininity dimension. Humane orientation, performance orientation, and future orientation are additions to the Hofstede model.

> **GLOBE study**
> the Global Leadership and Organizational Behavior Effectiveness study examined the effect of cultural variables on business practices. This study used nine dimensions to categorize cultures.

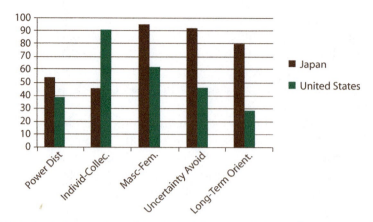

FIGURE 10.1 A Comparison of the United States and Japan Based on Hofstede's Five Dimensions

Because these data are more recent than the Hofstede study, and the dimensions more fine-tuned, we expect that to the extent they provide useful ways of characterizing country cultures that the GLOBE study will continue to become the standard for understanding cultural differences particularly in business. For comparison, Figure 10.2 shows the United States and Japan on the nine GLOBE dimensions. What is most notable about this comparison is that the differences between the two countries appear to have diminished since the Hofstede study, with only the in-group collectivism showing a large difference. However, the rating scales for the two studies are different, as were the subject population, so one must use caution in interpretation.

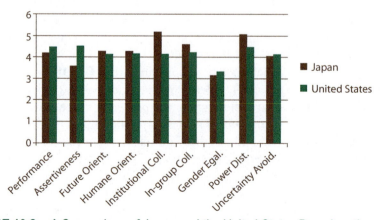

FIGURE 10.2 A Comparison of Japan and the United States Based on the GLOBE Dimensions

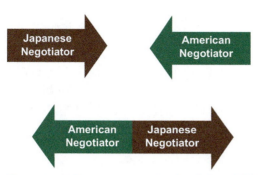

FIGURE 10.3   An Example of Overcompensating for Cultural Differences
First Row: The cultural schema that each negotiator has of the other leads them
to expect that there will be a large gap between the two and hence no settlement
zone. Second Row: Each tries to compensate for the other by moving in the other's
direction, and in so doing, they are not only farther apart than before, but moving in
the other direction!

Other studies seem to indicate both Japanese and U.S. negotiators are
sensitive to the cultural differences between the two, and when preparing to
negotiate, both sides tend to overcompensate for expected cultural differences. That is, in considering their intercultural schema for the other culture, negotiators from both cultures fail to consider that each will try to compensate
for the other's cultural negotiating style. The researchers call this phenomenon "schematic overcompensation."[11] See Figure 10.3 for a representation of
schematic compensation.

A number of other scholars have either built on or refined Hofstede's
work. Brett[12] reduces the cultural dimensions relevant to negotiation to
three—(1) individual versus collective orientation, (2) **egalitarianism** versus **hierarchy**, and (3) direct versus indirect—and examines these as they
relate to negotiators' goals, influence tactics, and type of communications,
respectively. We focus on the third dimension, direct versus indirect communications, next.

Not surprisingly, differences in communication styles can have a large
impact on global negotiations. Cultures who employ **direct communications**
(such as the United States) transmit their message in a very straightforward
way. The messages tend to be action-oriented and solution-minded.[13] And,
they are context free, which means one does not need to know the context to
understand the message. In negotiations, this means that parties are usually
not subtle; they will ask direct and pointed questions about interests, preferences, and priorities.

Cultures that value **indirect communication** (such as Japan) use a more
nuanced style. They consider it rude to ask directly for what they want.
Rather, they may make multiple proposals and expect the other negotiator to

Egalitarianism
a philosophy that
people should be
treated as equals.

Hierarchy
a belief system that
accepts unequal
distribution of status
and power.

**Direct and indirect
communications**
cultures with direct
communications
communicate in a
straightforward way
with action-oriented
words; cultures
who communicate
indirectly use a more
nuanced approach
and expect the
other to interpret the
meaning.

infer their preferences and priorities from the proposals made. Japanese, for example, feel it is rude to say "no" to a request and may instead say, "That would be very difficult." They may also say "yes" to a number of different proposals, but what "yes" means in indirect communication is, "I understand you" or "I hear you." Needless to say, there is a lot of room for miscommunication and misunderstandings in negotiation when parties use different styles of communication.

Brett categorizes Germany, the United States, Switzerland, and Scandinavian cultures as being direct communication cultures and Japan, Russia, France, Arabic, and Mediterranean people as embracing an indirect communication culture.[14] These groupings are consistent with the work of Hall, an anthropologist, who used the terms "**high- and low-context cultures**" to differentiate communication styles. High-context cultures place value on body language and nonverbal cues, whereas low-context cultures rely heavily on the spoken word.[15]

Time is another dimension where cultures differ. Hall defines two time systems: **monochronic time** (M-time) and **polychronic time** (P-time). Monochronic time characterizes most Western and low-context cultures (North Americans, Swiss, Germans and Scandinavians). These cultures treat time in a very linear way. Time is money and not to be wasted. Time is divided into units, and those on M-time cherish promptness. Moreover, M-timers prefer to deal with thoughts, issues, and so on, sequentially. High-context cultures are more likely to run on polychronic time, where human interactions are more important than sticking to schedules and timetables. Those on P-time are comfortable dealing with many things and people simultaneously. As negotiators, they are more likely to address issues in a seemingly haphazard way rather than sequentially. They are more likely to consider the big picture and are less concerned with the process with which agreement is reached. Rather than be frustrated by such differences, Americans need to accept that in global negotiations others may value time differently.

In their book, *Global Negotiation*,[16] Requejo and Graham provide the following insights into the ways different cultures view time.

- "Those who rush arrive first at the grave"—Spain
- "The clock did not invent man"—Nigeria
- "If you wait long enough, even an egg will walk"—Ethiopia
- "Before the time, it is not yet the time; after the time, it's too late"—France

We have discussed a number of dimensions along which cultures differ and have indicated where these are likely to make a difference in negotiations. In Box 10.1 we present a final perspective provided by Jeswald Salacuse:[17]

High- and Low-Context Cultures
high context cultures place value on body language, nonverbal cues, and the context in which something is said; low-context cultures rely on the spoken word regardless of the context.

Monochronic time (M-time)
cultures on M-time prefer to do things sequentially and in a linear fashion.

Polychronic time (P-time)
cultures on P-time are comfortable with focusing on the big picture and are less concerned with the process. They can skip from one thing to another without being concerned about sequence.

> ## Box 10.1 Salacuse: 10 Ways Culture Affects Negotiating Style
>
> 1. Goal—contract vs. relationship
> 2. Attitude—win-lose vs. win-win
> 3. Personal style—informal vs. formal
> 4. Communication style—direct vs. indirect
> 5. Time sensitivity—high vs. low (or monochronic vs. polychronic)
> 6. Emotionalism—high vs. low
> 7. Form of agreement—general vs. specific
> 8. Building an agreement—top-down vs. bottom-up
> 9. Team organization—one leader vs. consensus
> 10. Risk taking—high vs. low

Many of Salacuse's dimensions look familiar, as they appear in either Hofstede's study or the GLOBE dimensions. We expand on the five that are not: attitude, personal style, emotionalism, form of agreement, and building an agreement.

"Attitude" refers to how culture affects the way people characterize negotiations. Cultures that value assertiveness and competition are more likely to view negotiations as zero-sum distributive situations. Cultures that value harmony and egalitarianism will likely characterize negotiations as opportunities to create value for both sides.

"Personal style" is influenced by culture to the extent that hierarchical societies are more likely to be formal. For example, in countries such as Japan or China, one would never call someone by their first name unless they were invited to do so. Titles and formality reflect the values of these countries. On the other hand, negotiators from countries that value individualism are more comfortable with informality. Negotiators use first names, make themselves comfortable wherever they are, and are often insensitive to the fact that they may not be in a culture that values this approach.

"**Emotionalism**" refers to the level of comfort different cultures have with emotional displays. In most Mediterranean countries, displays of emotion are common. People gesture wildly, talk loudly, and are comfortable with displaying a variety of emotions. Cultures that value rationality and thoughtful discourse, such as Scandinavian countries and the United States, tend not to show emotions to the same extent when negotiating.

We have already touched somewhat on the "form of agreement." Legalistic countries, such as the United States, put a lot of value on the written contract, and the more specific the better. Eastern, and particularly Asian, cultures consider the value of the deal to be the relationship that is established between negotiators. A handshake or a very general agreement is acceptable. This is partially because in these countries, one's word counts for a lot and

Emotionalism
the extent to which different cultures are comfortable with showing emotion in social interactions. Cultures who value rationality and thoughtful discourse are less likely to show emotion.

Top-down and bottom-up agreements hierarchical cultures tend to dictate agreements from the top down. Egalitarian cultures trust individuals to create agreements from the bottom up.

not owning up to the agreement would lead to a loss of face. It is also because most other countries do not have legal systems that enforce written contracts in the fashion seen in other countries like the United States.

Finally, "building an agreement," that is, how the agreement is constructed, will depend on the extent to which a culture is hierarchical. Hierarchical cultures would build an agreement from the **top-down**. Even though those lower in status may be part of the negotiation team, in the end, those at the top will dictate the terms and form of the agreement. Countries that value egalitarianism and who put trust in individuals will be more likely to allow agreements to be constructed from the **bottom-up**.

Different Approaches to Understanding Culture

We have gone into considerable detail addressing various dimensions affected by culture, with a focus on the implications for negotiation. As a result we expect you now have a deeper of understanding of the challenges of cross-cultural negotiations.

Imagine that your business is sending you to another country to negotiate for the production of a new product line. Let us take China, for example. How do you go about preparing for such a negotiation?

Culture as a Learned Behavior

There are many layers to culture. Consider Figure 10.4. Think of culture as an iceberg with only the "tip" appearing above the waterline. This "tip" represents the behaviors we observe when we go to a country with a different culture. The first step to preparation is learning as much as possible about the appropriate business behavior in the country where you are going to do business. Many books and resources address behavioral dos and don'ts of global business. A particularly useful one is *Kiss, Bow, or Shake Hands*,[18] which covers business etiquette, negotiation norms, and so on. In that book, you will learn:

- about business hours, appropriate dress, how to address others (titles, etc.);
- that you will need a translator unless you know with certainty that all the people you are doing business with speak English;
- not to make business trips to China during the Chinese New Year, as everything is closed for at least a week before and after the festival;
- to bring business cards with your name and your business name in English and in Mandarin Chinese on the other side;
- to never put a person's business card in your wallet or back pocket;
- proper dining etiquette, like how to eat rice with chopsticks; and
- not to discuss business during a meals.

FIGURE 10.4   Culture Depicted as an Iceberg

Other books address gestures than can get you in trouble in certain counties, such as showing the sole of your shoe to an Arab or giving the "V" sign in South America. And there are many books on "How to negotiate with the [insert country of choice]." All of these books provide useful information, and if all you have time to do before negotiating in another country is to consult a book like this, it is certainly better than nothing; at a minimum, it will keep you from committing a major cultural faux pas. There is much more to know about cultural differences, however, than appropriate behavior.

Culture as Shared Core Values

A deeper understanding of culture is knowing the values and belief systems that lie beneath and drive the behaviors we observe. In the iceberg example, they support the behaviors we see but are not directly observable. In China, although the government is communist, most of the values and belief systems of the Chinese people are based on Confucianism and Taoism. These include preserving harmony and honoring reciprocal responsibilities in relationships.

A particular value of the Chinese is the concept of "**guanxi**," which means connections or relations between people. These can be social networks among family and friends, but with trust, they can also develop in business relationships. Understanding the guanxi networks of the person you will be negotiating with or even better creating a business relationship that develops into a guanxi network would be highly advantageous to your business prospects in China.

In their book, *Global Negotiation*, Requejo and Graham[19] discuss the following cultural values of the Chinese that can affect business negotiations:

- *Guanxi*—personal connections
- *Mianzi*—face or social capital
- *Shehui dengji*—social hierarchy
- *Rejni hexie*—interpersonal harmony
- *Qundai buanxi*—nepotism (in-group collectivism)

Guanxi
a term used in China to represent connections or relations between people. Having a guanxi network is key to getting deals done in China.

- *Zhengti guannian*—holistic thinking
- *Chikku nailao*—endurance or eating bitterness
- *Jiejian*—thrift
- *Linghe tanpan*—zero-sum negotiations
- *Jiao ta liangshi chuan*—threatening to do business elsewhere

It is beyond the scope of this chapter to delve into these; suffice to say that to the extent that a negotiator going to China has a deep understanding of these cultural values, they will be much more prepared than will those negotiators who have only a superficial understanding of acceptable behaviors.

Heterogeneity within Culture

The next level to understanding culture is to realize that all people in a country are not homogeneous. We understand that about our own country, as the United States, is a melting pot of people from many countries and cultures, albeit over the generations, most become more "Americanized." Still, we would have a hard time describing the "typical American."

We have a tendency to see people from other countries as being more similar to one another than they really are. Because of this perceived similarity, there is an unfortunate tendency to stereotype and assume what is true of one is true of all. We often fail to consider that in a country like China, there are many languages, people from a variety of ethnic backgrounds, different levels of education, different social statuses, and so forth.

As a global negotiator, it is not enough to know about typical Chinese behaviors and the values and belief systems that drive them; you must also try to learn more about the individual that will be sitting across the negotiation table. What area of China are they from? What language do they speak? What level of education does the other negotiator have? What is their status in the company? To the extent that you can learn more about the individual you will be interacting with, you will be far more prepared than simply knowing the stereotype of the typical Chinese business person

Culture in Context

Finally, understanding culture in the context you will be negotiating in gets to the core of international negotiations. Going back to our original premise that you will be negotiating in China to produce a new product line, here are some contextual issues you would want to know:

- Is the factory in a large city or a rural area?
- Does the factory use state-of-the-art technology?
- Are the workers paid a fair wage?
- Are there human rights issues that could cause problems when marketing the product back in the United States?

- Has my company done business with this factory before?
- Will the person I am negotiating with speak English?
- Have I interacted with this person or company before?

And, there are probably many more contextual issues that would differentiate this negotiation from one done by another American in another place in China. As in all negotiations, understanding the negotiation context improves your chances of success.

In sum, there are many layers and levels of understanding culture, and the deeper you go, the better off you will be in establishing mutually beneficial relationships. It is important to remember that in many countries, especially Asian countries, the relationship between the negotiators is the most important part of of the deal, not the contract.

What If They Are Coming Here to Negotiate?

Our discussion of culture and how to negotiate successfully in another culture has assumed that the negotiator is going to travel to the other country. Do these recommendations hold if the the other negotiators are coming to the United States (or your country)? It depends. Generally, negotiators follow the norms and standards of the country where the negotiation takes place. Sometimes, however, negotiations occur in neutral territory (especially political ones). Increasingly, the language for business negotiations is English regardless of where the negotiation takes place. That said, you would still be wise to understand the customs, norms, and values of the person you are negotiating with because it will still drive their negotiation behavior. It also makes sense to have an interpreter to keep you informed about what the other person is saying away from the table. Even if English is the language at the table, it will probably not be the language spoken when people caucus for discussions or for a coffee break.

Ethical and Legal Issues That Arise in International Negotiations

We discussed ethical issues in negotiation in Chapter 8. Your ethics shouldn't disappear just because you are negotiating elsewhere. We know, though, that not everyone shares our ethical standards, and this is more likely to be true when negotiating globally. It helps to know what the other negotiator's ethical standards are. It is also important to have a clear understanding of what your company's ethical standards are and if the company expects them to be adhered to regardless of where the negotiation takes place.

The question of "When in Rome, should you do as the Romans do?" is a question you should ask yourself *before* you are negotiating for your company in Rome. In many countries (such as Italy, Greece, and Brazil) bribery may be seen as a common practice. Thus, many negotiators would feel at a competitive disadvantage if they don't offer what others do.

Fortunately, there are some guidelines provided by the **Foreign Corrupt Practices Act** (FCPA). This act was signed into law by President Carter in 1977, and it was amended in 1998 by the International Bribery Act. The anti-bribery provisions prohibit:

> Making use of interstate commerce corruptly as in an offer or payment of anything of value to a foreign official, foreign political party, or candidate for political office for the purpose of influencing any act of that official in violation of the duty of that official, or to secure any improper advantage to obtain or retain business.[20]

Note that the FCPA refers only to bribery of government officials, not private citizens. The FCPA does draw a distinction between bribery and facilitation or "grease payments." The primary distinction is that "grease payments" are made to an official to expedite their performance of the duties they are already bound to perform. Said differently, this means that these payments are okay as long as they are used to get officials to do only what they normally do, just faster. They are not, however, allowed to get officials to do something that is unlawful.

The FCPA does allow certain payments to officials or businesses if the payments are permitted under the written laws of the host country. Before engaging in anything resembling bribery in another country, a negotiator should have a clear understanding of the laws in that country.

Who Is Subject to the FCPA?

The FCPA covers any U.S. or foreign corporation that has securities registered or that is required to file reports under the Securities and Exchange Act of 1934. As far as individuals go, the FCPA covers "any individual who is a citizen, national, or resident of the U.S. and any corporation and other business entity organized under the laws of the U.S. or having its principal place of business in the U.S."[21] In other words, if you are a U.S. citizen or resident, the FCPA act applies to you as well as to corporations. You may wonder if the FCPA has "teeth." It does. See Box 10.3 for some notable past cases. Additionally, it has become more common to see individuals prosecuted under the FCPA.[22]

What Behaviors Will Raise Concerns of the FCPA?

Following are some of the "red flag" warning signs and risk factors for FCPA issues:[24]

- Conducting business in countries with high corruption risk factors
- Cash or other unusual means of payment

Foreign Corrupt Practices Act
a law that details what is acceptable behavior in international negotiations and trade. It includes anti-bribery provisions that prohibit bribes to foreign officials or political parties in order to establish trade.

Box 10.3 Notable Cases Tried under the FCPA23

- Lucent Technologies—bribery in China
- Monsanto—bribing Indian officials
- Siemens—charged 1.6 million dollars, the largest fine in corporate history for corrupt payments to foreign officials in various Siemens' operating groups and subsidiaries around the world.

- KBR*—bribing Nigerian officials for contracts
- Halliburton—paid $579 million to the Justice Department and Securities and Exchange Commission for bribery and bid rigging in contracts around the world

* KBR (Kellogg, Brown, Root) is a subsidiary of Halliburton.

- Payments to family members of government officials
- Engagements with third-party agents with little or no apparent qualifications
- Payments to shell companies
- Unusual or excessive commissions or "success fees" paid to third parties
- Donations to special charities, institutions, or agencies on behalf of government officials
- Unusual processing or transactional fees
- Excessive entertainment, travel, or gifts
- Lax or improper record keeping
- Foreign clients or third-party agents who have had a history of improper business practices
- Insistence that a particular third-party agent be used
- Incomplete responses and/or objections to FCPA/compliance certification.

As in all negotiations, ultimately you are responsible for what you do and say. When you enter the international arena, your behavior is examined under a more powerful lens. Your reputation means everything.

CHAPTER SUMMARY

This chapter addressed negotiating with those who are "different" than you. We began with a discussion of gender issues in negotiation and highlighted research on this topic. We then turned to the many dimensions of culture that affect business and negotiation transactions. We discussed the different levels of understanding culture, from observable behaviors to culture in context with a specific focus on negotiating in China. The chapter began with a case describing a global negotiation that got off to a rocky start due to a lack of cultural sensitivity and ended with an examination of ethical issues that arise when negotiating globally and the laws that govern transactions between the U.S. and foreign countries.

Although it may be hard to imagine yourself as a global negotiator, as you become established in your careers, we can guarantee that the global economy will be an important influence on your working life, regardless of where you are and what you do. The sooner you accept this fact and prepare for it, the better business person you will be.

Questions/Exercises

1. Suppose you are travelling to Cozumel, Mexico for scuba diving over spring break. Because you can speak Spanish you decide to stay in a local hotel rather than at a large resort.
   a. What cultural differences will you expect to find at a local hotel? Consider such things as amenities in the room, interactions with the hotel staff, timeliness of responses to requests and so on.
   b. What will you need to consider as you plan to negotiate with a divemaster to take you out to the reefs for diving?
   c. How will you negotiate for local arts and crafts at the market?
2. How can ethnocentrism negatively affect a negotiator's preparation for a cross-cultural negotiation? In your answer consider such things as assumptions you make about appropriate behavior, concession making, information sharing and other aspects of the negotiation process.
3. Where does the United States rate on Hofstede's cultural dimensions?
   a. Do any of these ratings surprise you? Why or why not?
   b. How well do these ratings describe you as an individual?
4. What steps can you take to be sure that you achieve your goals in a mixed (male/female) dyad negotiation?
   a. If you are female are there particular errors you might be prone to make, and if so what can you do to avoid them?
   b. If you are male, consider the ways you might negotiate differently with a female than with another male. Should it be any different? Explain why or why not.
5. To what extent do you endorse the philosophy "When in Rome do as the Romans do?"
   a. Would your answer be different if you were representing a company you work for?
   b. How can you ensure that the company's goals are met without risking violating the FCPA?

Endnotes

1. Kolb, D. M., & Coolidge, G. G. (2001). Her place at the table: A consideration of gender issues in negotiation. In I. G. Asherman & S. V. Asherman (Eds.), *The negotiation source book* (2nd ed., pp. 251–268). Amherst, MA: HRD Press.

2. Kolb, D. M. (2009). Too bad for the women or does it have to be? Gender and negotiation research over the past twenty-five years. *Negotiation Journal, 25,* 515–531.

3. Babcock, L., & Lashever, S. (2003). *Women don't ask: Negotiation and the gender divide.* Princeton, NY: Princeton Press.

4. Bowles, H. R., Babcock, L., & Lai, L. (2005). Social incentives for gender differences in the propensity to initiate negotiations: Sometimes it does hurt to ask. *Organizational Behavior and Human Decision Processes, 103*, 84–103.

5. Small, D. A., Gelfand, M., Babcock, L., & Gettman, H. (2007). Who goes to the bargaining table? The influence of gender and framing on the initiation of negotiation. *Journal of Personality and Social Psychology, 93*, 600–613.

6. Riley, H. C., & Babcock, L. (2002). *Gender as a situational phenomenon in negotiation* (KSG Working Paper No. RWP02-037). IACM 15th Annual Conference. Retrieved from SSRN: http://ssrn.com/abstract=305159 or doi:10.2139/ssrn.305159.

7. Pradel, D. W., Bowles, H. R., & McGinn, J. L. (2005). When does gender matter in negotiation? *Harvard Business Review*, Prod. #: N0511D-PDF-ENG.

8. Hofstede, G. (2001). *Culture's consequences: Comparing values, behaviors, institutions, and organizations across nations* (2nd ed.). Thousand Oaks, CA: Sage.

9. Carrell, M. R., & Heavrin, C. (2008). *Negotiating essentials: Theory, skills and practices.* Upper Saddle River, NJ: Pearson Prentice Hall.

10. Javidan, M., Stahl, G. K., Brodbeck, F., & Wilderom, C. P. M. (2005). Cross-border transfer of knowledge: Cultural lessons from project GLOBE. *Academy of Management Executive, 19*, 59–76.

11. Adair, W. L., Taylor, M. S., & Tinsley, C. H. (2009). Starting out on the right foot: Negotiation schemas when cultures collide. *Negotiation and Conflict Management Research, 2*, 138–163.

12. Brett, J. M. (2007). *Negotiating globally: How to negotiate deals, resolve disputes, and make decisions across cultural boundaries* (2nd ed.). San Francisco: Jossey-Bass.

13. Ting-Toomey, S. (1988). Intercultural conflict styles: A face negotiation theory. In Y. Kim & W. Gudykunst (Eds.), *Theories in intercultural communications* (pp. 213–235). Newbury Park, CA: Sage.

14. Brett, J. M. (2007). *Negotiating globally: How to negotiate deals, resolve disputes, and make decisions across cultural boundaries* (2nd ed.). San Francisco: Jossey-Bass.

15. Hall. E. T. (1979, August). Learning the Arabs' silent language. *Psychology Today*, 45–53.

16. Requejo, W. H., & Graham, J. L. (2008). *Global negotiation: The new rules.* New York: Palgrave MacMillan.

17. Salacuse, J. W. (1999). Intercultural negotiation in international business. *Group Decision and Negotiation, 8*, 217–236.

18. Morrison, T. C., & Conaway, W. A. (2006). *Kiss, bow, or shake hands: How to do business in sixty countries.* Avon, MA: Adams Media.

19. Requejo, W. H., & Graham, J. L. (2008). *Global negotiation: The new rules.* New York: Palgrave MacMillan.

20. U.S. Department of Justice. (1977). Foreign Corrupt Practices Act. Retrieved from http://www.justice.gov/criminal/fraud/fcpa/.

21. U.S. Department of Justice. (1977). Foreign Corrupt Practices Act. Retrieved from http://www.justice.gov/criminal/fraud/fcpa/.

22. Bloomberg Finance L.P. *Bloomberg Law Reports, 2*, No. 12.

23. Sidley, A. (2010). Record prosecutions for FCPA violations in 2009. Retrieved from Sidley Updates, http://www.sidley.com/sidleyupdates/Detail.aspx?news=4296.

24. Marquet, C. T. (2011). Avoiding the pitfalls of the foreign corrupt practices act. Retrieved from http://www.marquetinternational.com/pdf/avoiding_the_pitfalls_of_the_fcpa.pdf.

Driving Defensively: Negotiating Your Way through Conflict, Emotional Situations, and Difficult Negotiators

You had been looking forward to this driving trip for some time—new and interesting places to visit, the chance to be with your friends, and the chance to get away from work for a while. The trip, however, has not been as much fun as you planned. You agreed to drive since you have a new four-door car. Two of your friends have been arguing with each other most of the trip. Your other friend seems to be overly critical of your driving. Instead of stopping at a fast-food restaurant for lunch today (as you had suggested), your three friends all demanded that you stop at a sit-down restaurant. They wanted to take a break and are tired of you dictating where to have lunch during the trip simply because you are the one driving the car. *"What's the big deal?"* you think. *"It's only lunch."* One and one-half hours later, you are finished with lunch and are now behind the schedule you planned for the day. You are getting tired of your friends and feel a bit cranky. *"Why can't we get along?"* you wonder.

Back on the interstate highway, the car and truck traffic is heavy. You are having a difficult time concentrating on the road with your friends' loud conversations and their music blasting in the car. The car ahead of you is barely driving the speed limit. You are finally able to pass this driver. As you pull into the passing lane, from out of nowhere comes a large SUV. The SUV driver flashes his lights at you and tailgates your car until you speed up and return to the right lane. Your heart is racing. The SUV driver shakes his fist at you as he passes and seems to be very angry. Now you are mad. *"What a reckless jerk,"* you think. You are still upset as the SUV driver zooms off. Your friends, sensing you are upset worked up, tell you to slow down. You are still driving 10 miles over the posted speed limit, thinking about what you will say to the SUV driver if you are able to catch up with him. As you plan "pay back" for this reckless driver's behavior, the unmistakable flashing lights of a police car catch your attention. You pull over to the side of the road to talk to the police officer and to receive what will likely be a speeding ticket—another unexpected expense of your trip. What a disaster. *"My friends better help pay for this ticket,"* you think. *"They caused me to be distracted. It was not my fault."*

This car trip example reflects on several issues that present themselves in negotiations: (1) conflict between negotiators and their stated positions, (2) the impact emotion has on the way negotiators behave during a negotiation, and (3) problems associated with working with a difficult negotiator. We will address these issues in this chapter.

CHAPTER OBJECTIVES

- To understand the different sources of conflict and how they impact on a negotiation
- To understand how emotion affects the negotiation process and the ability of negotiators to identify interests underlying negotiation positions
- To understand how establishing rapport will help a negotiator deal with emotional, angry, and difficult negotiators

KEY TERMS

Interpersonal conflict	Intrapersonal conflict	Mirroring
Intergroup conflict	Defend-attack cycle	N.I.C.E. approach
Intragroup conflict		

CHAPTER CASE

You own an upscale salon and spa called "Bentleys." Bentleys caters to both men and women. Due to the negative turn in the economy and the increased number of salons in the community, your revenue has fallen by 15% in each of the past two quarters. You bought Bentleys two years ago from your Aunt Sheila.

Bentleys' stylists have traditionally received quarterly bonuses ranging from 5% to 10% of the revenue generated from their customers. Of the five Bentleys stylists, two have been hired within the past six months and the other three have been with Bentleys for five years. The quarterly bonus plan was referenced in the offer letters given to each of your stylists; however, because of the significant change in Bentleys' revenue during the past two quarters, you have decided to implement a new bonus plan.

You plan to negotiate with the stylists as a group, meaning that any negotiated change affects all of the stylists. Changing the current bonus plan at this time will be difficult. Three stylists have complained about problems they are having paying their bills. Other stylists have complained about your lack of success in attracting new clients to Bentleys. This will not be an easy negotiation.

■ ■ ■ ■

Sources of Conflict in Negotiations

Interpersonal conflict
Conflict that may arise between people who have different goals and interests.

Conflict can occur in different ways during a negotiation. In a distributive bargaining situation, conflict may arise over the negotiators' attempt to distribute value—who "wins" the negotiation. Conflict may occur in an integrative negotiation when negotiators are unable to find the right combination of proposals to satisfy their different interests. There may be a clash of personalities; a laid back and cooperative negotiator may have difficulty working with a confrontational transaction-oriented negotiator (**interpersonal**

conflict). Two departments in a company facing budget cuts may compete for the same limited organizational resources (**intergroup conflict**). Conflict within a negotiation team may occur if the spokesperson agrees to bargaining proposals without first checking with the members of the negotiation team (**intragroup conflict**). An agent representing a principal in a negotiation may feel conflicted when her personal values seem to be at odds with the principal's directives (**intrapersonal conflict**).

Negotiation skills can be used to manage or resolve conflict that occurs during negotiations or conflict that occurs in a wide variety of everyday disputes: disputes between employees in the workplace, disputes between family members, disputes between businesses and customers, disputes between a company and its suppliers, or disputes between business partners. Unresolved conflict can create significant costs for a business: lost customers, employee turnover, bad management decisions, morale problems, lost work time, legal costs, reputational harm, unnecessary job restructuring, the loss of investors, and diminished shareholder value.[3,4] Sources of conflict can turn on personality/relationship differences, value differences, having too much or too little information, differences in organizational titles, power differences, or differences over underlying interests.

The filters used to process information may cause negotiators to see the sources of their conflict differently. While one negotiator may see her insistence on a particular issue as a completely legitimate request, the other negotiator may view the negotiator as being unreasonable. It is easy to shy

Intergroup conflict
Conflict that may occur between groups of people caused by shared and different interests and goals.

Intragroup conflict
Conflict that may develop within a group of people due to their different interests and goals.

Intrapersonal conflict
Conflict a negotiator may feel due to his or her own contradictory feelings or interests.

Box. 11.1 An Example of Intragroup Conflict in the Movies

The movie, *A Civil Action* (1998), centers on a lawsuit filed by attorney Jan Schlictmann and his law firm on behalf of several families living in Woburn, Massachusetts, against Beatrice Foods and W.R. Grace. Schlictmann's small law firm incurs heavy costs in terms of both money and time preparing for trial. The lawyers in the firm encourage Schlictmann to settle the case. Schlictmann and the lawyers in his firm meet in a memorable scene to negotiate a settlement with lawyers from Beatrice Foods and W.R. Grace. Schlictmann offers to settle the case for $25 million, a figure that seems to be acceptable to the lawyers from Schlictmann's law firm and to the lawyers representing the two companies. Schlictmann then, to the apparent surprise of the lawyers from his law firm sitting at the table, states the families want "another $25 million to establish a research foundation to study the links between hazardous waste and illness and $1.5 million per family annually for 30 years." This settlement proposal is worth $320 million. As Schlictmann increases his settlement offer beyond the initial $25 million, the lawyers from his firm appear confused and give Schlictmann looks that can be read to mean, "What are you doing? We did not agree to that." The offer is rejected by the W.R. Grace and Beatrice Foods attorneys. By the end of the movie, Schlictmann's law firm goes out of business, Schlictmann declares bankruptcy, and the lawsuit is settled for $8 million.

Box 11.2 Conflict and Defend-Attack Behavior

The fall 2010 elections led Wisconsin Republicans to take control over the state assembly and senate. Voters additionally elected a Republican governor, Scott Walker. Facing a budget deficit, Governor Walker proposed a "budget repair bill," in February 2011, which required state employees to contribute 50% of their annual pension contribution for the state retirement system and to contribute additional money (at least 12.6% of the premium cost) for their health insurance coverage. The "budget repair bill" also significantly changed Wisconsin law that allowed state employees to join labor unions and to bargain collectively with their employers.

Governor Walker framed his "budget repair bill" as a necessary response to the state's budget deficit. He emphasized that changes in employee contributions for pensions and health insurance premiums brought Wisconsin state employees more in line with private sector employees. Opponents of the governor's budget repair bill described it as a way of "busting" the state employee labor unions and "stripping" state employees of their legal rights. Others described the "budget repair bill" as a "war" on the Wisconsin middle class and an "assault" on workers.

The weeks following Governor Walker's proposed "budget repair bill" were highlighted by statements and actions taken by both sides reflective of a defend-attack cycle of behavior.

Supporters of Governor Walker attempted to get the "budget repair bill passed." The bill passed the Wisconsin assembly and was sent to the Wisconsin senate. Fourteen Democrats from the senate left the state of Wisconsin to deny the senate the necessary quorum needed to pass the bill. Governor Walker asked Wisconsin state troopers to find and arrest the 14 senators and bring them back to the state capitol in Madison. Republican lawmakers began to assess monetary fines to the 14 Democrats for each day that they stayed out of Wisconsin.

Thousands of protestors came to the Wisconsin state capitol building and occupied the building both day and night. Governor Walker threatened to lay off state employees. More protestors came to Madison. They chanted, "Kill the bill." Both sides accused the other of distorting facts and being influenced by "outside forces" (i.e., out-of-state corporate interests in the case of Governor Walker and out-of-state labor unions in the case of the protestors).

In a late-night session, Republicans used a parliamentary maneuver and passed the collective bargaining changes included in the "budget repair bill." Protestors were seen crying in the capitol building after the vote. They chanted "Shame, shame, shame," as legislators left the capitol building. Governor Walker was compared to a "third-world dictator" and called a "corporate shill." Opponents filed lawsuits claiming the process by which the bill was passed violated Wisconsin law. Petitions to recall legislators who supported the bill were circulated and signed. Said one Madison attorney, "This is going to unleash a tsunami of litigation."[1] Added a Wisconsin lawmaker, "It's honestly past the point of being rational."[2]

away from conflict at the bargaining table, either breaking off the negotiation or ignoring the source of the conflict and moving on to a different issue. Other times, the conflict may cause the negotiators to be even more positional in their thinking, leading to an escalation of the conflict by both negotiators who engage in **defend-attack** behavior—defending their positions and attacking those offered by the other person. This back-and-forth or tit-for-tat behavior motivated by underlying conflict between negotiators is illustrated in Box 11.2 Conflict and Defend Attack Behavior.

Returning to the conflict situation that opened this chapter, it would be useful to anticipate different points of conflict with the Bentleys stylists before talking to them about changing the bonus plan:

Personality/Relationship Differences: You did not hire three of the stylists working at Bentleys. They have a personal loyalty to the former owner (your Aunt Sheila) and periodically make comments like, "That's not the way Sheila used to do it" and "We never had that problem when Sheila was here." These three stylists never seem to support your ideas for Bentleys—new signage, the creation of a social media site, and the addition of a massage therapist. You have to admit, though, they are good at what they do and they have a large number of clients. Still, they don't seem to trust your judgment. On the other hand, you have been hesitant to include them in your plans to change Bentleys.

Value Differences: You are closer in age to the two most recently hired stylists than the three stylists who were at Bentleys when you bought the salon. You like talking to the two recently hired stylists and on occasion have gone out for drinks with them after work. The three senior stylists all have families (you don't) and believe it is inappropriate to socialize with you outside of work time. While you have your undergraduate business degree, none of the stylists has a four-year degree, although they all graduated from a very well regarded stylist school. Another problem from your perspective is their lack of respect for you since you are not a licensed stylist.

Interest Differences: The stylists want to be financially secure and to be paid fairly for their work at Bentleys (**tangible interest**). You want to be seen by the stylists as a knowledgeable entrepreneur, someone who can make sound business decisions (**intangible interest**). The stylists will likely want input in the way that the bonus structure is modified (**intangible interest**) as well as the reasons why the bonus structure must be changed (**tangible interest**). Because of your knowledge of Bentleys' financial situation, you believe the stylists should defer to your decision on the appropriate bonus structure (**intangible interest**).

In addition to reviewing the possible points of conflict with the Bentleys stylists, you will need to consider the appropriate conflict handling/negotiation style for this situation. We reviewed different types of conflict

Defend-attack cycle
At a point of impasse in a negotiation, or where negotiations break down due to lack of progress or communication between the negotiators, negotiators frequently spend time defending their last proposals and criticizing the other negotiator's proposals. This negative "back-and-forth" exchange frequently leads both negotiators to become angry and more adamant in demanding that the other negotiator change his or her last proposals.

handling/negotiation styles in Chapter 2: accommodating, avoiding, collaborating, competing, and compromising. Since you want to reach an agreement with the stylists that best serves Bentleys' interests and maintain a good working relationship with them, a collaborating approach will likely work best in this situation.

> **TAKE AWAY:** *Conflict may occur at various times during a negotiation. Negotiation skills are used to manage and resolve conflict. Understanding the different types of conflict, as well as the possible sources of the conflict, are key to effectively managing and resolving conflict.*

The Role of Emotion in Negotiations

As we have discussed in this book, negotiations tend to go through a series of stages: preparation, rapport building-information trading, deal making, and closing. A negotiator's emotions will change during progression through these stages. During the preparation stage, a negotiator may be excited, nervous, or even fearful. In the rapport-building and information-trading stages, a negotiator may feel positive about the working relationship being created with the other negotiator. On the other hand, a negotiator may be intimidated by the other side's threats or feel suspicious about the other side's motives due to a lack of trust. During the deal-making and closing stages, a negotiator may feel positive about the progress made at the negotiation table or happy about the outcome. Conversely, a negotiator can be upset about reaching a sticking point (impasse) during the deal-making stage or become angry during the closing stage if he or she feels "cheated" by an unfair outcome.

Building Rapport with Someone Who Is Emotional

In Chapter 5, we explained the difference between rapport, a genuine personal relationship with the other negotiator, and schmoozing, a superficial attempt to find a connection with the other negotiator. We frequently trust people we view as similar to ourselves – something referred to as the "similarity principle" – which, in turns causes us to look for similar or shared experiences with the other negotiator. Unfortunately, the similarity principle may cause us to look for superficial shared experiences. On the other hand, a genuine personal connection (**rapport**), allows the negotiator to better understand the other side's positions and interests; allows the negotiators to feel comfortable asking clarifying questions, which reduce misunderstandings at the negotiation table; and improves the chances the negotiators will feel committed to fully implementing a negotiated agreement. As stated by Fisher and Ury in *Getting to Yes:*

> *A working relationship where trust, understanding, respect, and friendship are built up over time can make each new negotiation smoother and more efficient. And people's desire to feel good about themselves, and their concern for what others will think of them, can often make them more sensitive to another negotiator's interests.*[5]

Rapport allows a negotiator to better understand an emotional reaction by the other negotiator. An effective negotiator may, for example, be able to identify why the other negotiator is so intent about reaching an agreement on a particular issue because he or she has been in a similar situation. The better a negotiator is at identifying the emotion expressed by the other negotiator, "the stronger the rapport."[6]

Although a small thing may trigger an emotional outburst in negotiation—the room temperature may be too hot or too cold for a negotiator's liking or the negotiators are spending too much time talking about what seems to be an unimportant or "throw away" proposal—the emotional outburst is generally motivated by a very strong underlying interest. Anger can serve as a "neon sign" pointing to something that the other negotiator cares deeply about.

TAKE AWAY: *Building rapport with someone who is angry and upset can be challenging. A person's emotions, however, offer a clear signal about what is important to them.*

BIn the movie, *Charlie Wilson's War* (2007), Central Intelligence Agency (CIA) officer Gust Avrakotos meets with his supervisor, CIA Director of European Operations John Slattery, to talk about why Avrakotos was not promoted to the position of Helsinki, Finland, Station Chief. Avrakotos, becoming increasingly more annoyed, tells Slattery, "The Helsinki job was mine," "Promises were made," "I have been with the company 24 years," and "I've spent the last three years learning Finnish." Slattery, likewise becoming increasingly annoyed, tells Avrakotos that he was passed over for the position because he lacked "proper diplomatic skills" and was "coarse." A profanity-laced argument ensues between Avrakotos and Slattery, ending when Avrakotos leaves and breaks the window glass of Slattery's office. Avrakotos certainly had a tangible interest in being promoted to the Helsinki Station Chief position and the triggering event in his argument was Slattery's decision to bypass Avrakotos for the promotion. The intensity of Avrakotos'

Box 11.3 Schmoozing versus Rapport

A good example of the difference between schmoozing and building genuine rapport can be seen in the movie, *The Insider* (1999), and the negotiations between Lowell Bergman of the *60 Minutes* television program and former Brown & Williamson Vice President for Research and Development Jeffrey Wigand. Bergman is tasked with convincing Wigand to go on *60 Minutes* to talk about how tobacco companies were "lying" to the public about the addictive qualities of cigarettes. Wigand, however, had signed a severance agreement with Brown & Williamson that included a confidentiality clause prohibiting Wigand from talking to people about his employment with the company. If Wigand went on *60 Minutes* and talked about his employment with Brown & Williamson, he could be sued by the company for breach of contract and lose the severance money and health insurance coverage the severance agreement provided to him and his family.

During a meeting with Bergman at a Japanese restaurant, Wigand commences with small talk, saying, "The Internet said you did graduate work at Wisconsin and then went to UC La Jolla with Professor Herbert Marcus."

Bergman corrects Wigand's pronunciation of the professor's name ("Marcuse"), saying, "He was my mentor and a major influence on the New Left in the late 60's and on me personally."

Wigand responds, "Next to your father?"

Bergman, in a rather testy manner says, "My father? What the hell's that got to do with my father?"

Taken aback, Wigand tells Bergman, "My father was a mechanical engineer, the most ingenious man I ever knew."

Bergman, even more agitated, says, "Well, my father left us when I was five years old. He was not the most ingenious man I ever knew. Let's get back to Brown & Williamson."

Wigand's attempt to build rapport based on his knowledge of where Bergman went to college and his (Wigand's) assumption that they had a shared admiration for their fathers failed. He did not do enough homework about Bergman's mentor (Marcuse) and assumed Bergman respected his father as much as he (Wigand) did. Rapport was, however, later established in this scene when Bergman "talks tough" to Wigand, emphasizing the importance of what *60 Minutes* was asking Wigand to do ("blow the whistle" on the activities of Brown & Williamson) and how he (Bergman) had "been out in the world giving my word and backing it up with action." To a person like Wigand, who values the truth and needs someone to stand up with him, Bergman's words helped establish a bond between the two men that ultimately leads Wigand to agree to appear on *60 Minutes*.

reaction (the yelling, the profanity, and ultimately his breaking the office glass in Slattery's office) was, however, driven by his intangible interests in being respected for his loyalty to the CIA ("I have been with the company 24 years") and in having promises made by Slattery's predecessor about the Helsinki job kept ("Promises were made" and "I've spent the last three years learning Finnish").

Many negotiators see emotion and anger at the bargaining table as either an intimidation tactic or the sign of an "irrational" negotiator. Telling an emotional or angry person to "calm down" or "get a grip on yourself" will actually cause the emotional or angry person to become even more upset because you are inferring that they are "out of control" and are not thinking rationally. Emotions can, however, help us to better identify things that are important, which, in turn, leads to better decision making.[7-10] While fears and feelings of nervousness may cause us to act impulsively, our emotions may actually play an important part in our abilities to think and behave in a "rational" manner. Think about how the anxiety of driving in a new city, driving during a thunderstorm, or driving with a driving instructor, can cause you to focus even more on the task of driving.

In order to build rapport with someone who is upset, angry, or emotional, a negotiator must match the intensity of the other person. This does not mean losing control of your own emotions; rather you want to show you are equally passionate about the issues being discussed. This may seem somewhat counterintuitive in that we usually assume that the best way to respond to someone who is emotional is to simply listen until he or she is "talked out." People who are upset want to know that their concerns are being understood (that you care about why they are upset) and will lead to some type of constructive response.

> **TAKE AWAY:** *Establishing rapport with an angry or emotional negotiator takes time, patience, and the good sense not to tell the other negotiator to "calm down" or "be rational." The more a negotiator listens during the negotiation, the more the negotiator controls the situation. Indeed, angry or emotional people may be very rational—in their eyes, there may be a very rational reason for their emotional response.*

When faced with the chore of building rapport with someone who is angry or emotional, think of a kayaker paddling in white-water rapids. The kayaker cannot simply float through the river rapids or sporadically paddle. Instead, the kayaker must furiously paddle to match the speed of the rapids. The kayaker becomes in sync with the pace of the rapids and eventually paddles out of the rapids into calmer waters.

An angry or emotional person wants to know that you understand their interests and the intensity of the underlying feelings for those interests. This can be accomplished by direct eye contact, **mirroring** the other person's gestures (that is, if the person is leaning toward you and using hand gestures to make a point, then you should lean forward and use hand gestures to emphasize your points), and matching the intensity of the person's emotions with questions that show you understand (or are trying to understand) their interests. Taking notes will allow you to control the pace of the conversation.

Mirroring
Similar to mimicry, mirroring means matching the other negotiator's body language, degree of eye contact and level of passion for a particular issue to establish (or reestablish) rapport.

Acknowledging what you hear the other person say ("As I understand it, you have been placed on hold the last two times you called our customer service department"); pausing after the person speaks, which gives you the chance to process what you hear and allows the other person to "fill the silence" with additional information; and summarizing the person's key points ("You are concerned about delays in our production schedule and what seems to you to be an increased amount of damaged product in our recent shipments, is that right?") will demonstrate to the angry or emotional person that you are concerned about understanding their interests.

Matching intensity does not mean trying to "out yell" the other negotiator. It means using intense language ("That is very *important* to you isn't it?" "As I understand it, you don't feel you were treated *fairly* by this car dealership," "You seem to be very *concerned* about the children who walk past this work site on their way to school") to show your understanding of where the other person is coming from and why they are upset.

The use of intense language and mirroring of behavior is seen in the movie, *The Goodbye Girl* (1977). In *The Goodbye Girl,* Paula McFadden and her daughter are living with an actor (Tony) in New York City. Tony leaves New York to film a movie, dumping Paula in the process. Paula is an unemployed dancer who continues living in the apartment. Unbeknownst to Paula, Tony had sublet the apartment to a fellow actor named Elliot Garfield. Elliot paid Tony $600 for the apartment. When Elliot arrives at the apartment, he is equally surprised to find Paula and her daughter. They negotiate over who should stay in the apartment. Elliot tells Paula, "Look, I'm sorry about this." He continues, "I don't blame you for being hostile. I think I get the picture. Tony rented me the apartment and split with the money, right? And you and your daughter got dumped on." Paula sticks to her position that she should stay in the apartment. Elliot steps closer to Paula, raises his voice, and says, "So what's the deal? I mean I got a lease here. You going to honor it or what?" He threatens to go to court: "Look, I don't want to get legal. Legal happens to be on my side." Standing in close proximity to each other and still using raised voices, Paula and Elliot continue to argue about who should stay in the apartment. Elliot ultimately asks, "Can we make a deal?" He reminds Paula that she "has a daughter to think about" and emphasizes, "We're both in a bind, the two of us." They ultimately agree to share the apartment.

The Goodbye Girl shows two upset and irritated people who are in a predicament due to no fault of their own. They are both emotional. Neither trusts the other person. Paula's anger about the situation reflects several underlying intangible interests, most notably the need for security and recognition for the fact that she had been treated poorly by Tony. Elliot matches Paula's level of emotion by using direct eye contact, speaking quickly, and acknowledging her right to "be hostile" because she—like him—was "dumped on" by Tony. Once Paula believes Elliot truly understands why she is upset, she is able to reach a point where she can properly consider the one option they have in the situation—to share the apartment during the term of Elliot's sublease.

The Use of Apologies

The words of an old hymn ask, "Keep me from saying words that later need recalling."[11] A negotiator may need to acknowledge the other negotiator's emotions—why that person is feeling and acting a particular way, why they are upset or angry—as an important first step in building rapport. Telling someone, "I'm sorry," acknowledges that you understand he or she is upset. William Ury, co-author of *Getting to Yes,* explains the value of an apology in emotional negotiations:

> . . . [C]rushing an opponent is not the right answer. We often over-look the simple power of an apology . . . What . . . people most often want is the recognition that they *have been wronged. Only when that acknowledgement has been made will they feel safe in nego-tiating. An apology thus creates the conditions for a constructive resolution of the dispute.*[12]

Effective apologies include recognition of the emotional impact of the action on a person, an expression of regret, and a commitment not to repeat the negative action.[13] To someone who has stubbornly maintained a particular position during a negotiation, a position that is proving to be unworkable, receiving an apology may give them the chance to back down from that position without being publicly embarrassed or losing face.

Assume your first meeting with the Bentleys stylists did not go well. When you presented your proposed changes to the bonus structure—to freeze all bonuses for the next two quarters and establish the same 5% bonus plan for all of your stylists—the three senior stylists all jumped to their feet, called you "greedy," and left the shop. You were mad when they left (who likes to be called "greedy" after all?), and they were certainly upset with your proposed changes to their bonus plan. An apology from you may reopen the communications with these three stylists, people you want to continue working for Bentleys. Talking to the three stylists, you could, for example, make the following statement:

> I know how important you three have been to Bentleys success. Our customers come here because of the great service you provide. We are all interested in continuing the success that my Aunt Sheila

started when she opened Bentleys. Aunt Sheila told me that I should bounce ideas off the stylists when I took over the shop. I did not do that before considering changes in our bonus system. I apologize for not talking to you three first about the reasons why I think this is something we need to do. Given the way I presented this to you, I understand why you were upset. I should have shown all the stylists our recent financials, so everyone can see our current situation. What ideas do you have that would allow us to meet our expenses while still providing our stylists with a fair bonus?

Handling a Difficult Negotiator

Negotiation experts Ron Shapiro and Mark Jankowski have written a book titled *Bullies, Tyrants, and Impossible People: How to Beat Them Without Joining Them.* They propose a four-step approach to effectively deal with "difficult, angry, irrational, emotional, demanding, close-minded, tyrannical, illogical [and] rude" people.[10] This four-step approach goes by the acronym of **N.I.C.E.**:[14]

Neutralize your emotions: Because dealing with difficult people can be emotional, and difficult people do things to cause us to react, the N.I.C.E. approach advocates that you keep your emotions "in check." This can be accomplished by focusing on the issues you have with the difficult person instead of on the normal human reaction of striking back. Shapiro and Jankowski offer several other tricks to neutralize emotions: "slowing your pace, lowering your voice, changing your physical environment, taking a deep breath, relaxing your shoulders, smiling, putting your finger to your lips, asking questions, listening and, counting silently."

Identify the type: There are three different types of difficult people—the situationally difficult, the strategically difficult, and the simply difficult. Situationally difficult people are difficult because of something that happened to them (a bad encounter with a boss, a car accident, money trouble, relationship break-up, etc.). A strategically difficult person is someone who believes being difficult is the best way to get desired results. They favor hardball tactics in negotiations—good cop/bad cop, intimidation, ultimatums, false deadlines, bluffing, and so on. Simply difficult people are just that; "they are difficult" by nature. They refuse to make concessions in negotiations and "just keep ratcheting the tension higher and higher."

Control the encounter: The different types of difficult people require different approaches to deal with them. A situationally

N.I.C.E. approach
Negotiation experts Ron Shapiro and Mark Jankowski propose an approach to working effectively with an angry or "difficult" negotiator. They use the acronym of N.I.C.E to explain this approach: Neutralize your emotions; Identify the type of difficult negotiator you are dealing with; Control the encounter; and Explore the options.

Box 11.4 Responding to an Angry Person

Master negotiator Roger Dawson offers three suggestions for dealing with an angry person (co-worker, customer, vendor, etc.):

1. **Establish Criteria:** Find out exactly what the other person wants you to do. "Get the angry person committed to a position."
2. **Exchange Information:** Ask for information and "don't jump to conclusions" about the other person's motives or interests.
3. **Reach for Compromise:** Look for things the other person values and for things that you would be willing to trade (your concessions).

Source: Dawson, R. (1999). Secrets of power negotiating for salespeople (pp. 204–208). Franklin Lakes, NJ: The Career Press.

difficult person, for example, may respond positively when you try to see things from their perspective. Shapiro and Jankowski recommend trying to empathize with the person, ask questions to obtain information, and allow the other person to vent and reassure the person that steps can be taken to improve their situation. Empathy means acknowledging what the other person has to say (or why they are upset), not necessarily agreeing with them. For the simply difficult person, Shapiro and Jankowski recommend evaluating the person's source of power/leverage, identifying your own "counterbalancing" power/leverage (e.g., another job offer), and communicating the consequences of the simply difficult person's behavior (e.g., "If you keep this up, I will leave this company and you won't have anyone with my level of experience left in the department").

Explore the options: Dealing with difficult people may lead to impasses. To get break the impasse—get "unstuck"—alternative solutions or options must be developed. This requires getting the other person involved in the brainstorming process. For example, ask, "What would you do if you were on my side of the table?" or "What would be wrong with doing it this way?"

In this chapter, we have outlined ways for you to identify different sources of conflict in a negotiation. We have also looked at ways that emotion affects a negotiation and how you can establish rapport with an angry or emotional negotiator. What happens though when you cannot resolve the conflict? What happens when you cannot break an impasse with the other negotiator? We will answer these questions in the next chapter.

■ ■ ■ ■

CHAPTER SUMMARY

Conflict and emotion are important parts of the negotiation process. Both can signal strong underlying interests that must be addressed in order for the negotiators to reach an agreement. Unfortunately, many negotiators see such conflict or emotion as something to run from, rather than an opportunity to both build a better connection with the other negotiator and identify new areas of agreement that can bring value to both negotiators. Effective negotiators know emotions and conflict cannot be turned off and on like a water faucet. To establish a connection with someone who is angry or emotional, a negotiator must take steps to understand the intensity of the person's feelings and demonstrate to that person—by asking questions, paraphrasing, and acknowledging their concerns—that they"get it." The acknowledgment piece—recognizing the other person has a right to be upset or angry—is an important first step in dealing with an emotional or angry negotiator, customer or, family member.

Questions/Exercises

1. You are the customer service manager at the Big Box Home Repair Store. Two months ago, Big Box ran an advertisement for "free carpet installation." Customers paid for their carpet order from Big Box, but the installation work done by Big Box employees was done "for free." This promotion has been very successful for Big Box. There has, however, been some problems with the ordering of the carpet. To make this promotion "pay out" for Big Box, the company entered into an agreement with a new "low-cost" carpet vendor. This new vendor has been late with several deliveries and has sent carpet orders to Big Box that have not matched up with the customers' orders. You are not quite sure if the problem is with the vendor or with your staff in the carpet and flooring department who take room measurements from customers and then email the carpet orders to the vendor.

   You have just received a telephone call from a notoriously difficult customer.

   This customer is a well-known news anchor on the local television network, owns a very expensive home, and is known around town as being a "cheapskate." He has done business with Big Box several times, each time calling to complain to you about the service and each time asking for some sort of "discount" on the work. This particular customer is on his way to Big Box to talk to you. Apparently, the carpet order sent to his house is the wrong color, and this customer wants a "huge discount" because of the delay caused by "your incompetence." How are you going to handle this customer?

2. You are the CEO of a small company that provides in-home nursing care to physically disabled clients. Last week, one of the company's nursing assistants, Elmira Whittington, told a nursing supervisor she no longer wanted to be assigned to provide care for Mack Brown, one of the company's long-time clients. According to the nursing supervisor, Elmira reported Brown

called her an "old hag" and asked that she be reassigned from his care because he wanted to see some "eye candy." Elmira responded by slapping Brown's face. Elmira is 52 years old and has worked for the company, without any prior incidents, for five years.

The nursing supervisor, Janet Evans, insists that Elmira be disciplined for violating the company's work rule that prohibits the "physical abuse" of clients. Elmira refuses to be assigned to care for Brown and demands she receive an apology from him. From what you have been told, Elmira is still "mad as hell." You are scheduled to meet with Elmira in 15 minutes. This will be the first time you have met Elmira. How do you propose to establish rapport with Elmira? Assume Elmira opens the meeting up with you by saying, "I don't know how you can help me. You have no idea how hard it is to work with these clients. Also, what do you know about being 52 years old?" How will you respond to Elmira's comments?

3. You are the owner of a catering business. Yesterday, one of your employees made a delivery to the XYZ Company for its annual shareholders' meeting. This is the first time you had done a catering job for XYZ. You would like to continue to do catering work for XYZ but were concerned when your employee told you about an altercation he had with the XYZ maintenance manager when the employee returned to XYZ to pick up serving platters. The employee parked in the visitor's parking lot in front of XYZ's administrative office building, entered the building to pick up the serving platters, and was met at the parking lot by the maintenance manager. According to your employee, the maintenance manager yelled at him for parking

in the visitor's parking lot, called him an "an idiot for not knowing enough to park in the back near the loading dock," and kicked the side of the van, causing a large dent just above your company's logo on the driver's side door. Your employee is threatening to "go to the cops." You have an estimate from the local body shop for $650 to fix the dent in the door of your van. The other employees in your business want you to "stand up" to the XYZ maintenance manager. You are worried about losing the chance to have repeat business with XYZ. As luck would have it, the XYZ maintenance manager left you a telephone message saying that he will be stopping by in 15 minutes to "go over some problems he has with your company." What are your interests? What do you anticipate to be the interests of the XYZ maintenance manager? Write out, in three to five sentences, what you plan on saying to the maintenance manager when you meet with him.

4. In the 1946 holiday classic movie, *It's a Wonderful Life*, customers of the Bailey Building and Loan managed by George Bailey are panicked about keeping their money with Mr. Bailey's business and rush into the Bailey Building and Loan to get their money back. (This "bank run" scene is available on YouTube - https://www.youtube.com/watch?v=PGLeMdlYN60). Mr. Bailey ultimately manages the anxiety and conflict felt by his customers. Identify the concepts presented in this chapter that Mr. Bailey used to resolve this conflict situation with the customers of the Bailey Building and Loan.

5. William Ury, co-author of the work *Getting to Yes: Negotiating Agreement without Giving in*, author of the book, *Getting Past*

No: Negotiating with Difficult People, and well-known expert on negotiation and conflict management, gave a TedTalk on negotiation conflict (https://www.youtube.com/watch?v=6xCkhV7zhuw; https://www.ted.com/talks/william_ury_the_walk_from_no_to_yes). Listen to Ury's Ted Talk. What lessons about dealing with conflict in negotiation did you learn from listing to Ury? How would you describe Ury's suggestion of "going to the balcony"? What implications does "going to the balcony" have for negotiations?

Endnotes

1. Barbour, C., & Treleven, E. (2011, March 26). Collective bargaining law published despite court order blocking it. *Wisconsin State Journal*. Retrieved from http://host.madison.com/wsj/news/local/govt-and-politics/article_f22629e6-572a-11e0-ab2f-001cc4c002e0.html.

2. Barbour, C., & Spicuzza, M. (2011, March 16). After weeks of divisiveness, lawmakers extend an olive branch. *Wisconsin State Journal*. Retrieved from http://host.madison.com/wsj/news/local/govt-and-politics/article_f7210d02-4f83-11e0-9f91-001cc4c002e0.html.

3. Dana, D. (2001). *Conflict resolution* (pp. 18–29). New York: McGraw-Hill.

4. Sutton, R. I. (2007). *The no asshole rule: Building a civilized workplace and surviving one that isn't* (p. 36). New York: Warner Business Books.

5. Fisher, U., & Patton. (1991). *Getting to yes: Negotiating without giving in* (2nd ed., p. 19). New York: Penguin Books.

6. Moeller, L., & Christensen-Szalanski, J. (2010). *Making the puzzle pieces fit: How to identify interests and resolve conflict* (2nd ed., p. 95). Dubuque, IA: Kendall Hunt/Conflict Press.

7. Batson, C. D., Shall, L. L., & Oleson, K. C. (1992). Differentiating affect, mood and emotion. In M. S. Clark (Ed.), *Emotion: Vol. 13.*

Review of personality and social psychology (pp. 294–326). Newbury Park, CA: Sage.

8. Clore, G. L. (1992). Cognitive phenomenology: Feelings and the construction of judgment. In L. L. Martin & A. Tesser (Eds.), *The construction of social judgments* (pp. 133–163). Hillsdale: NJ: Erlbaum.

9. Damasio, A. R. (1994). *Descartes' error: Emotion, reason, and the human brain.* New York: Putnam.

10. Gross, J. J. (1978). Emotion regulation: Past, present, future. *Cognitive and Emotion, 13*(199), 551–573.

11. Heermann, J. (1978). O God my faithful God. *Lutheran Book of Worship* (p. 504), Minneapolis: Augsburg Publishing House.

12. Ury, W. (2007). *Getting past no: Negotiating in difficult situations* (p. 61). New York: Bantam Books.

13. Fisher, R., & Shapiro, D. (2005). *Beyond reason: Using emotions as you negotiate* (p. 15). New York: Penguin Group; and Kellerman, B. (2006, April). When should a leader apologize and when not? *Harvard Business Review,* 73–81.

14. Shapiro, R. M., & Jankowski, M. A. (2005). *Bullies, tyrants, and impossible people: How to beat them without joining them* (p. 9). New York: Three Rivers Press.

12

Who do You Call when you are Lost, Stuck in Traffic, or when your Car Breaks Down?: Using Third Parties in Negotiation

This has been a great trip. There have been absolutely no problems. You have driven through a large city, one that you have never visited before. It would be great, you think, to spend some time in the city and take a bus tour of the sights. Maybe next time; for now, you need to stay on schedule.

You are on the way to your destination. At that exact moment in time, you see a long line of cars stopped in front of you on the road. You did not plan for this traffic jam and have no idea how long you will be stuck in traffic.

An hour later, you escape the traffic jam. Skipping a dinner break allowed you to make up for time lost during the traffic jam. You are back on schedule, 50 miles from your destination. Finally, the end is in sight. Suddenly, your engine light begins to flash. You slow down and pull your car off to the shoulder of the road. The driving map application on your phone, suggested a final route for your trip along a relatively quiet state highway. There does not seem to be a gas station or repair shop in sight. You are not handy with cars, so you will need someone to take a look at your engine.

When you are in a new city, you may hire someone—a taxicab driver, private driver or a bus driver—to drive you around. They have a greater knowledge of where to go and how to get there in the city than you do.

When you have a flat tire, or when your car breaks down, you might call a friend, or use your cell phone to search for a local mechanic or take advantage of the services of a motor club like the American Automobile Association. Sometimes you need the assistance of other people to help you reach your final destination.

In negotiations, you may need to hire someone (an agent) to represent you in a particular negotiation. Like a taxi driver, private driver or bus driver transporting you around unfamiliar city streets, the agent may have a greater knowledge of the type of negotiation you are involved with. Hiring the agent to represent your interests will, hopefully, lead to a better outcome compared to what you could negotiate for yourself.

Despite your best plans, road blocks and unanticipated problems—traffic jams, flat tires, and flashing engine lights—can occur during a driving trip. You may need the help of a mechanic to get you back on the road. In negotiations, similar unanticipated problems can occur—changed economic circumstances of the parties involved in the negotiation, a clash of personalities at the bargaining table, changing BATNA, and so on. You may need the help of someone who can help you reach an agreement with the other negotiator (a mediator) or someone who can help you resolve a dispute (arbitrator) with the other party.

In this chapter we will review the occasions when an agent may be used in a negotiation, steps negotiators can take to break a deadlock (impasse) and other third-party options (mediation and arbitration) that negotiators may use to facilitate an agreement or resolve a dispute.

CHAPTER OBJECTIVES

- To understand the circumstances under which an agent may be used to represent a party in a negotiation
- To understand what steps can be taken to break a negotiations impasse
- To understand how mediation and arbitration can be used to break negotiation impasses or to resolve conflict between parties

KEY TERMS

Agents and principals	Mediation	Arbitration
Ury's breakthrough strategy	Shuttle diplomacy	Arbitration award
Court trial/litigation	Caucuses	

■ ■ ■ ■

The Use of Agents in Negotiation

We have provided an overview of how to improve your negotiation skills through preparation and understanding relevant negotiation strategies. As we have discussed, many negotiation situations cannot be avoided, and even the most inexperienced of negotiators must be ready to negotiate on short notice. There are, however, some situations when it makes sense to consider hiring someone to represent your interests in a negotiation. In these situations, you direct the other person to negotiate for you. You control the other person's authority (what they can or cannot agree to) to negotiate on your behalf and whether or not to accept any agreement the other person negotiates for you. In this relationship, you hold the position of **principal** and the other person is your **agent**.

Agents and principals
Principals employ other people, called agents, to represent the principals' interests in a negotiation.

An agent has a legal duty to act in the best interests of the principal. The agency relationship is generally created by an agreement between the principal and the agent. A homeowner, for example, may enter into a contract with a real estate agent to sell his or her house. The contract may be for a set period of time, such as 90 days, and the homeowner agrees to pay a commission to the agent based on the final selling price of the house. The homeowner tells the agent his or her desired selling price. The agent, who has expertise in knowing the market rate for home sales in the homeowner's community, works with the homeowner to identify an asking price and a settlement range. The agent shows the house to prospective buyers and attempts to persuade the buyers and their real estate agents to accept the homeowner's asking price or at least make a counteroffer that falls within the homeowner's settlement range. The agent is obligated to present any offer received from the prospective buyers to the homeowner. The agent works with the prospective buyers and their realtors until a deal can be reached or the parties reach a point of impasse.

A homeowner who has bought and sold several homes over the years may not need the help of a real estate agent in the house buying-selling process. Likewise, a homeowner who plans to sell his or her house to a friend or relative for an agreed-upon price may not see the need to use a real estate agent.

There are, on the other hand, several reasons why a homeowner would want to employ a realtor to help buy or sell a house. First, the homeowner may not have much experience in buying or selling a house. The realtor has expertise the homeowner lacks—knowledge about the market rate for homes in the area, experience with other realtors, and an understanding of the house buying-selling process. Second, the homeowner may not have sufficient time to advertise the house or to look for potential houses to buy; that becomes the job of the agent. Last, the realtor is not emotionally invested in the house they are hired to buy or sell. A prospective buyer of a house, who "falls in love with the house" and "has to have it," may not be able to keep a level head when it comes to negotiating a reasonable price for the house. The agent can step in and be the "voice of reason" for the prospective house buyer. Sellers of homes may overvalue their homes because of the work they have done on the house or the memories they associate with the house. The house seller may not appreciate hearing criticisms about the choice of paint color in different rooms or comments about features of the house that would have to be updated if the prospective buyer purchased the house. These comments may be very upsetting to the seller. The realtor would, however, understand that such comments are made by prospective buyers as a way to have the seller lower the asking price.

Box 12.1 Scott Boras: Sports Agent Extraordinaire

Scott Boras had dreams of playing major league baseball. Three knee surgeries while he was playing in the minor leagues led Boras to retire in 1978, short of reaching the major leagues. After retiring, Boras went to law school, graduated with his J.D., and started practicing medical malpractice law in Chicago. While Boras was working in private law practice, a high school classmate who was playing major league baseball asked Boras to negotiate his player's contract. Boras negotiated that contract and then negotiated a five-year $7.5 million contract for a former minor league teammate. Other baseball players hired Boras for their contract negotiations. Today Boras is known as the most powerful agent in major league baseball, representing players such as, Stephen Strasburg, Gerrit Cole, Jose Altuve, and Bryce Harper. During Major League Baseball's 2019 winter meetings in San Diego, Boras negotiated three contracts for players Gerrit Cole, Stephen Strasburg and Anthony Rendon for the approximate amount of $814 million.

Boras is known as a hard-line negotiator who uses player statistics in different and innovative ways to demonstrate what he considers to be the true market value of the players he represents. He earns a 5% commission on negotiated contracts. New York Yankees General Manager Brian Cashman said of Boras: "Scott's a seller and we're the buyer. He's willing to take chances, and his clients are willing to take chances with him." Boras says, "My job isn't to create the market. My job is to define the market." Boras follows his "four Ps" in negotiations: preparation, passion, persistence, and prayer. Former major league general manager Bill Bavasi described Boras as "very prepared, very smart and very patient. He's not afraid to take a good player and wait." Said former player Jorge Fabregas, "[Boras] pushes teams to where they've never been pushed. If I'm a player, I want him on my side."

Many major league teams try to avoid selecting players in the annual draft who are represented by Boras. He has been described as "baseball's most hated man" and been criticized by team management for what they consider to be "outrageous" contract demands. Los Angeles Angels of Anaheim team owner Arte Moreno has had difficult negotiations with Boras. When asked to comment on Boras, Moreno said, "My mother always told me, 'If you can't say anything nice, don't say anything at all.'"

Boras has described his role as an agent as follows: "I want the player to play where he wants to play and do what he wants to do. That's my job. If my client has ideas and methods and ways to get things done, my job is providing information and facilitating his interest in getting a deal done."

Sources: Benjamin, M. (2004, May 2). Go-to-guy: Agent Scott Boras is changing the business of baseball. U.S. News & World Report. *Retrieved from http://www.usnews.com/usnews/biztech/articles/040510/10eeagent.htm; Kepner, T. (2007, December 3). Agent to the superstars has soft spot for the "common" player.* New York Times. *Retrieved from http://www.nytimes.com/2007/12/03/sports/03iht-BORAS.1.8568182.html?_r=1; Newhan, R. (1998, December 15). The deal makers.* Los Angeles Times. *Retrieved from http://articles.latimes.com/1998/dec/15/sports/sp-54327; and Arte Moreno cool on Scott Boras, but Boras salutes Angels. (2011, January 27).* Los Angeles Times. *Retrieved from http://latimesblogs.latimes.com/sports_blog/2011/01/scott-boras-arte-moreno-angels-jered-weaver.html; Young, J., (2019, December 13). "Sports Agent Scott Boras says Huge MLB Contracts Prove 'Moneyball' Model doesn't Work," CNBC.com, https://www.cnbc.com/2019/12/13/agent-scott-boras-says-big-mlb-contracts-prove-moneyball-doesnt-work.html.*

The parties in many types of negotiations use agents to represent their interests. Literary agents represent authors in negotiations with publishing companies. Agents represent athletes in negotiations with sports teams and actors negotiating for roles in movies and television programs. Experienced consultants may represent companies or labor unions in collective bargaining. Lawyers represent companies in business transactions, such as the resolution of a lawsuit or the merger and acquisition of another business.

TAKE AWAY: *Agents are used in a negotiation because of their specialized expertise to help the parties save time in reaching an agreement and to give the parties sound advice in negotiations in which the parties are emotionally invested.*

Box 12.2 When or Why Should You Use an Agent in Negotiations?

For their expertise
- Agents may have substantive knowledge that you lack.
- Agents have expertise about the process in certain domains.
- Agents may have special influence with important people who are involved with the deal.

For their emotional detachment

For tactical flexibility

For status or balance, if the other side is using an agent or lawyer, you may want to use one too

---

The use of agents in negotiations does come with some disadvantages. The most obvious disadvantages are that of cost, control over the negotiation process, and possible miscommunication between the agent and the principal.

Scott Boras negotiated a record-setting $252 million contract for baseball player Alex Rodriguez with the Texas Rangers baseball team. He had known Rodriguez since the early 1990s, when Rodriguez was in high school. Boras represented Rodriguez when he was traded from the Rangers to the New York Yankees. Boras earned commissions based on the amount of the contracts he negotiated for Rodriguez. It was also Boras who announced during the 2007 World Series that Rodriguez was opting out of his record $252 million contract and leaving the Yankees to be a free agent. As a free agent, Rodriguez could negotiate to play for any team in major league baseball.

The Yankees refused to negotiate with Boras after he announced that Rodriguez was opting out of his contract. Rodriguez, however, still wanted to play with the Yankees. As the Yankees continued to play hardball in their negotiations, Rodriguez took it upon himself to change the tone of the negotiations by negotiating the outline of a deal directly with the Yankees—without Boras' help. Rodriguez later said that opting out of his contract with the Yankees was "a mistake that was handled extremely poorly" and that his goals "were not aligned" with the approach Boras was taking in the negotiation.[1] Rodriguez added, "If I had to do it again, I would've called Hank [Yankees Senior Vice President Hank Steinbrenner] from Day 1 and negotiated myself."[2] Rodriguez ultimately agreed to a new 10-year $275 million contract with the Yankees. He later ended his player-agent relationship with Boras.

Rodriguez's former Yankees teammate, Hall of Famer Derek Jeter's contract negotiations also illustrates how agents affect the negotiation process. Jeter the Yankees' team captain, one of the best players of his generation, and a favorite player of many baseball fans. His 10-year $189 million contract with the Yankees ended after the 2010 season. Jeter had one of his poorest seasons as a baseball player in 2010. He was also one of the older players on the Yankees. Jeter's agent proposed a new contract at $23 to $24 million per year for four or five years.[3] The Yankees countered with a three-year contract offer for $15 million each year.[4] Jeter did not want to take a pay cut under his new contract. Frustrated with the pace of the negotiations, Jeter's agent was quoted as saying he was "baffled" by the team's negotiations proposal:

> *There's a reason the Yankees themselves have stated Derek Jeter is their modern-day Babe Ruth. Derek's significance to the team is much more than just stats. And yet, the Yankees' negotiating strategy remains baffling.*[5]

The Yankees responded to Jeter's agent by encouraging Jeter "to test the market and see if there's something he would prefer other than this. If he can, fine. That's the way it works."[6] Baseball fans commented on the "nastiness" of the negotiation and the public "war of words" between Jeter's agent and the Yankees.[7] Although he was not quoted in the media, Jeter did use his agent to communicate frustrations with the Yankees' hardball negotiations and to gain support from baseball fans to improve his leverage. On December 4, 2010, Jeter and the Yankees agreed to a new three-year contract that paid Jeter nearly $16 million a year, making him the highest paid player at his position (shortstop) in the major leagues at that time.[8] Jeter finished his 20-year playing career with the Yankees in 2014.

TAKE AWAY: *While a principal is ultimately responsible for outcomes negotiated by his or her agent, tactics taken by the agent may affect the pace of the negotiation and affect the principal's relationship with the other negotiator.*

> ### Box 12.3 Potential Problems with Using Agents in Negotiations
>
> They can be expensive.
>
> They add additional communication links, making the negotiation more complex and leaving room for misunderstandings.
>
> Their interests may not be aligned with the principal's interests; they might use negotiation tactics that the principal finds unacceptable.
>
> They keep the principals from communicating directly with each other.

Finding Ways to Bypass Negotiation Roadblocks

A negotiator who has planned for a successful negotiation and who has established a good working relationship with the other negotiator may still encounter different roadblocks to reaching a negotiated agreement. A negotiation that is going along smoothly may come to a sudden and frustrating halt. An effective negotiator must be able to determine the cause of the impasse and find ways to bypass the roadblocks to a negotiated agreement.

Suppose that you plan on taking two summer school courses. Your parents have paid for your tuition since your first year at the university. You have generally lived at home during the summers and worked at various summer jobs to pay for the cost of your books. By taking two courses this summer, you will be able to take a manageable schedule of courses during the upcoming fall semester (which is important so that you can maintain your 3.5 grade point average) and graduate next May. You also do not want to move back home this summer, as several of your friends will be taking summer school courses on campus. The two courses you need to take during the summer term are also not available online. Your parents object to you taking summer school courses and believe you would be better off living with them and working this summer. You think, *"I don't understand my parents. If I don't take summer courses, I won't graduate next May. Another semester of school will cost them far more than the $2,000 I would make this summer. They are being so unreasonable."*

William Ury, a co-author of *Getting to Yes,* wrote a follow-up book titled *Getting Past No,*[9] which builds on the principles summarized in *Getting to Yes* and proposes a "breakthrough" strategy to help negotiators overcome negotiation roadblocks. Ury notes that negotiators frequently exhibit one of three common reactions at the point of impasse: strike back, give in, or break off the negotiation.[10] Negotiators may get angry, stop listening to the other negotiator, and assume there is no way to bridge the gap between the parties'

Ury's breakthrough strategy

Negotiation expert and mediator William Ury has developed a breakthrough strategy to help negotiators work through an impasse in their negotiations. Ury's breakthrough strategy consists of the following steps: Don't React—Go to the Balcony; Don't Argue—Step to the Other's Side; Don't Reject—Reframe; Don't Push—Build Them a Golden Bridge, and Don't Escalate—Use Power to Educate.

last offers. Ury suggests that the negotiators view each other as partners engaged in joint problem solving. To that end, Ury proposes the following five-step **breakthrough strategy**:

- **Don't React—Go to the Balcony:** Negotiators at a point of impasse may be upset with the other negotiator because of positions taken or things said during negotiations. "Going to the balcony" means taking a break from the negotiation so that the negotiator can regain their "mental balance" and see the remaining issues in the negotiation with a more "detached" view, much as an audience member would watch a play from the balcony of the theater. This could include "pause and say nothing" in response to an attacking statement from the other negotiator, summarizing your understanding of the negotiator's last offer (something Ury calls "rewinding the tape"), or taking a break from the negotiations.

- **Don't Argue—Step to the Other's Side:** A negotiator can overcome the doubts or suspicions of the other negotiator by listening to what they have to say. At a point of impasse, negotiators frequently stop hearing (or paying attention to) what the other negotiator has to say. The negotiators may have also made wrong assumptions about the interests of the other party. Acknowledging the other negotiator may have some legitimate reasons to have said "no" to your last offer, showing that you have made the attempt to see things from the other negotiator's perspective, or making an apology can go a long way to restart a stalled negotiation. It is, after all, harder to break a negotiations impasse with someone you don't like or know very well.

- **Don't Reject—Reframe:** It is common that negotiators see their impasse in light of positions instead of looking beyond those positions ("We won't reach any kind of agreement unless you waive your 5% rush fee for last minute orders") to discover the underlying interests. Rather than continuing to tell the other negotiator "no," a negotiator using Ury's breakthrough strategy reframes the conversation by referencing what he or she understands the other negotiator's interests to be: "As I understand it, you are interested in finding a company that will ship parts to you with less than 24 hours' notice without charging a rush fee. We normally charge a 5% rush fee on orders placed with less than 24 hours' notice. Could we look at the possibility of waiving the rush fee and agreeing to a longer-term agreement than what you have been proposing?" Hidden or unmet interests can also be uncovered during this step of the breakthrough strategy through the use of open-ended ("What am I not understanding about your last offer?" "Are there other options we have missed?") and "why" questions ("Why is it important to you that we include a non-compete clause in my employment contract?").

- **Don't Push—Build Them a Golden Bridge:** Ury identifies several obstacles to agreement that present themselves in a negotiation: unmet interests, a negotiator's fear of "losing face," the notion that a proposal on the bargaining table is not their idea, or the feeling of the other negotiator that they have received too much information at one time to make a decision ("too much, too fast").[11] A negotiator who has not moved from their r last position may need a way (i.e., Ury's "bridge") to go from that position to a new proposal that will result in an agreement. Remember that the other side must achieve something in the negotiation in order to say "yes" to your proposals. A bridge could take the form of an explanation for a change in the negotiator's position that would allow the other negotiator to "save face," or it could be an additional concession to sweeten the deal. Management negotiators in contract talks with a labor union may, for example, offer an explanation for a change in the union's position that will be acceptable to the union members: "We know that you have consistently proposed a 5% across-the-board wage increase. That may have been reasonable when we started negotiations. However, since that time, the company's largest customer has declared bankruptcy. As you know, we are in a different economic situation now. A 2.5% across-the-board wage increase is more in line with the current economic climate and what we are able to pay after losing our largest customer's business." Labor union negotiators could sweeten a deal with a company that has been rejecting the union's proposal to add an additional holiday to the list of the employees' paid holidays by proposing that employees not receive the additional holiday day until the second year of their new collective bargaining agreement.

- **Don't Escalate—Use Power to Educate:** The final step in Ury's breakthrough strategy is to point out to the other negotiator what could happen if the two of you cannot reach an agreement. A negotiator, for example, could ask the other negotiator questions such as, "What do you think will happen if we can't reach an agreement?" or "Considering how long we have been negotiating, and how close we are, what will your board of directors think if we can't reach an agreement and you have to start all over in the process of finding a new supplier?" or "If we can't work this out, we are going to have to file a lawsuit. I am not sure spending time in court and money on lawyers is something that is an attractive option for either of us." This step requires that a negotiator understand their BATNA and have a sense of the other negotiator's BATNA as well.

How could you use Ury's breakthrough strategy to reach an agreement with your parents about taking summer school courses so that you could graduate next May? The first thing you would do is to take a "time out" from your discussions with your parents; that is, **go to the balcony**. This may mean that you tell them, "Let's talk about this tomorrow." Now that you are no longer in the discussion, take a step back and review how the negotiation has gone so far. How did you approach your parents? What kind of mood were they in when you talked to them? Could you have picked a better time to talk to them? Did you talk to your parents when they were together? Should you have spoken to your parents individually? If you spoke to your parents by phone, would a face-to-face meeting have worked better?

The second step would be to try to see things from your parents' perspective; that is, **step to their side**. Why are they upset by the prospect of you taking summer school courses? Have you had this conversation with them before? If so, what did they say? How in the past have you made decisions about your course work? Were your parents involved in the decision? If so, how was this situation different? What are your parents' reasons for objecting to your taking summer school courses? Can you understand why and how those reasons may be legitimate?

The third step, **reframing**, will require you to have a follow-up conversation with your parents. That conversation may start out as follows: "Mom and Dad, I appreciate the support you have given me during college. I know that my success at school is important to you. I also want to make sure I make the right decision about taking summer school courses. Can you please tell me again why you would prefer I come home this summer and find a job instead of taking summer school courses at the university?"

In order to **build a golden bridge** between your parents and your goal of taking on-campus summer classes, you will need to identify the common interests you have with your parents. "Mom and Dad, I know how important it is to you that I do well in school. The courses I will be taking next fall will be difficult. I will need to spend more time studying for those courses than what I have spent on study time in the past. If I can finish those two courses this summer, then I can focus on my more difficult courses this fall and keep my grade point average around 3.5. When we last spoke, I was not very clear about what courses I was planning to take this summer and the reasons why I am proposing to take summer school." If the reason why your parents object to your taking summer school does turn on your ability to pay for the cost of your books (instead of their concern that you won't be coming home over the summer or a concern that you were making the decision about summer school without their input), you could offer another option to them: "Mom and Dad, as I understand it, you are concerned that if I don't work this summer, then I won't be able to pay for my books next year. Here is an idea. Why don't I try to work part-time this summer while I am taking my two courses? These two courses are offered in the evening. I could try to find work at the university recreation center teaching swimming lessons in the mornings and then take the two classes during the evenings. Although I won't make as much money as last summer when I worked full-time, I will have my course work done at the end of the summer and have earned enough money to pay for my fall semester's books."

If you have not convinced your parents to pay for your summer school, you could **use your power to educate**, the fifth and final step of Ury's break-through strategy. At this step, you would want to share your BATNA with your parents and raise questions about what could happen if you don't take summer school: "Mom and Dad, I really have appreciated your paying for my tuition. If we can't reach some sort of agreement about me taking summer school, it's going to be difficult for me to maintain my 3.5 grade point average and still graduate by next May." Another approach would be to tell your parents, "If we can't come to some sort of agreement about summer school, then I may have to take out a short-term loan. I know we have talked about not borrowing money to pay for my education, but I believe it's that important for me to take these two courses this summer."

> **TAKE AWAY:** *Every negotiation includes sticking points. Sometimes those sticking points lead to breakdowns in the negotiations. Negotiators may, at a point of impasse, engage in defend-attack behaviors and blame the other negotiator for the lack of an agreement. Effective negotiators acknowledge this human tendency to "strike back" and take steps to avoid making a difficult situation worse and look at ways to bypass the roadblock in their negotiation.*

Box 12.4 Using a "Change of Scenery" to Break a Negotiation Impasse

Negotiation expert Ron Shapiro suggests that negotiators try to "change the scenery" of their negotiations in order to break an impasse:

"If you've been meeting at your office, offer to go to theirs. Settings can be intimidating, stifling, stale, or negative. Being on your turf may create a sense in the other party that they've already given just by being there. In addition, either or both parties can get tired of staring at the same walls. Imaginations and energies wane. After too much time passes without progress, the negotiators may subconsciously associate the surroundings with lack of progress . . . Just by going to their office or a neutral site, you will change the dynamics of the negotiation . . . *Moving sometimes feels like movement.* It may not be logical but attitudes shift with locales."

Source: Shapiro, R., & Jankowski, M., with Dale, J. (2001). The power of nice: How to negotiate so everyone wins—especially you! (rev. ed., p. 210). New York: John Wiley & Sons.

■ ■ ■ ■

Using a Third Party to Help Break Negotiation Impasses—Mediation and Arbitration

Even the best negotiators understand there are situations that call for the help of an outsider—a third party—to help them find common ground with another negotiator or to bring some final resolution to an ongoing dispute. Sometimes the use of a third party to help with negotiations is required by the law (as in the case of many public sector labor-management disputes between state governments and unionized state employees) or by contract (where the parties have agreed to resolve their disputes through litigation, arbitration, or mediation). Other times, the parties voluntarily agree to have a third party help them to overcome negotiation sticking points that have led to an impasse.

Box 12.5 One Way to Resolve a Dispute

Major league baseball players went on a 232-day strike from August 12, 1994, until April 2, 1995. The players went on strike and stopped playing baseball games because they could not reach an agreement with the owners of the Major League teams for a new collective bargaining agreement. The strike caused cancellation of the 1994 World Series, delayed the start of the 1995 season, and angered baseball fans across the country. One fan was then-Ohio Congressman James Traficant. Congressman Traficant offered a rather unique suggestion to help the owners of the Major League Baseball teams and the Major League Players Association break their negotiation impasse:

"Negotiators should be locked in a room with no windows and no air conditioning and should be fed baked beans, hard-boiled eggs and chocolate kisses. In eight hours, they will be pleading, 'Play Ball!'"

Source: 1994–95 Major League Baseball strike. Retrieved from http://en.wikipedia.org/wiki/1994%E2%80%9395_Major_League_Baseball_strike; and Litke, J. (1995, February 9). Baseball's combatants—Lock 'em in a room. Retrieved from http://articles.sfgate.com/1995-02-09/sports/17795012_1_president-clinton-rep-james-traficant-heart-strings.

As we have discussed in this chapter, at a point of impasse in a negotiation, the parties frequently engage in defend-attack behaviors, defending the proposals they have made in the negotiations and attacking the other negotiator (and their proposals) as being unreasonable and the cause for the breakdown of negotiations. Negotiators at this point are frustrated and stop talking to each other. There may be threats of ending negotiations, employees going on strike, companies locking out employees, or lawsuits. This type of "tough talk" is seen in remarks National Football League Players Association

Executive Director DeMaurice Smith made in January 2011 to NFL player representatives about their negotiations with the NFL owners:

> *We are at war! Nobody gets strong without fighting. Nobody stays strong without fighting. Nobody negotiates their way to strength. Nobody talks their way to a good deal. Nobody sits down and just has miraculous things happen.*[12]

Although we will be focusing in this chapter on two primary forms of third-party intervention, mediation and arbitration, third-party approaches can range from the very informal (a parent trying to resolve a dispute between her two daughters) to the very formal (a breach of contract lawsuit—a **court trial**—between two companies involving a complex business transaction). The third party can be a friend, roommate, neighbor, or someone formally trained as a mediator, arbitrator, or judge. The parties determine the process that the third party follows and the amount of control the parties will have over the outcome. A comparison of different third-party approaches is shown in Figure 12.1.

In **mediation**, the negotiators select a third party (the mediator) who works to bring the negotiators back to the bargaining table. The mediator identifies the issues in dispute and helps the negotiators focus their energies on finding new proposals rather than continuing defend-attack behaviors that negatively affect their ability to work together. The mediator controls the process of the mediation—the process by which they try to facilitate an agreement between the parties—but the negotiators determine whether they reach

Court trial/litigation
Disputes in the American legal system are resolved through court trials, where evidence and testimony are presented to a judge or to a jury. The judge or jury uses this evidence and testimony to decide who wins the court trial and what the winning party should receive for a remedy. Litigation is a general phrase used to describe the process by which lawsuits are filed and ultimately decided.

Mediation
A form of alternative dispute resolution (ADR) that involves a neutral third-party working with two sides in a dispute (or the negotiators in a negotiation that has reached an impasse) to try to identify common interests.

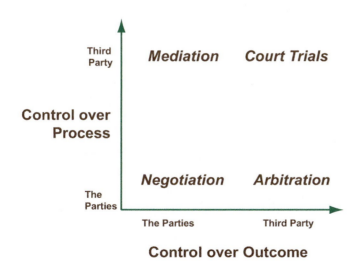

FIGURE 12.1   Different Third Party Approaches

an agreement (the outcome). Mediation is also a confidential process, meaning that what is said to the mediator remains private, allowing both sides to say what they need to say and to vent emotions.

When the parties select a third party in **arbitration** (the arbitrator) to resolve a negotiation impasse, they control the process the arbitrator will follow—the issues to be decided, the standards the arbitrator will use in making a decision, the evidence to be considered by the arbitrator, and the timing of the hearing before the arbitrator—but the arbitrator controls the outcome. Unlike mediation, which is a form of assisted or facilitated negotiation, arbitration in many respects looks like a court trial before a judge. Arbitration is also, in most cases, a private process, meaning the arbitration hearing is not open to the public and, unlike a court's decision, the arbitrator's written award is shared only with the parties and not made public.

The specific aspects of mediation and arbitration are discussed in greater detail in the following sections.

Mediation

Mediation allows negotiators to determine their own outcome. The mediator lacks the authority to force the parties to reach an agreement. Their job is try to address the problems in the parties' relationship, discover interests, and help create proposals that give the parties the chance to reach an agreement. The mediator is considered to be "neutral" because they do not have an association with either party or a vested interest in a particular outcome favoring one side or the other. Mediation is appropriately used in situations when the continuing relationship between the negotiators is important: child custody issues between divorcing parents, disputes between a company and its unionized employees, border disputes between neighboring countries, product quality issues between a manufacturer and its customers, and payment disputes between a construction contractor and its subcontractors.

There are several benefits of mediation. A mediator:

- maintains control over the process, which will hopefully lead to a negotiated agreement by the parties;
- works to control the emotions of both parties;
- allows both parties a chance to say what they what to say—to "be heard"—while maintaining confidentiality of what they tell the mediator;
- builds the parties' understanding of the other side's concerns and interests;
- helps to search for solutions that are acceptable to both parties;
- motivates the parties to settle through discussions about the parties' BATNAs in the event an agreement cannot be reached; and

Box 12.6 Managers as Mediators

Mediators used to help negotiators break an impasse or to resolve a dispute are generally neutrals, meaning they don't have an association with either party or have a specific interest in a particular outcome. The skills that mediators use to facilitate agreements can be used by managers to resolve workplace disputes with employees they supervise, to build consensus on new policy changes, or to brainstorm with staff. Specifically, managers can help disputing employees identify goals and interests, uncover their priorities, establish a framework and ground rules for discussions, level the playing field between employees at different organizational levels (allowing both to be equally heard), and open communication channels. Managers can use similar skills in chairing multi-party meetings by creating meeting agendas, identifying the decision standard (i.e., majority vote or group consensus), and working out steps for implementation of any agreed-upon items.

- creates the framework of an agreement on resolved issues that both sides are committed to carry out and implement.

Mediators use different techniques to help the parties reach an agreement. A mediator may meet the parties together in a joint session to review the different issues and then separate the parties into different rooms. At that point, the mediator shuttles back and forth between the parties with different proposals, pushing each side to identify what it is they want and challenging the parties to consider the alternatives if an agreement cannot be reached. This approach is frequently called **shuttle diplomacy;** a third-party representative of one government is traveling between different countries and acting as a mediator in a dispute between two or more countries. Other mediators keep the parties meeting face-to-face as much as possible, allowing the parties to take short breaks (often times referred to as **caucuses**) with their negotiating team to discuss different proposals.

Oftentimes a mediator's "reality check"—"Do you understand how costly a lawsuit would be if you can't resolve this issue?" or "What do you think your customers will do if the employees go on strike and your assembly line is shut down for weeks?"—convinces the parties to reevaluate their positions and look for areas of possible concession. American diplomat Dennis Ross explained the value of reality checks in his attempts to mediate agreements during Middle East peace discussions:

Mediating requires each side to adjust its behavior to what a deal is going to require. Mediation requires constant explanation of what the reality is, and how both sides have to adjust to it. It requires explaining the needs of one side to the other—something that is never appreciated.[13]

Shuttle diplomacy
This is a type of mediation when the mediator keeps the two sides separated from each other and the mediator goes back and forth with questions and proposals for each side.

Caucuses
Parties to a negotiation or to mediation may take a "time out" during the negotiation or mediation when they can meet with the members of their own team to review proposals made during the negotiation or mediation or to consider a proposal made by the other side that requires additional time to review.

Regardless of the approach the mediator takes, the process of mediation does tend to flow through a series of different steps:

- Opening remarks by the mediator describing the goals of the mediation (to reach an agreement), their role (an interested but neutral facilitator, not a judge who will make a ruling at the end of the mediation), and the mediation process
- Initial discussion of issues in dispute and the parties' respective positions on those issues—their opening statements
- Summary of the issues in dispute and discussion of the agenda for the mediation
- Exploration of the parties' interests and positions; an opportunity for the parties to see the dispute from the other side's perspective
- Mediator-led brainstorming of ideas for new proposals, including proposals suggested by the mediator
- Achievement of an agreement that satisfies as many of the parties' interests as possible
- Summary of the parties' agreement

TAKE AWAY: *Mediation is a third-party process that allows the parties to a negotiation dispute or impasse to reach an agreement with the help of a neutral facilitator (the mediator). Mediation is best used in negotiation or conflict situations when the ongoing relationship is important and the parties' impasse or conflict has had a negative impact on the parties' relationship.*

Arbitration

Arbitration is related to the negotiation in two ways. First, the threat of turning control of the outcome of a negotiation over to a third party provides incentive for the negotiators to reach an agreement on their own. An arbitrated resolution to an impasse may lead both parties to be unhappy—a prospect that may motivate both sides to find a voluntary negotiated outcome. Second, arbitration is a process that negotiators can use as an end point if they are unable to reach an agreement. The negotiators determine what the issues the arbitrator will decide and the arbitrator's authority to resolve the parties' impasse or dispute. The parties' control over the process of the arbitration while giving control over the outcome to the arbitrator is generally viewed as a better alternative than a court trial.

Arbitration is best used when the parties need a final resolution. An employee who is fired from her job may want a third party's decision about whether her firing by the employer was proper or legal. A divorcing couple who cannot agree on division of marital property—a house, jointly purchased artwork, or the family pets—may need the help of a third party to determine how their property should be split up.

Like a court trial, an arbitration hearing is an adversarial process in that one party is ultimately recognized as a winner in the dispute. Evidence supporting their positions is presented by the parties to the neutral third-party arbitrator, who makes a final and binding decision that resolves the parties' dispute. Arbitration resembles a court trial in that the arbitrator acts like a judge, receiving evidence and making a decision based on that evidence. Arbitration does have some advantages over the litigation process of resolving a lawsuit through court trial:

- Arbitration is less expensive than a court trial because it usually does not take as much time and may or may not require the use of lawyers to present the case before the arbitrator.
- Arbitration is generally a private process, meaning that arbitration hearings are not, like a court trial, open to the public to watch, nor is the arbitrator's decision made public like the decision of a court judge.
- Arbitration provides the parties with control over the process; they select the arbitrator based on their particular expertise and experience and create rules by which the arbitrator hears evidence and makes a decision. By contrast, the rules for court trials are established by legislative bodies or the judicial system, and judges are generally assigned to court cases instead of selected for the case by the parties themselves.
- **Arbitration awards** can be appealed to court on a very limited basis (usually the standards for court review involve evidence of bias by the arbitrator in favor of one party or the other, the arbitrator exceeding their authority, or some other form of misconduct by the arbitrator) compared to a court decision, which may be appealed through different levels of the judicial system.

State law in many states requires that public sector employees, such as school teachers, maintenance employees, police officers, firefighters, and so on, who reach impasses with state government employers during negotiations for new collective bargaining agreements submit their disputes to an arbitrator for resolution rather than go on strike. Oftentimes, business partners agree to arbitrate their disputes instead of going to court.

The American Arbitration Association maintains lists of arbitrators; parties can select an arbitrator from these lists to resolve disputes between businesses or disputes between employers and labor unions representing their employees. A standard arbitration clause in a contract between two businesses would look like the following:

Any controversy or claim arising out of or relating to this contract, or the breach thereof, shall be settled by arbitration administered by the American

Arbitration
A form of alternative dispute resolution (ADR) that involves a neutral third party hearing evidence from the two sides to a dispute and making a decision as to which party is right and which party to the dispute is wrong. The parties in arbitration generally select the arbitrator themselves and create the procedural rules the arbitrator must follow in hearing the evidence and making his or her decision.

Arbitration award
The decision an arbitrator makes in an arbitration case is called an award. While an arbitrator can give the parties an oral decision, frequently parties want the arbitrator to provide a written justification and analysis for their decision.

Box 12.7 King Solomon—Arbitrator

King Solomon served as an arbitrator when faced with resolving a dispute between two women who both claimed to be the mother of the same child. One of the women told King Solomon that the other woman had accidentally smothered her child and now was claiming to be the mother of her child. The other woman denied this claim. As described in the Bible (1 Kings 3:23–28), King Solomon resolved this dispute as follows:

Then the king said, "One says, 'This is my son that is alive, and your son is dead'; while the other says, 'Not so! Your son is dead, and my son is the living one.'" So the king said, "Bring me a sword," and they brought a sword before the king. The king said, "Divide the living boy in two; then give half to one, and half to the other." But the woman whose son was alive said to the king—because compassion for her son burned within her—"Please, my lord, give her the living boy; certainly do not kill him!" The other said, "It shall be neither mine nor yours; divide it." Then the king responded: "Give the first woman the living boy; do not kill him. She is his mother." All Israel heard of the judgement that the king had rendered; and they stood in awe of the king, because they perceived that the wisdom of God was in him, to execute justice.*

Arbitration Association under its Commercial Arbitration Rules, and judgment on the award rendered by the arbitrator(s) may be entered in any court having jurisdiction thereof.[14]

The costs of arbitration are usually shared by the parties. The arbitrator's authority is limited by the parties' agreement to arbitrate their dispute. Discovery, which is used in court trials (interviewing possible witnesses, making demands for copies of relevant documents, etc.), and the various motions filed before a court trial to either limit the issues in the case or have the case dismissed before it is decided by a judge or jury are generally used on a limited basis in arbitration. Arbitration hearings can be scheduled in a matter of months rather than years, as is the case with court trials. An arbitrator is also required to issue his or her written decision, called an **award**, within 30 to 60 days after the end of the arbitration hearing.

TAKE AWAY: *While arbitration has many advantages over a court trial, it is still based on an adversarial process in which one side ultimately will win the case and the other side will lose. The win-lose outcome in arbitration will not help the parties to resolve any problems they have in their relationship. Mediation, by contrast, allows the parties to agree to outcomes that may include more than just the payment of money (e.g., one side offering an apology to the other), provides the parties with the chance to fix any relationship problems they have, and may result in an outcome that both sides see as a win.*

■ ■ ■ ■

CHAPTER SUMMARY

Negotiation is an ever-changing process. Some negotiations require expertise or experience of an agent. Other times, deals that are close to being complet-ed can become "unglued" at the last moment, causing negotiation impasses. Although a changed strategy may help a negotiator break the impasse, new tactics may not be enough. A negotiator may need to step back from the nego-tiation—go to the balcony—to take a fresh look at the circumstances leading up to the impasse. The help of a third party may be necessary when negotia-tors cannot break an impasse on their own. Mediation is a process designed to assist parties in finding a voluntary solution to their negotiation impasse. Yet other times, negotiators need a final and binding resolution to their impasse or dispute. While going to court is a possibility, arbitration is generally con-sidered a more efficient and less costly option for the negotiators who need the closure that comes with a final decision to their dispute.

Questions/Exercises

1. Assume you have been offered a job by a company located in Plano, Texas. You cur-rently live in Florida and will be graduat-ing from college in a month. The human resources manager of the Texas company wants to talk to you about the terms of the proposed employment contract, which includes a non-compete provision, mean-ing that if you quit your job with the company, you won't be able to work for one of its competitors for a minimum of one year. If you take the job in Texas, you will also need to buy a new car (your job will require a significant amount of car travel) and find an apartment to rent. Would it make sense in any of these three negotiations—the negotiations over the terms of your employment contract, the negotiation for a new car purchase, and the negotiation of locating an apartment in Dallas—to use the services of an agent? Why or why not?

2. You have a one-year lease with an apart-ment rental company. The lease prohibits

pets and includes a provision that requires a $500 "pet violation" if you keep a pet in your apartment. Last month, your grand-mother asked you to watch her pet Brit-tany spaniel dog for a weekend when she was out of town. You agreed. Although you did not have any problems with your grandmother's dog, several residents in your apartment complex saw you walking the dog in the parking lot and reported you to the apartment rental company. Yester-day you found a written "pet violation" notice from the apartment rental company manager tacked to your apartment door. The notice said that you owed $500 for having a pet in your apartment. You don't have the $500 necessary to pay the pet violation charge; however, you do have $150 in cash you could use to pay the charge. This morning you called the apart-ment rental company manager. She did not have much time to talk to you but did say she expected you to pay the full $500 pet violation charge. To your surprise, the apartment rental company manager did agree to meet with you tomorrow. What steps can you take to persuade the apartment rental company to not charge you for the pet violation fee? If you cannot reach an agreement with the apartment rental company manager, do you believe mediation would be an appropriate form of alternative dispute resolution (ADR) to resolve this dispute?

3. Your parents have been talking to your grandfather about selling his house. Your grandfather has been having trouble living by himself and agreed to move from his house to a residential care facility. He also agreed in conversations with your parents to list his house with a real estate agent, with the hope of selling the house to help fund his stay in the residential care facility. This morning, the real estate agent came over to your house to have your grandfather sign the listing agreement with the agent's office. Just as your grandfather was ready to sign the agreement, he looked at the real estate agent and your parents and said, "This is not right. I have lived in this house most of my life. You can't take it from me." He has refused to sign the listing agreement and is not speaking to your parents. Is your grandfather's response understandable? If so, why? How might you use Ury's breakthrough strategy to break the impasse between your parents and grandfather?

4. You built a house on a lot next to land owned by friends of your family—the Brown family. This is your dream house. You believe your family will live in the house for the next 20 years. Before you purchased the lot and built your house, the Brown family had planted a row of trees (at an expense of $10,000) on what they thought was their side of the property line. After you built your house, the Browns discovered that the trees they planted were actually on your side of the property line. Yesterday, Mr. Brown asked you to reimburse him for half of the cost of planting the trees ($5,000) since the trees "improved the value of your property." You believe that Mr. Brown is being completely unreasonable since it was Mr. Brown who made the mistake as to the location of his property line. Mr. Brown has contacted a lawyer and seems insistent that you pay for at least half the cost of planting the trees. Assume that you cannot reach an agreement with Mr. Brown and that you will need the help of a third party. Under these facts, would you prefer mediation or arbitration as a means of resolving this dispute?

5. Stevens Aviation considered suing Southwest Airlines over use of the phrase "Just Plane Smart," a phrase Stevens had trademarked and a phrase Southwest had been using in its advertisements. Instead of going to court over Southwest's use of Sevens' "Just Plane Smart" trademarked phrase, Stevens CEO Kurt Herwald proposed a different form of ADR to legendary Southwest CEO Herb Kelleher. The dispute between Stevens and Southwest was resolved on March 20, 1992 at an event called "Malice in Dallas." How was this trademark dispute resolved?

Endnotes

1. Rodriguez finalizes $275M deal with Yankees. (2007, December 13). *ESPN.com*. Retrieved from http://sports.espn.go.com/mlb/news/story?id=3153171.

2. Rodriguez finalizes $275M deal with Yankees. (2007, December 13). *ESPN.com*. Retrieved from http://sports.espn.go.com/mlb/news/story?id=3153171.

3. Schmidt, M.S. (2010, November 26). Jeter said to be asking $23 million to $24 million a year. *The New York Times*. Retrieved from http://bats.blogs.nytimes.com/2010/11/26/jeter-said-to-be-asking-for-23-to-24-million-a-year/.

4. Schmidt, M.S. (2010, November 26). Jeter said to be asking $23 million to $24 million a year. *The New York Times*. Retrieved from http://bats.blogs.nytimes.com/2010/11/26/jeter-said-to-be-asking-for-23-to-24-million-a-year/.

5. Lupica, M. (2010, November 21). Derek Jeter's agent Casey Close says Yankees public hardball with shortstop is "baffling." *New York Daily News*. Retrieved from http://www.nydailynews.com/sports/baseball/yankees/2010/11/21/2010-11-21_derek_jeters_agent_casey_close_says_yankees_public_hardball_with_shortstop_is_ba.html.

6. Lacques, G. (2010, November 23). Cashman dares Derek Jeter to test the free agent market. *USA Today*. Retrieved from http://content.usatoday.com/communities/dailypitch/post/2010/11/brian-cashman-derek-jeters-contract-has-to-be-a-fair-salary/1?csp=34.

7. Kepner, T. (2010, November 23). What's baffling is the nastiness of Jeter talks. *The New York Times*. Retrieved from http://www.nytimes.com/2010/11/24/sports/baseball/24kepner.html.

8. Vecsey, G. (2010, December 5). Jeter deal done: Now comes the hard part. *The New York Times*. Retrieved from http://www.nytimes.com/2010/12/06/sports/baseball/06vecsey.html?_r=1.

9. Ury, W. (1993). *Getting past no: Negotiating in difficult situations.* New York: Bantam Books.

10. Ury, W. (1993). *Getting past no: Negotiating in difficult situations* (pp. 32–36). New York: Bantam Books.

11. Ury, W. (1993). *Getting past no: Negotiating in difficult situations* (pp. 107–108). New York: Bantam Books.

12. Pappu, S. (2011, January 22). Quarterback for at team of 1,900. *The New York Times*. Retrieved from http://www.nytimes.com/2011/01/23/business/23nfl.html?_r=1.

13. Ross, D. (2007). *Statecraft and how to restore America's standing in the world* (p. 230). New York: Farrar, Strauss and Giroux.

14. American Arbitration Association. (2010). *Commercial arbitration rules and mediation.* Retrieved from http://www.adr.org/sp.asp?id=22440#A2.

The End of the Road—Where We've Been and Future Journeys

By now you have read all the chapters, had the opportunity to role-play several negotiations, and gained additional negotiation practice through the online portion of the book. Congratulations, you have completed your driver's education course and passed your driving test. Below we briefly summarize the road we have traveled.

Chapter 1: Recognizing You Are on the Road

In this chapter, we identified the reasons why people say they "hate to negotiate." We gave you a definition of "negotiation" and used that definition to describe the many types of situations where negotiation skills are necessary and important. We ended the chapter by considering the traits possessed by effective negotiations.

Chapter 2: What Type of Driver Are You?

In Chapter 2, we reviewed different negotiation styles and discussed the circumstances (using the dual-concerns model) when each type of negotiation style may be appropriate. We described the concept of social motivation and presented an exercise that helped to determine whether you are an individualist, a competitor, or a cooperator as a function of your preferences for resource allocations between you and another person. We also emphasized in concluding the chapter, the importance of your working relationship with the other negotiator and discussed the role that assumptions and stereotypes may play in negotiations.

■ ■ ■ ■

Chapter 3: What Kind of Trip Are You Taking? The Short versus the Long Haul

Chapter 3 distinguished distributive (short-haul) bargaining from integrative (long-haul) negotiation. Distributive bargaining tends to occur when relative strangers are negotiating over a single issue and a fixed pie of resources is to be divided. A variety of hardball tactics used in distributive bargaining situations were identified. Negotiations terminology, such as "aspiration level," "BATNA," and "reservation price," was presented to help you establish a point of reference for negotiations. As we ended the chapter, we discussed the value of concessions in the negotiation process, and reviewed the reciprocity and fairness norms.

■ ■ ■ ■

Chapter 4: The Adventure of Cross-Country Driving: Principles of Integrative Negotiation

In this chapter, we drew an analogy between integrative negotiation and a cross-country driving trip. We discussed the fact that integrative negotiation situations typically involve multiple issues that the negotiators value differently. Integrative negotiations, unlike distributive bargaining discussed in Chapter 3, are not typically one-time interactions. The difference between "positions" and "interests" was examined. Approaches to uncover the other party's interests were discussed. We also presented a system for quantifying a multi-issue negotiation and showed how bundling offers can create value, as contrasted with compromising (i.e., "splitting the difference") on every issue. The chapter concluded with a discussion about the Pareto frontier and how outcomes that fall below it "leave money on the table."

■ ■ ■ ■

Chapter 5: Planning Your Road Trip: Planning and Preparation for Successful Negotiations

Chapter 5 identified the different stages of a successful negotiation: preparation, rapport-building, information-trading, deal-making and closing. We discussed the importance of preparing for negotiation success and outlined a road map that negotiators can follow to prepare for a successful outcome. The difference between "tangible" and "intangible" interests was explored. In addition, we emphasized the difference between developing meaningful rapport with the other negotiator and "schmoozing." Chapter 5 concluded with a discussion about different negotiation strategies, and how negotiators can best match those different strategies to specific negotiation situations.

Chapter 6: Reading the Road Map, Billboard Signs, and Detours: Creating Value in Negotiations

Chapter 6 discussed the difficulties negotiators have in identifying interests. We examined the reasons why many negotiators accept the first offer that is close to their bottom line/reservation price and why negotiators miss opportunities that add value to their negotiated agreements. We also reviewed the type of questions negotiators can ask during the different stages of a negotiation to identify interests and discussed ways to generate additional value-added options through brainstorming. The chapter concluded by exploring ways negotiators can close a deal and the necessary steps they should take once an agreement is reached to make sure they have a clear understanding of what they agreed to when the negotiation is completed.

Chapter 7: What If You Are Driving a Scooter and They Are in a Semi-Truck? Power, Leverage, and Influence in Negotiation

This chapter focused on the ways we can get people to say "yes" to us, even if we seem to have less advantage or power than the other person does. We discussed different kinds of power, and distinguished "power" from "leverage." We examined interests, rights, and power as three different approaches to resolving disputes and considered transaction costs, satisfaction with the outcomes, the effect on relationships, and the likelihood of the dispute reoccurring as ways of evaluating these three approaches. The chapter concluded with an introduction to Cialdini's six principles of influence.

Chapter 8: What If They Don't Obey the Rules of the Road? Trust, Ethics, and Reputation in Negotiation

Chapter 8 dealt with those drivers who do not always obey the rules of the road. We discussed the importance of building trust in negotiation and why it is difficult to regain trust once it is broken or lost. We learned how to analyze situations that might lead a negotiator to behave in untrustworthy ways and examined different ethical theories to provide a framework for understanding ethical and unethical behavior in negotiations. We ended the chapter with a discussion about the importance of building a reputation for honesty and protecting that reputation at all costs.

■ ■ ■ ■

Chapter 9: Objects in the Mirror May Be Closer than They Appear: Perceptions, Biases, and Communication in Negotiation

Chapter 9 discussed the ways in which our perception colors and filters the information that we take in and how that can influence judgments we make about others in negotiations. We also considered how framing effects can cause us to reverse our preferences as a function of whether options are presented as potential gains or losses. A number of cognitive biases and heuristics were discussed to demonstrate how they have the potential to affect negotiation behavior negatively. We discussed what, how, and why information is communicated in negotiation. We ended the chapter with a discussion of the pros and cons of using various types of communication channels for negotiations.

■ ■ ■ ■

Chapter 10: Understanding What It Is Like to Drive on the Other Side of the Road: Gender and Cultural Differences in Negotiation

In this chapter we addressed negotiating with those who are "different." We initially presented a discussion of gender issues in negotiation and highlighted research on this topic. We then turned to the many dimensions of culture that influence business and negotiation transactions. We discussed the different levels of understanding culture, from observable behaviors to culture in context, with a specific focus on negotiating in China. The chapter ended with an examination of ethical issues that arise when negotiating globally and laws that govern transactions between U.S. businesses and those operating in other countries.

■ ■ ■ ■

Chapter 11: Driving Defensively: Negotiating Your Way through Conflict, Emotional Situations, and Difficult Negotiators

Chapter 11 explained how conflict and emotion are important parts of the negotiation process and how both signal strong underlying interests that must be addressed in order for the negotiators to reach an agreement. We explored the defend-attack cycle in conflict situations. We discussed how effective negotiators understand conflict and emotion at the bargaining table can be used to establish rapport with the other negotiator and identify new areas of possible agreement. We ended this chapter by talking about the important role effective apologies can play in resolving conflict and steps that a negotiator can take to respond to a "difficult" negotiator.

Chapter 12: Who do You Call when you are Lost, Stuck in Traffic, or when your Car Breaks Down?: Using Third Parties in Negotiation

Chapter 12 noted that negotiation is an ever-changing process and explained how some negotiations require the expertise or experience of an agent. We also talked about the ways negotiators can try to jump-start a stalled negotiation process by using Ury's breakthrough strategy. We ended this chapter by identifying the differences between mediation and arbitration, and discussed when the use of each of these types of alternative dispute resolution processes may be helpful to resolve a dispute or negotiations impasse.

Concluding Author Comments

We have enjoyed having you along for the ride. You have earned your license to negotiate. Apply the rules you have learned in this book to new and different negotiations that you come across in the future. Look to take the scenic route in your travels—the negotiation path that will allow you to find the most value in your negotiated outcomes. Good luck.

Terry L. Boles, Ph.D.
Lon D. Moeller, J.D.
S. Beth Bellman, Ph.D.

Glossary

Assumptions: are often made about individuals based on stereotypes, or other imperfect information. In negotiation it is important to check out your assumptions before assuming they are true.

Accommodation: a conflict handling style where the individual gives in to the other. This is not an effective style in a one-time negotiation; however, if there is an ongoing relationship between the negotiators, one can (and should) accommodate the other if the issue is relatively unimportant and the relationship matters a lot.

Active listening: This type of listening involves a negotiator reflecting back exactly what they believe the other person said. It serves two important purposes, it lets the other person know you are paying attention to what they say, and it allows them to correct any misunderstandings.

Agents and principals: Principals employ other people, called agents, to represent the principals' interests in a negotiation.

AL: stands for aspiration level. This is a high target that a negotiator sets for him- or herself for the negotiation.

Anchoring and adjustment: a decision bias where in uncertain situations people will be influenced by an "anchor" to make their decision, and even if they know the anchor may not be accurate, they do not adjust away from the anchor sufficiently.

Arbitration: A form of alternative dispute resolution (ADR) that involves a neutral third party hearing evidence from the two sides to a dispute and making a decision as to which party is right and which party to the dispute is wrong. The parties in arbitration generally select the arbitrator themselves and create the procedural rules the arbitrator must follow in hearing the evidence and making his or her decision.

Arbitration award: The decision an arbitrator makes in an arbitration case is called an award. While an arbitrator can give the parties an oral decision, frequently parties want the arbitrator to provide a written justification and analysis for their decision.

Authoritative standards and objective information: Authoritative standards and objective information, such as agreed upon market rates, or the opinion of an expert source accepted by both negotiators, can be used by negotiators to better explain or justify their bargaining proposals.

Availability bias: this bias occurs when people overestimate the frequency of an event or occurrence based on how easily they can recall instances of the event.

Avoiding: a conflict handling style where the individual is uncomfortable with conflict and avoids confrontation altogether. This style only makes sense if the issue is unimportant to both negotiators. Avoiding the conflict rarely makes it go away.

Bargaining goals: A negotiator must plan to be successful by identifying specific and desired outcomes in his/her negotiation. These specific outcomes are called bargaining goals and represent outcomes that may exceed what the negotiator may generally expect to achieve in the negotiation.

Bargaining zone: the bargaining zone is the distance between the two negotiators opening offers. This is the zone in which bargaining takes place.

BATNA: stands for the "Best Alternative to a Negotiated Agreement." A BATNA is a reference point that is outside of the negotiation. It is what you will get if you don't get agreement in the current negotiation it might be the status quo, or another outside offer. Having a good BATNA gives you power in the negotiation.

Bogey: a contentious tactic where a negotiator pretends something or some issue is important to him or her, but it is not. This tactic is often employed so that the negotiator can then "concede" on the issue (which really isn't a concession at all) and get something of value in return.

Boulwarism: A negotiation technique in which a negotiator makes an initial "take it or leave it" first and only offer in negotiation. This technique is named after the approach developed by former General Electric Vice President Lemuel Boulware for collective bargaining with General Electric's labor unions.

Boundary spanners: individuals who are extremely influential because they have social ties that span many different social networks.

Brainstorming: Creative negotiations proposals can be identified during the preparation stage or during the deal-making stage of a negotiation by having negotiators suggest possible ideas without criticizing or evaluating the ideas. This technique is called brainstorming. When the brainstorming is completed, the negotiators indicate their preferred ideas and may work together to rank the ideas that meet as many of their interests as possible.

Bundling issues: when there are multiple issues in a negotiation it is often helpful to "bundle" like issues together and offer them as a package. For example, in an employment negotiation a recruiter might make an offer that bundles benefits, retirement, and vacation days together.

Call to action: when persuading someone this is the moment when you ask them to respond. In infomercials it is when they ask you to "pick up the phone."

Caucuses: Parties to a negotiation or to mediation may take a "time out" during the negotiation or mediation when they can meet with the members of their own team to review proposals made during the negotiation or mediation or to consider a proposal made by the other side that requires additional time to review.

Celebrating the deal: Once an agreement is reached, both negotiators should congratulate each other and celebrate the fact that they were able to negotiate an agreement.

Chicken: an extreme tactic that forces the other to show his or her hand. The nuclear arms race is an example of the game of chicken.

Claiming value: this is the amount of the resource being negotiated that is claimed by a negotiator. Negotiators who focus on claiming value are looking to claim as much as possible for themselves.

Coercive power: a way to force compliance by being able to punish the other if they don't act in the desired manner.

Communication channels: the different ways in which people can communicate and therefore negotiate. These channels include face-to-face, phone, email, text or chat, and video conferencing. Communication channels vary in the richness of what can be communicated.

Compatible issues: when there are multiple issues in a negotiation there is a tendency to think that the parties want different things on all the issues. There may, however, be several compatible issues in the negotiation. In an employment negotiation both parties may want the job candidate to be in a certain location and doing a certain type of job. Recognizing compatible issues can help negotiators build integrative agreements.

Competing: a conflict handling style where the negotiator looks out for his or her own interests and cares little about the relationship with the other person. Competitors like to "win" and they do well in one-time negotiations, but less so when there are multiple issues and the relationship with the other is important.

Compliance: getting another person to do what you want them to do.

Compromise: is meeting someone halfway. If there is only a single issue to be negotiated and the negotiators' positions are diametrically opposed, compromise is probably the only feasible solution. Compromisers value equality and fairness.

Concessions: A concession is a change or modification in a proposal a negotiator has previously made in the negotiation.

Creating value: value is created when parties make trade-offs among issues rather than simply compromise on all issues. Creating value is often called "expanding the pie."

Cultural sensitivity: the extent to which individuals are aware of the cultural norms, and belief systems of the individuals with whom they are interacting.

Dual-concern model: a two-dimensional model that plots conflict handling styles as a function of level of concern for own outcomes and interests (Assertiveness) and as a function of the concern for the other's outcomes and interests (Cooperativeness).

Conflict handling styles: the different approaches that individuals take to resolve conflicts or to handle negotiations. Most people have a preferred style, but a good negotiator can adapt their style to the situation.

Contentious or hardball tactics: these are tactics that negotiators may use to claim as much value for themselves as possible. These tactics are used to undermine, fool, or confuse the other negotiator.

Court trial/litigation: Disputes in the American legal system are resolved through court trials, where evidence and testimony are presented to a judge or to a jury. The judge or jury uses this evidence and testimony to decide who wins the court trial and what the winning party should receive for a remedy. Litigation is a general phrase used to describe the process by which lawsuits are filed and ultimately decided.

Deception: giving information that implicitly encourages people to draw false conclusions.

Defend-attack cycle: At a point of impasse in a negotiation, or where negotiations break down due to lack of progress or communication between the negotiators, negotiators frequently spend time defending their last proposals and criticizing the other negotiator's proposals. This negative "back-and-forth" exchange frequently leads both negotiators to become angry and more adamant in demanding that the other negotiator change his or her last proposals.

Direct and indirect communications: cultures with direct communications communicate in a straightforward way with action-oriented words; cultures who communicate indirectly use a more nuanced approach and expect the other to interpret the meaning.

Door-in-the-face: a persuasion technique where you ask someone for a very large request—one they are likely to say "no" to. Then after they say no you come back with a smaller request (what you hoped to receive all along) and they are more likely to say "yes" to it that if you had not asked for the larger request first.

Egalitarianism: a philosophy that people should be treated as equals.

Emotionalism: the extent to which different cultures are comfortable with showing emotion in social interactions. Cultures who value rationality and thoughtful discourse are less likely to show emotion.

Endowment effect: this is an effect whereby the value of an object can change as a function of whether or not it belongs to you. People tend to "endow" things and ideas that are their own with added value over the same object or idea generated by another person.

Essential competition: the type of competition where there can only be one winner. In business it can be when there is a very small niche market and there is not room for two competitors, thus it is essential that one must "win." Some will be tempted to use unethical tactics when there is essential competition.

Ethics of consequence: a utilitarian or pragmatic approach to ethics. It assumes the individual will choose the action that produces an outcome that does the least harm and the most good.

Ethics of principle: a relativist approach to ethics that is grounded in the prevalent culture. It assumes that people are rational and will do the right thing to produce an outcome that is consistent with the culture. A "do unto others" approach.

Ethics of purpose: is an absolutist approach to ethics that views people as basically good and suggests they will use a good means to reach a good end.

Ethnocentrism: the tendency to believe that one's own culture, belief system, ideas, etc. are centrally important and correct and all other groups are measured in relation to one's own.

Expert power: the power that another negotiator may have over you if they are an expert in an area you know nothing about.

Exploding offer: An exploding offer is a proposal made during the **closing** stage of a negotiation that has a specific time limit for acceptance. This proposal will not be available to the other negotiator once the stated time period expires.

Fairness norms: there are many norms of fairness. The most commonly used are equity, equality and need.

Fixed pie assumption: this assumption is that the size of the resource to be divided (or the negotiation "pie") is fixed. This assumption is often false; as integrative negotiation can often increase the size of the pie by adding issues that allow both negotiators to find a way to agree to an outcome that satisfy both of their interests.

Foot-in-the-door: a persuasion technique where you get someone to say "yes" to a small request, and then later ask them for a larger request that is consistent with the small request you made earlier. This technique relies on normative leverage.

Foreign Corrupt Practices Act: a law that details what is acceptable behavior in international negotiations and trade. It includes anti-bribery provisions that prohibit bribes to foreign officials or political parties in order to establish trade.

Framing effects: these effects occur when a situation is described in terms of what you stand to gain versus what you stand to lose. People are much more sensitive to and influenced by loss frames, and they are more risk-seeking in the domain of losses.

GLOBE study: the Global Leadership and Organizational Behavior Effectiveness study examined the effect of cultural variables on business practices. This study used nine dimensions to categorize cultures.

Good cop/bad cop: when negotiating with a partner, one takes the hard line and puts extreme pressure on the other side, leading them to believe that a deal may not even be possible, then the "good cop" comes in and makes a concession that allows the cop duo to receive what they had hoped for all along.

Ground rules: The rules, by which a negotiation will proceed, as discussed and agreed-upon by both negotiators, are called ground rules.

Guanxi: a term used in China to represent connections or relations between people. Having a guanxi network is key to getting deals done in China.

Halo effect (and horns effect): this effect occurs when we only know one good (bad) thing about another person and then generalize this information to other attributes of the person without good reason. If someone is nice (mean) you may also assume they are smart (stupid).

Hierarchy: a belief system that accepts unequal distribution of status and power.

High- and Low-Context Cultures: high context cultures place value on body language, nonverbal cues, and the context in which something is said; low-context cultures rely on the spoken word regardless of the context.

Highball/lowball: a contentious tactic where a negotiator makes a first offer that is extremely high (if they are the seller) or low (if they are the buyer), in the hopes of convincing the other negotiator that their own goals are un-achievable.

Identity-based trust: trust in another person that is based on a shared identity— like same religion or same sorority. You do not actually know or have personal experience with the individual, but you trust them due to your shared dentity.

Individualism—Collectivism: one of Hofstede's dimensions—individualists value independence, free will and individual rights. Collectivists value close ties between individuals and an individual's identity is tied to the group.

Institutional-based trust: the type of trust you have in someone because you know the institution or organization they represent has structures or policies in place that require their members to act in trust-worthy ways.

Integrative negotiation: a negotiation where parties attempt to integrate their interests. To do so, parties must be willing to share their interests, and be able to prioritize the issues to be negotiated, so they can concede on low-priority issues in order to claim more value on high-priority issues.

Interests: are the underlying reasons for the position a negotiator takes. For example, the reasons for an applicant's asking for a starting salary of $60,000 are unpaid college loans, need for a new house and new car, etc. *Positions* are singular; *interests* are multiple.

Interests (tangible and intangible): Tangible interests represent things that a negotiator wants or needs that are tangible, and generally easy to identify, such as money, a new job, or a specific price in a sales transaction. Intangible interests, on the other hand, are things a negotiator may want or need which are less obvious, things such as recognition, respect or fair treatment.

Intergroup conflict: Conflict that may occur between groups of people caused by shared and different interests and goals.

Interpersonal conflict: Conflict that may arise between people who have different goals and interests.

Intimidation: a tactic that seeks to undermine the other negotiator's confidence, often by providing false or dubious information.

Intragroup conflict: Conflict that may develop within a group of people due to their different interests and goals.

Intrapersonal conflict: Conflict a negotiator may feel due to his or her own contradictory feelings or interests.

Irrational escalation of commitment: this bias occurs when people get into bidding wars and end up paying more for something than it is worth. Additionally, people may honor sunk costs and continue to throw "good money after bad" even when the evidence suggests it is a losing cause.

Knowledge-based trust: the type of trust that develops when you know the other person and have had some prior interactions with them such that you can be confident in predicting their behavior.

Legitimate power: power that comes with the position you hold in an organization or society.

Leverage: unlike power, which tends to be static and positional, leverage is dynamic and situational. Leverage increases to the extent you have what they need. Your BATNA can also provide you with leverage.

Long-term orientation: one of Hofstede's dimensions. Those high on this dimension value tradition and hard work and do not expect immediate rewards. Those low on this dimension seek immediate gratification and are concerned with looking good to others.

Loss aversion: people are much more sensitive to losses than they are to gains of the same size. Loss aversion can be explained by the subjective utility curve in Prospect Theory.

Mediation: A form of alternative dispute resolution (ADR) that involves a neutral third-party working with two sides in a dispute (or the negotiators in a negotiation that has reached an impasse) to try to identify common interests.

MESO: an acronym for "Multiple Equivalent Simultaneous Offer." If a negotiator has done a multi-attribute utility analysis of the issues then he or she can bundle some of the issues and offer two bundles simultaneously that are of equal value to him or her. This signals a willingness to be flexible in the negotiation; it also helps discover where the trade-offs in the negotiation might be.

Mimicry: Rapport can sometimes be established with the other negotiator by matching ("mimicking") the other negotiator's body language, degree of eye contact or passion about issues discussed during the negotiation.

Mirroring: Similar to mimicry, mirroring means matching the other negotiator's body language, degree of eye contact and level of passion for a particular issue to establish (or reestablish) rapport.

Moment of power: according to Cialdini, this moment is right after someone says "thank you" to you. It is your opportunity to take credit for what you did, and remind the other that they would do the same for you. This evokes the norm of reciprocity.

Monochronic time (M-time): cultures on M-time prefer to do things sequentially and in a linear fashion.

Multi-attribute utility analysis: a process of weighting the issues in a negotiation (weights must add to one) and then assigning a numeric value to the options within each issue. This process forces a negotiator to prioritize the issues and allows the negotiator to quantify the issues and option, thereby helping him or her see where the trade-offs might be.

Mutual gains bargaining: another term for integrative negotiation that is often used in collective bargaining. The focus is on both parties doing the best they can in the negotiation.

Negotiation: a process that helps two or more people work together to achieve goals and solve problems.

Nibble: this is a tactic that attempts to "nibble" away an agreement that has already been struck. After selling you a big ticket item at a reduced price the other negotiator may then try to add on extras like an extended warranty, which brings the price back up to what you would have originally paid.

N.I.C.E. approach: Negotiation experts Ron Shapiro and Mark Jankowski propose an approach to working effectively with an angry or "difficult" negotiator. They use the acronym of N.I.C.E to explain this approach: Neutralize your emotions; Identify the type of difficult negotiator you are dealing with; Control the encounter; and Explore the options.

Normative leverage: a type of leverage that plays on the other's norms and values. If you make an offer that is consistent with the other person's norms and values, it will be difficult for them to say no to your offer.

Norm of reciprocity: a nearly universal norm which says that "if you do something nice for me, then I must do something nice for you." This norm plays an important role in negotiations both for concession making and for information sharing.

Objective information: all the reference points set in a negotiation should be based on objective criteria. A BATNA, for example, isn't what you hope or dream you can get elsewhere, it is what you already *know* with certainty that you can get elsewhere.

Overconfidence: once individuals have generated an answer to a question that has been posed, they are more confident than they should be that their answer is correct. This is especially true when they are asked to make estimates about something that they are aware they really don't know the answer to.

Polychronic time (P-time): cultures on P-time are comfortable with focusing on the big picture and are less concerned with the process. They can skip from one thing to another without being concerned about sequence.

Positions: a position is a stand taken in a negotiation, like "I must have a salary of $100,000." Positional bargaining can lead to impasses if a negotiator will not move from his or her position.

Post-settlement settlements: if negotiators have negotiated in good faith and feel they have done the best they could given the information they had, they may agree that if either party can suggest another settlement that is better for at least one of the parties and no worse for either, that they will agree to the new settlement. For this process to be effective, negotiators have had to build trust; also it is important to put a limit on the time for suggesting new settlement options.

Power gap: In most negotiations, neither party can force the other to accept negotiation proposals. This power gap between the negotiators requires that a negotiator convince the other side to accept his or her proposals through the use of proposals that relate to the other negotiator's interests.

Preference reversals: are related to framing effects in that people will give responses that are intransitive depending on how the question is framed. That is, they will reverse their preference as a function of whether the question is posed in terms of possible gains or possible losses.

Principled negotiation: a term used by Fisher and Ury in *Getting to Yes,* which advocates deciding and negotiating on issues based on their merits (and the importance of those issues to each negotiator) rather than haggling over each issue, assuming that both negotiators have the same level of interest in achieving their stated position for each issue in the negotiation.

Priorities among issues: when there are multiple issues in a negotiation a negotiator should be able to prioritize among them.

Problem solving/collaboration: this style works best when negotiators care a lot about their own interests AND they value the relationship with the other negotiator. This strategy works well when there are multiple issues to be negotiated and negotiators have different preferences and priorities over the issues.

Prospect theory: a subjective utility theory that shows individuals' psychological value for money is not linear. Most people have a utility curve that is concave in the domain of gains and convex in the domain of losses, and the slope is steeper in the domain of losses, which can account for loss aversion.

Rapport: Effective negotiators establish a personal connection with the other negotiator by asking questions, sharing information and building a trusting and sincere working relationship. This personal connection is called rapport and allows both negotiators to share information and trust that negotiated agreements will be implemented and followed by both sides.

Reactive devaluation: is the tendency to undervalue the concessions that other negotiators make.

Reference points: there are many reference points in the negotiation process. They serve as benchmarks for a negotiator to assess how well they are doing in the negotiation. One may be the goal for the negotiation, another the bottom line, or what one can get elsewhere, or what someone else received.

Referent power: the power of the crowd. One way to accrue power is to find like-minded others and join together to increase your power.

Relation-based trust: when you have a strong pre-existing relationship with the other person you can predict their trustworthy behavior with accuracy. In this type of relationship you can freely share information and assume the other will not exploit you.

Representativeness heuristic: a decision heuristic where judgments about persons or events are made based on how well the person or event fits into a prototypical or stereotypical category. If enough features of the person or event fit the category, we tend to overgeneralize and assume all the characteristics of the category fit the person.

Reward power: a way to force compliance by controlling rewards.

Role reversal: During preparation for a negotiation, or as a means of identifying new options at the bargaining table, a negotiator may try to see the negotiation from the other negotiator's perspective and anticipate what the other negotiator wants or needs. This technique is called role reversal.

RP: stands for "reservation price," which for a buyer is the most he will pay or for a seller the least she will accept. In preparing for a negotiation you should establish what your RP will be before coming into the negotiation so you don't pay too much (the winner's curse) or accept too little.

Schmoozing: Unlike a personal connection established with the other negotiator (rapport), schmoozing is a tactic used by some negotiators to emphasize similarities (real or pretend) with the other negotiator.

Selective attention: the tendency to focus only on information in our environment that is consistent with what we already believe or know. This can lead to biased information processing where decision makers ignore information that is inconsistent with prior beliefs and only attend to self-confirming evidence.

Selective disclosure: in negotiation, this means you don't disclose all your information, rather you share only that information that it is in your best interest to share.

Self-fulfilling prophecy: a situation where you assume something is true of an individual (like, they are competitive) and you treat them in a way consistent with that assumption (you act competitively toward them) and by doing so bring out the very behavior you assumed to be true (they act competitively toward you because you acted competitively toward them).

Shuttle diplomacy: This is a type of mediation when the mediator keeps the two sides separated from each other and the mediator goes back and forth with questions and proposals for each side.

Single-issue negotiations: a negotiation where there is one issue being negotiated—like the price for a car. These negotiations are often referred to as "distributive" negotiations in that the resource being negotiated (usually money) must be divided or distributed in some way.

Social motives: reveal one's preferences for distributions of resources between oneself and another person. The three primary social motivations studied are cooperation, competition and individualism.

Sources of power: one way to force compliance is to have power over another person. There are many sources of power; several are listed below.

Splitting the difference: A popular closing technique during negotiations is to have both negotiators to agree to accept on the mid-point between their last proposals to reach an agreement.

Stages of a successful negotiation: Preparation, rapport-building, information-trading, deal-making and closing.

Stereotypes: beliefs about a group or culture that are based on generalized knowledge that are assumed to be true of any individual from that group or culture. The problem with stereotyping is that the central tendency of any group is usually not true of any one individual from that group, yet people interact with the person as if it was true.

Sweetener: A sweetener is a small proposal or concession that is made during the **closing** stage of negotiation to persuade the other negotiator to agree to a final offer.

Top-down and bottom-up agreements: hierarchical cultures tend to dictate agreements from the top down. Egalitarian cultures trust individuals to create agreements from the bottom up.

Traits of effective/successful negotiators: genuine, flexible, ethical, an active listener, and curious. This is not an exhaustive list, but a negotiator who has these five traits is well on their way to being a successful negotiator.

Transaction costs: the costs associated with using a power- versus rights- versus interest-based approach to negotiation.

Trust dilemmas: are mixed-motive situations where there are short-term incentives to compete. To move the other person toward thinking long-term you must focus on the future of the relationship, increase communication, focus on joint outcomes and institute accountability.

Uncertainty avoidance: one of Hofstede's cultural dimensions—the level of comfort a society's members have with unstructured situations. Those high on this construct are more rule-bound and controlling, whereas those low are more tolerant of diverse perspectives and less troubled by ambiguity.

Ury's breakthrough strategy: Negotiation expert and mediator William Ury has developed a breakthrough strategy to help negotiators work through an impasse in their negotiations. Ury's breakthrough strategy consists of the following steps: Don't React—Go to the Balcony; Don't Argue—Step to the Other's Side; Don't Reject—Reframe; Don't Push—Build Them a Golden Bridge, and Don't Escalate—Use Power to Educate.

Win-lose: an outcome of a negotiation where one person gets what they want and the other person receives nothing (or very little).

Win-win: an outcome of a negotiation that gives both parties what they want.

Win-win negotiations: integrative negotiation, principled negotiation, and mutual gains bargaining are all forms of win-win negotiations.

Zero-sum game: a game where one person must win and one must lose. If negotiation is viewed as a zero-sum game, then it is assumed both parties want the same thing and only one can have it. There is no room for compromise or finding a solution that will satisfy both people.

Zone of potential/possible agreement: this zone is defined by the reservation prices of the seller and the buyer. If a buyer's RP is more than the seller's RP—there is a positive bargaining zone. If the buyer's RP is less than the seller's RP there is no positive bargaining zone and agreement will be unlikely.

Index